Thomas Erskine

The Brazen Serpent, or Life through Death

Edition 3

Thomas Erskine

The Brazen Serpent, or Life through Death
Edition 3

ISBN/EAN: 9783744746687

Printed in Europe, USA, Canada, Australia, Japan

Cover: Foto ©Thomas Meinert / pixelio.de

More available books at **www.hansebooks.com**

THE
BRAZEN SERPENT

OR

LIFE COMING THROUGH DEATH

By THOMAS ERSKINE, Esq., Advocate

AUTHOR OF 'REMARKS ON THE INTERNAL EVIDENCE FOR THE
TRUTH OF REVEALED RELIGION'

'Out of the eater came forth meat;
Out of the strong (the oppressor) came forth sweetness.'
JUDGES xiv. 15.

THIRD EDITION

EDINBURGH: DAVID DOUGLAS
1879

NOTE BY THE PUBLISHER.

This Volume is an exact reprint of the Second Edition (1831), with the exception of part of a paragraph on p. 203 and the four paragraphs which follow, as these were deleted by the author in a copy preserved for his own use.

CONTENTS.

CHAPTER I.
GOD THE LIFE.

PAGE

The object of religion is, that the life of God should be manifested in man. This life of God, or life from above, is the Holy Spirit dwelling in man, .   1

CHAPTER II.
CHRIST THE HEAD.

On the Doctrine of Christ's Headship as contrasted with the doctrine of substitution.

Connection between the atonement of Christ and the sanctification of his Church.

Jesus the Revealer of the Father, declaring the true love and the true righteousness in acting and suffering, . . 40

CHAPTER III.
CHRIST THE RESURRECTION.

The release of Christ from the prison of the grave (God's testimony to the remission of sins), considered in connection with the day of grace.—See Note, p. 88.

The day of grace preparatory to the day of judgment.

The dispensation of Christ contrasted with the dispensation of Adam.

Fulness of the gospel provision and man's consequent responsibility, ... 84

CHAPTER IV.

CHRIST THE CONQUEROR.

The victory of Jesus shadowed out in the brazen serpent.
The present forgiving love of God through Christ and his glory to be revealed, the faith and hope of the Gospel.
The true humanity of Jesus, ... 126

CHAPTER V.

CHRIST THE KING.

Christ exalted to the right hand of power. His exaltation manifested on earth by kingly power in his members.
The work of the Spirit. On prayer. On the coming judgments, ... 182

CHAPTER VI.

GOD THE SOVEREIGN.

A higher good brought out of the destruction of evil, and a good which could only thus have been produced, the revealed purpose of God in the history of man.
This principle set forth in the brazen serpent, and contained in the gospels preached to Adam, Noah, and Abraham.
Noah and Abraham types of the election. Men are elected not to the shedding of the blood, which is the atonement, but to the sprinkling of the blood, which is the purging of the conscience (1 Pet. i. 2).
Comparison between the good marred in Adam and the good given in Christ, ... 229

On Love, Personal Assurance, etc., . 283

THE BRAZEN SERPENT.

CHAPTER I.

GOD THE LIFE.

The third chapter of John's Gospel is one of the key chapters in the Bible. "All Scripture is given by inspiration of God, and is profitable for doctrine, for reproof, for correction in righteousness;" but there are some passages which, in an especial manner, serve to unfold the mysteries of the kingdom of God, by setting them before us in their very elements. And such a passage is that which records our Lord's conversation with Nicodemus on the subject of the new birth. To the matter contained in that passage I would now direct my reader's attention.

"There was a man of the Pharisees, named Nicodemus, a ruler of the Jews: the same came to Jesus by night, and said unto him, Rabbi, we know that thou art a teacher come from God: for no man can do these miracles that thou doest, except God be with him." It is evident from this account that Nicodemus had already heard Jesus speak in public to the people, and that he had been much struck by his doctrine, as well as by the miraculous power that accompanied it, and gave testimony to it as the doctrine of that God whose power upholds and controls all things. Nicodemus must have had his interest very much excited with regard to Jesus before he could have been induced to seek this interview. His coming by night shows at once his anxiety to understand something more of his doctrine, and his sense of the obloquy to which he might expose himself by such a step, if known; yet when he comes, he does not ask any particular question about the doctrine which had so struck him,—he seems just to cast himself generally and without reservation on this new teacher, who carried with him such high credentials, trusting that the spirit which was mighty in Jesus to perform miracles would also direct him to suit his instructions to the need of his disciple. But though he does not himself explain what his difficulties were, yet, from the answer which Jesus gave him, we may gather that they were connected with something which he had heard on the nature of the kingdom of God and the character of its subjects. He must have heard some such discourse as the sermon on the mount, in which the spiritual character of the kingdom was set forth, and the nature of true blessedness explained to consist in the possession of that spiritual character: "Blessed are the poor in spirit, for theirs is the kingdom of God: blessed are the meek; blessed are the pure in heart." Or he might have heard him claim for God the love of the heart, and condemn every thought, word, and action as sinful, which did not proceed from this love; or he might have heard him say, Love your enemies, do good to them that hate you, pray for them that despitefully use you and persecute you, that ye may be like your Father in heaven, who loves his enemies, and does good to them that hate him. We can easily suppose the feeling of a conscientious man on hearing such things from a teacher whose divine authority he could not disallow, whilst he was at the same time quite conscious that he was neither poor in spirit nor pure in heart, and that in very truth he had not towards God a feeling which he could honestly call love, and that he did not and could not love his enemies,—we can easily, I say, suppose him feeling great anxiety, and reasoning thus with himself: If this be the only true blessedness, and the only recognised character of the heirs of the kingdom of God, it is perfectly certain that I, as I now stand, have neither part nor lot in the matter. And then we may suppose him setting about endeavouring to love God, and to be poor in spirit, and to love his enemies, and then finding that all his endeavours were absolutely nothing, and that he did not love a particle more for all the painful and conscientious efforts that he made. What is he to do? If the demand on him were to fast, or to go through the temple service, or to give a certain portion, or the whole, of his goods to the poor, or even to his enemies, he could meet the demand; he could do anything which required only the tongue or the hands, or the feet to do it, but he could not command his feelings, he could not love by trying to love. And yet a miraculously accredited messenger from heaven had declared that, in this character of holy love, and in it alone, consisted true blessedness, and the capacity of seeing or entering the kingdom of God. He thus felt himself, by the declaration of God, excluded from that good thing on which the expectation of the whole nation of Israel was fixed—on God's best blessing; for thus they always rightly regarded the kingdom of God, however erroneous their notions as to its nature might be. In this his extremity of ignorance and helplessness, there remained no resource but to apply to Jesus himself, and this he accordingly did. "Rabbi, we know that thou art a teacher come from God, for no man can do these miracles that thou doest, except God be with him." Thou bearest God's credentials, and, in God's name, thou hast made claims on me which I cannot disallow, but which I cannot meet; I have tried, but find I can do nothing; divine Teacher, teach me. "Jesus answered and said unto him, Except a man be born again," or be born *from above* (as it is literally translated on the margin), "he cannot see the kingdom of God." In this answer Jesus recognised the difficulty which Nicodemus felt, but he did not remove it; for he only told him that it was quite true, that as he *then* was, it was absolutely impossible for him to do those things which he had been trying to do; that these things were the actings of a principle of life altogether different from that which he had at present, and that until he had that life, which was a life from above, all efforts to do them must, in the nature of things, be as vain as the efforts of one kind of tree to bring forth the fruit of another kind of tree. By thus recognising his difficulty, and assuring him that it was a real difficulty, however, he gave him this important information, that it was vain to expect by any system of discipline to train up that nature or principle of life which he had by his first birth into a fitness for the kingdom of God, or into a character of true blessedness, or a capacity of doing any of those things which belong to the kingdom of God. Except a man be born from above—except a man get the life from above, an entirely new principle of life—he cannot see the kingdom of God. If you would have a branch bring forth fruit different from the natural fruit of the tree, you must first infuse a new sap, for the old sap must produce the old fruit; it can produce no other. A selfish and unholy nature cannot produce the fruits of holy love; a holy loving nature must be infused. Effort, however conscientious and persevering, is absolutely nothing here; a new nature must be infused or nothing is gained—even a holy loving life from above, which would do these acts spontaneously. To the paramount importance of acquiring this life, Nicodemus's attention was thus directed by our Lord's answer; but still the question remained, how it was to be acquired; and so he replied, "How can a man be born when he is old? can he enter the second time into his mother's womb, and be born?" How is this new life to be had? "Jesus answered, Verily I say unto thee, except a man be born of water and (or rather *even*) the Spirit, he cannot enter into the kingdom of God; that which is born of the flesh is flesh, and that which is born of the Spirit is spirit. Marvel not that I said unto thee, Ye must be born again; the Spirit breatheth where he will, and thou hearest his voice, but canst not tell whence he cometh nor whither he goeth: so is every one that is born of the Spirit." Nicodemus was hereby informed that this new life is no modification of that fleshly life which we have by our natural birth, but an entirely different subsistence,—that it is a spiritual life; and as the source of fleshly life is the flesh, and every stream from that source partakes of its nature, so the source of this new life is the Spirit, and every stream from that source, in like manner, will partake of its nature.[1]

[1] I may just observe that the word translated *wind* in the 8th verse, is the word translated *Spirit* through the rest of the chapter, and indeed through the rest of the New Testament. The only reason that can be given for this translation here is, that the translators supposed that there was a reference in the passage to the sovereign election of God in the regeneration of sinners. But the real reference is to that which is said in the third verse: "Except a man be born from above, he cannot *see* the kingdom of God." The life and movement of the kingdom of God is the Spirit; and no one can see or comprehend the actings of the Spirit except he have the Spirit in him. No one can understand or sympathise with human things except he have a human spirit in him, and no one can understand or sympathise with divine things except he have a divine spirit in him. There are three aspects in which everything on this earth may be regarded: first, the way in which it strikes the outward senses, viz., its outward form; second, the way in which it strikes the intellect, viz., its place in that system of things which our reason apprehends. Now these are two aspects under which we all naturally regard the objects and events about us; for we have two orders of faculties just suited to these two

This information did not throw any light on the way of obtaining the life from above, it only shut up Nicodemus more absolutely to the conclusion that, as he then stood, he knew nothing about the kingdom of aspects. But there is a third element in everything, which is neither discernible to our outward senses nor our intellect, and that is *God*,—his power in making and sustaining the thing, and his purpose in placing it where it is. This is the kingdom or reign of God in the affairs of this world; and as this reign is the acting of the Spirit of God, it cannot be seen or comprehended by any one who has not the Spirit of God in him, who is not born of the Spirit. The Spirit of God in a man, therefore, is the power in him, which corresponds to, and is necessary for the understanding of, the kingdom of God in the universe—that third and chief element in everything. The time is approaching when that kingdom will make itself most palpable and visible even to the outward senses and intellect. It is at present working underground, so to speak, but it is soon to explode, and then all the kingdoms of the earth will become before it like chaff on the summer threshing-floor. *Now* it cometh not with observation, but *soon* it will come even as the lightning, which makes itself awfully visible over the whole earth.

"The Spirit breatheth where he will." In him we live, and move, and have our being. He is about us like the air we breathe; nothing excludes his presence, but he is not discernible except by his own indwelling power. "And thou hearest his voice." Nicodemus had heard the word of the kingdom, but he understood it not; he knew not whence it came, nor whither it went. And as the Spirit is, so is every one that is born of the Spirit; he is not understood by the world, but he sees and understands the kingdom of God. The kingdom of God in a man is the life of God, or the Spirit of God in him; and the possession of this life constitutes him a part of the glorious kingdom which is to be revealed at the appearing of Jesus Christ. The not having this life prevents him from seeing the kingdom now, and excludes him from it, and exposes him to be dashed in pieces by it, which is the wrath to be revealed at the appearing of Jesus Christ. Whilst, therefore, a man is without this life, there is nothing between him and the coming wrath but *time*.

God, and was entirely unqualified either for its duties or its blessedness. My dear reader, be honest with yourself on this matter. Have you peace and joy in God? Do you love God and man—yea, your enemies? If you say, "I endeavour to have peace and joy in God, and I endeavour to love God and man as far as I can." If you say, "I know that I have not these fruits, but I have done all that I can to have them. I am sure that my efforts have been sincere and persevering." I answer—listen to what our Lord saith, "Except a man be born from above, he cannot see the kingdom of God." You are making your efforts at the wrong place, for instead of endeavouring to get the right sap, you are endeavouring to bring forth the right fruit without the right sap. "Verily I say unto thee, Ye must get a life from above." And marvel not that it should be so. If blessedness evidently consists in peace, joy, love, and if you find that you cannot acquire these things by any efforts of that life which you have at present, it is quite reasonable to conclude that, in order to acquire them, you must first have another life, a new principle of life. Reader, let me press it on you—you must have a spiritual life in you before you can do a single action which is not rebellion against the kingdom of God. And don't deceive yourself by thinking that that life can be in you without your being aware of its presence; as well might a lighted candle be unrecognised in a dark room. That new life is light and the old life is darkness. If you don't know that the life is there, it is because it is not there. And if it is not there, you are yet without God, without Christ, without hope.

Thus shut up to the necessity of having this new life, but not knowing wherein it consisted, nor how it was to be obtained, Nicodemus demanded, "How can these things be?" The answer to this question must necessarily be the gospel or good news to man; for the possession of the life is a participation of the blessedness and character of the kingdom of God, as the want of it excludes from that blessedness and character.

Had our Lord said no more to Nicodemus, had he not explained to him how he was to get this new life, he would have left him, if possible, in a worse state than he found him. But he did say more; he explained the mystery; he told what the life was, and how it was to be acquired. He answered the all-important question, "How can these things be?" but not till he had blamed this master in Israel for his ignorance on a subject of which God had already spoken through the law and the prophets. "If I have told you earthly things, and ye believe not, how shall ye believe if I tell you of heavenly things?" And yet unless I tell you of them you can never know them; no one else can tell you, "for no man hath ascended up to heaven save the Son of Man who is in heaven." The earthly things, of which he had already spoken, related to the absolute necessity of a man's being born from above, or getting a life from above, before he was capable of seeing the kingdom of God, or of being the heir of that kingdom. The heavenly things of which he had yet to speak related to the fountain of that new life in the heart of God, and to the channel through which it was conveyed to the soul of man. The answer to the question, How can these things be? must therefore contain the heavenly things. And these are accordingly set forth in the fourteenth and four following verses.

Our Lord begins his explanation of the nature of the *life*, and of the mode of its communication, by referring to a fact in the Jewish history, which, like many other facts in that history, was typical of good things to come: "As Moses lifted up the serpent in the wilderness, so must the Son of man be lifted up, that whosoever believeth in him might not perish, but might have eternal life"—*the life from above*. Let us shortly consider the circumstances of the fact referred to, as they are narrated in Numbers xxi. 5, etc.: "And the people spake against God, and against Moses, Wherefore have ye brought us up out of Egypt to die in the wilderness? for there is no bread, neither is there any water; and our soul loatheth this light bread. And the Lord sent fiery serpents among the people, and they bit the people, and much people of Israel died. Therefore the people came to Moses, and said, We have sinned, for we have spoken against the Lord, and against thee; pray unto the Lord that he take away the serpents from us. And Moses prayed for the people. And the Lord said unto Moses, Make thee a fiery serpent, and set it upon a pole: and it shall come to pass, that every one that is bitten, when he looketh upon it, shall *live*. And Moses made a serpent of brass, and put it upon a pole; and it came to pass, that if a serpent had bitten any man, when he beheld the serpent of brass, *he lived*." Now our Lord tells Nicodemus that there is something in this history which shadows out the way of obtaining the life from above, or the everlasting life. May his own blessed Spirit guide us to the right understanding of it!

The sin of the people recorded here is the sin of questioning and denying God's love and faithfulness in bringing them out of Egypt, " Wherefore have ye brought us out of Egypt to die in the wilderness?" They were punished by having fiery serpents sent amongst them, who bit many of them, so that much people of Israel died. In this distress they came to Moses, and confessed that they had sinned, and said, " Pray unto the Lord that he take away the serpents from us." Moses prayed, and God heard and answered, but instead of taking away the serpents, he desired Moses to set up a brazen serpent on a pole, with the assurance that the very sight of it should have the effect of counteracting the poison of the bites, and thus *renovating the life* of those who had been bitten. " It shall come to pass, that every one that is bitten, when he looketh upon it, *shall live*."

Nicodemus had asked *how* he was to get the new *life from above?* and Jesus told him that the way of getting it was shadowed out by the way in which the bitten Israelites got their tainted life renewed, according to this history. The life of which our Lord spoke was the life of the soul, whilst the life which was restored by the sight of the brazen serpent was the life of the body (and this difference must be well attended to), but still in both cases it was *a life* that was to be renovated or acquired.

In the case of the Israelites, it was not the favour of God, nor the forgiveness of God, which they were to gain by looking at the serpent, it was *life*. When the serpents were first sent amongst them, they naturally regarded them as a sign of God's anger, and at that time they asked Moses to pray to God for a deliverance. They understood that the serpents had been sent as a punishment of sin, and they confessed their sin and asked forgiveness. The prayer was answered by the command to Moses to set up the serpent of brass. This was the form in which it pleased God to send them deliverance. This was the form in which he chose to manifest his love and his forgiveness. And all who understood the order that had been given to Moses, would necessarily recognise in it, that God indeed loved them and had forgiven them, and they would look to the serpent, not for love, nor for forgiveness, but for that *healing*, that *life*, of which it was the appointed channel.

If any one of the Israelites, after the lifting up of the serpent, had asked Moses to pray that God would give them forgiveness and deliverance in this calamity, that man would have been denying that God had already, in the lifting up of the serpent, given them a deliverance, and manifested his forgiving love to them. To such an application most assuredly Moses would have made answer by asking the man if he had not heard of the brazen serpent? for if he had heard of it, that he was treading under foot God's manifested love, and was doing despite unto the Spirit of grace, for that in the serpent God had already given health and a cure, and now if any man in the camp remained uncured, it was because he would not be cured. Let us suppose the Israelite replying to Moses, "I don't know whether God loves me or has forgiven me, and therefore I don't know whether he will give the serpent the power of healing me; assuredly I am not yet healed." Moses might have answered, "Has God excepted any man from a participation in this wondrous gift? Is it not for the whole nation, and specially for *every one that is bitten?* And is not the gift of this healing ordinance to this whole nation of rebellious murmurers, a demonstration of God's love and forgiveness to them all, and consequently to each one of them all? What else but love and forgiving love could have induced him to give them such a gift? As to your not being cured, the reason is that you have not looked at the serpent according to God's commandment. God has loved and forgiven the people whether they look at the serpent or not, but if they will not look at it, they cannot be healed, they cannot be saved from the effects of the poisonous bites, they cannot have their *diseased and tainted life renovated.*" If the man had said, "That love and that forgiveness are of little value, which leave me in this diseased state;" do you not think that the wrath of Moses would have waxed hot against him, and that he would have pronounced him a despiser of the riches of the goodness of God? Before the serpent was lifted up, the people might have asked Moses to pray for God's forgiving love as a thing which they had forfeited, and which might most righteously have been withheld from them. But after the serpent was lifted up, a petition for mercy or forgiveness, which meant anything else than an acknowledgment of their own absolute unworthiness—a petition for mercy and forgiveness in short, which arose not from a humbling sense of a compassion which faileth not, but from a doubt whether mercy and forgiveness had really been extended to them, such a petition could only have been considered as an expression of presumptuous unbelief, for it would have been a direct denial that God had given them a deliverance by puting a healing virtue in the serpent so lifted up.

It would have been an offence of the same nature as their refusal to go in and take possession of the promised land, although God had told them that he had given it to them as their inheritance; and let me here direct the attention of my readers to the language of the Spirit of God in narrating that transaction. God was angry with the people for their unbelief, and threatened to destroy them; and Moses prayed for the people just by repeating over God's proclamation of his own *name:* "The Lord God, merciful and gracious, forgiving iniquity, transgression, and sin, but by no means clearing the guilty;" and God answered, "*I have pardoned* according to thy word" (that is, according to his own great name which Moses had only repeated); "but as truly as I live, . . . they shall not see the land which I promised to their fathers" (Numbers xiv.). Compare this history with the third chapter of the Epistle to the Hebrews, where it is recorded for our admonition that these men, *these very pardoned men, could not enter into the promised land because of unbelief.* Even so Moses might have answered an unhealed Israelite who was doubting or cavilling about God's forgiving love to himself: "God hath pardoned thee, but thou canst not be healed—thy poisoned life cannot be renovated—without looking at the serpent; it is not God's love nor his pardon that thou art to get by looking at the serpent, but health and renovated life. His love and his pardon were manifested in the appointment of the serpent, as gifts already bestowed; they were given unconditionally, but health depends on looking at the serpent." God's command to Moses to lift up the serpent was, in fact, a declaration on the part of God that he had forgiven the people, and that he loved them and desired for them that they should be healed. He commanded it to be raised up *not that* he might love the people who should look at it, and so be healed, *but because* he loved the people, and desired for them that they should be healed. Whosoever remained unhealed, remained so in consequence of frustrating the counsel of God against himself, for the serpent was certainly lifted up for the whole people, for thus said the Lord, "And it shall come to pass that *every one* that is bitten, when he looketh upon it, shall live." In that appointment, there was embodied a love and a forgiveness, and a purpose of healing for every one that was bitten.

As I am fully persuaded that the confounding or identifying of the *pardon* with the *life*, has been and is a most fruitful source of error in religion, I must beg the reader's particular attention to the strongly marked distinction which is made between them in this history. There cannot be stronger evidence for anything, than that the serpent lifted up, in the circumstances of the case, contained a demonstration to the Israelites, not only of a love on the part of God to them, but of a forgiveness already past. If any one feels a doubt on this subject, let him only consider the following case: In Athens, it is well known that certain criminals were punished by being compelled to swallow poison. Now, let us suppose that the government of the state were in possession of a medicine which was a perfect and infallible antidote to the poison. Let us further suppose, that after having condemned a certain individual, and compelled him to swallow the poison, they had sent him the antidote before the poison had time to injure him. I ask whether this would not have been really a forgiveness, and whether the forgiveness would not have been dated from the time of their sending him the antidote, rather than from the time of his taking it? And I ask also, whether the man's refusal to take the antidote could be justly regarded as at all annulling the pardon granted by the state; that is, whether it would be right to say that the state had not really pardoned him until, or unless, he took the antidote. By this act the government certainly withdrew their condemnation, and made his death, if he did die, the effect of his own choice, and not of their sentence. They certainly, by this act, relieved him, as far as their power went, both from the guilt and the punishment of his offence. Assuredly he would die if he did not take it; but it could not be said that he died under the sentence of the law; he died a pardoned man. His refusal to take the antidote prevented the *forgiveness* from becoming *life* in him, but it could not make him unforgiven. And if, after the rebellion of a city, the government had first condemned them all to drink the poison, and afterwards had sent the antidote, it would have been the same thing as telling them that they were all guilty and all forgiven.

The *forgiveness* of the state, as a past thing, was testified by and embodied in the gift of the antidote; the *life* could only be had by taking the antidote. The *forgiveness* is an act of the state and a manifestation of its character altogether independent of the will of the prisoner; the *life*, or the enjoyment of it, depends upon his will.

When the brazen serpent was lifted up, God's antidote was given to every Israelite, and in that antidote his forgiveness as a past thing was testified and embodied. That was the date of the pardon; it was no longer in prospect or in offer; it was passed into an act, although the *life* of the body depended on looking on the serpent, and the *healing* of their distrustful murmurings, which was the renewed life of their soul, depended on their seeing or believing the character of God's forgiving love revealed in the ordinance.

For it is of importance to remember that God had a purpose of healing souls by this ordinance as well as bodies. And it is of great importance to observe the different ways in which these two healings were effected. I believe that the confounding of these two things is almost as general and as hurtful as the confounding of *the pardon* with the *life*.

We are told in the history that the people had murmured against God as if they had been brought up out of Egypt just to perish in the wilderness. Their souls were discouraged. They had denied that God had dealt with them as a loving father, they disbelieved his love, and hence they could not trust themselves in his hands, but were in a state of enmity and apprehension and suspicion towards him. This was their sin, the *disease of their souls*. God first sent fiery serpents amongst them. This judgment no doubt would convince them that they had offended one who was able to punish, and that they had been foolish to murmur against omnipotence; but as it rather agreed with the tenor of their murmurings, namely, that they had been brought into the wilderness to perish, it could not convince them that the ground of their murmuring was false, and therefore it could not heal the *disease of their souls*, which arose from a disbelief of God's love. Nothing but a demonstration of love, forgiving love believed, could heal this disease, and that could not fail to do it.

Every Israelite, therefore, who saw in the serpent lifted up a demonstration of God's forgiving love, even in the midst of his expressed disapprobation and displeasure at their sin, would have his soul healed, and every one who failed to see this in it, would remain unhealed in soul, however much he might be healed in body. It is evident that nothing less than the belief of a love in God which had already forgiven them, could have healed that murmuring distrust which was their sin and their disease. For even although they had discovered that God had brought them out of Egypt in love, and thus that their former murmurings were wicked and unreasonable, yet unless they knew that *these murmurings also* were forgiven, they would still have reason to fear that God's purpose *now* towards them was not a purpose of love but of anger. Nothing short of the belief of a love which had forgiven *all*, and which even in punishing their offences, and subjecting them to privations and hardships, did not cease to be love, fatherly love,—nothing short of the belief of such a love could support the confidence of persons circumstanced as the Israelites were. For they were not only daily exposed to the difficulties of the wilderness; they were destined, in very truth, to die in the wilderness, and that on account of sin. In such circumstances, nothing could really heal the spirit of murmuring and sustain confidence, but the belief of a love which, whilst it retained all its tenderness, could manifest itself even in the infliction of sufferings, by making these sufferings the channels of blessing.

Those who believed in such a love would have their souls healed by it, for it would itself enter into them and become *their life*, supporting them under the afflictions of the wilderness, and carrying them forward peacefully to meet the death which was denounced on them, in the hope of a better resurrection. If any of them were enlightened by the Spirit to catch a glimpse of the crucified Saviour in the serpent lifted up, they would then see the **full** display of *that love*, a love which manifested itself in afflicting, and torturing, and slaying the beloved One, that afterwards it might highly exalt him. But those among them who saw nothing of this character of love would of course have no support under the weariness of the wilderness, and under the pressure of the penal death awaiting them, but would remain in a state of hopeless anxiety and unsanctified sorrow and spiritual death.

To make a demonstration of the existence of this manner of love was assuredly the purpose of God in causing the serpent to be lifted up as an ordinance of healing, instead of immediately removing the living fiery serpents from the people. This plague of serpents might be regarded by them as the general symbol of all their wilderness afflictions, and now, although they were not removed in answer to their prayer for deliverance, but still allowed to remain as a memorial of God's displeasure against their distrustful murmuring, yet in that lifeless figure of their dreaded enemy, suspended as a trophy on the pole, not merely deprived of his power to harm, but by the mighty power of God converted even into an ordinance of healing to the very persons whom he had bitten, they would recognise a loving assurance from God, that he would finally overcome all their enemies, and remove all their sorrows, and cause them all to work for their everlasting salvation, yea, that he would make them perfect through sufferings. " Behold, happy is the man whom God correcteth; therefore despise not thou the chastening of the Almighty : for he maketh sore, and bindeth up; he woundeth, and his hands make whole " (Job v. 17).

The truth declared in the serpent lifted up, thus contained an ample provision for the wanderers in the wilderness. They had many sorrows, and they felt that they were all merited; but this blessed truth converted every sorrow into a well of salvation, because it revealed the forgiving love of God healing sin through a sorrow which was to be turned into joy. It thus also condemned their sin as indeed exceeding sinful, by showing them that it was love itself which condemned and which punished them.

The spirit which breathes through a great many of the Psalms, is just the spirit which would necessarily be produced by the belief of such a love as this. Thus, in the 130th Psalm, the speaker, who I believe is no other than our Lord Jesus Christ, our glorious Head, says, "Out of the depths have I cried unto thee," and then the third verse, "If thou shouldest mark iniquities, O Lord, who shall stand? but there is forgiveness with thee, that thou mayest be feared." As if he had said, If these depths were really the inflictions of an unforgiving God, who could endure them, and what could be learned from them but despair? but they come from a Father's hand, from a forgiving love; and the knowledge of that changes their character, and not only gives support under them, but makes them medicinal to the soul, a wholesome training in thy *fear* and *trust;* for *trust* is often the meaning of *fear*, when it is spoken of as a right thing, as is evident from Psalms xxxi. 19; xxxiii. 18; xl. 3; cxlv. 19, in all of which instances *fear* is put as the parallel to *trust*. See a remarkable instance of this meaning of *fear* in Isaiah lx. 5. And this surely is the only *fear* which could be produced by forgiveness; "There is forgiveness with thee that thou mayest be feared." We have reason to believe that the 90th Psalm was written by Moses, in the midst of these wilderness afflictions, and it breathes precisely the spirit or life which I have been describing. Especially it seems to me that the 11th verse can only be rightly interpreted by comparing it with the 3d and 4th of the 130th Psalm: "Who knoweth the power of thine anger? Even according to thy fear, so is thy wrath." That is, "Who understandeth thine anger? He only who has thy fear, he only understandeth the nature or purpose of thine anger." Now who is it that has the fear of God? He only who sees the forgiving love of God: "There is forgiveness with thee that thou mayest be feared." The purpose of affliction is only understood by him who sees God's forgiving love in it: "So teach us to number our days, *that* we may apply our hearts unto wisdom." He who sees love in the affliction, learns wisdom from it; whilst to him who sees nothing but displeasure in it, it is the sorrow of the world, working death. This view of the passage agrees with the principle of the brazen serpent, and with the title of the Psalm, "A prayer of Moses, the man of God." The 3d chapter of the Lamentations is full of this same spirit; the expression in the 42d verse, "Thou hast not pardoned," means just, Thou hast not removed the affliction, or the fiery serpents are allowed to remain; but the brazen serpent, the symbol of healing through suffering, is lifted up, and he who caused it to be lifted, is the same yesterday, to-day, and for ever. His way in this dispensation is still to make perfect through suffering. And so when we read in his word of his *wrath* and his *anger*, let us remember that there is a forgiving love in them all, which makes them "according to this fear;" that is, which makes them healing or medicinal. The Psalmist says, "*O Lord God of my salvation*, thy wrath lieth hard upon me, thy fierce wrath goeth over me, thy terrors have cut me off" (Psalm lxxxviii. 1, 7, 16). This fierce wrath is the wrath of God *his* salvation. Can that be a wrath of hatred? Impossible.

Hatred can never heal. Nothing but forgiving love can heal—a love which has forgiven, and afflicts not willingly but to sanctify.

Now, my dear reader, mark how admirably the principle of a love, manifesting itself in punishment, is brought out in the serpent lifted up as the ordinance of healing. Had the appointed object been Moses's rod, no one would have wondered; for the people had been accustomed to see great things done with it. But this would not have explained the *manner* of God's love, his forgiving love to sinners. For the things done with that rod had been all evidently for the deliverance of Israel; it had been stretched over the Red Sea, and a way was opened through the waters; it was again stretched out, and Pharaoh and his host were overwhelmed by the sea returning to his strength. The rod had been always employed evidently in their favour. So if a loaf of manna had been appointed as the object to be looked at, it would have been an acknowledged friend, employed in a friendly office. But the serpent was their enemy; he had bit the people, and much people of Israel had died. And therefore he was chosen as the ordinance of healing, that God might thereby shadow forth his manner of love which he bears and exercises to sinful men. It is not a love which supports under affliction, but a love which uses affliction, yea penal affliction, to accomplish its purposes of blessing. It is not a love to which we may look away from the infliction of our Father, as if love were his right hand, and justice were his left, but a love which we can discover in the infliction which tells us of the evil of sin, and of the necessity of its eradication. Till this love is known, men hide their sin from themselves, and almost succeed in their endeavours to think that they are more sinned against than sinning.

But let us now consider wherein lies the difference of principle between these two healings—the healing of the body and the healing of the soul. Both were produced by the serpent lifted up, but in very different ways; so different that they might even be separated from each other, so that a man's soul might be healed when his body died; or the body might be healed when the soul remained unhealed or dead.

Now mark, the body of the man was healed by looking at the serpent, in consequence of a sovereign appointment of God, which had connected the healing with the looking, in a way perfectly unintelligible to us. There was no necessity for his believing anything about the serpent, or having a single thought about it, or even having heard of it. If any of his friends, without saying a single word to him on the subject, had placed him so as to see the serpent, he would have been healed. This is clear from the record: "And it came to pass, that if a serpent had bitten any man, when he *beheld* the serpent of brass he lived" (Numbers xxi. 9). So that it is misapprehending the matter altogether, to say that it was not enough *to know* that there was a brazen serpent, which had the power of healing, or *to believe* it, but that it was further necessary *to look* at it, for *this last* alone was necessary.

Then the soul of the man was healed of his distrustful murmurings by the serpent lifted up, when he *understood* by it that there was a forgiving love in God, which was quite consistent with heavy displeasure against sin, and with the infliction of much sorrow and suffering on account of it, and which made use of that sorrow and suffering, to fulfil its own gracious purposes of putting away sin, and making man partaker of God's holiness. The man might understand all this without ever looking at the serpent; he might be so situated that he could not be carried to see it, or he might be blind, and thus he might die of the bites, but his *soul was healed*. His body *died*, but his soul *lived*. His soul was healed by perceiving God's true character. The disease of his soul consisted in believing a false suggestion concerning God's character, namely, that he had not brought the people out of Egypt in love, otherwise he would not have allowed them to suffer from the want of water, nor would he have confined them to that *light bread;* and his healing, or the life of his soul, consisted in knowing the true character of God's love towards man, which seeks to make man a partaker of its own holiness and its own blessedness, and trains him to this in a way of trial which may humble self and show the vanity of the creature. This is the life, and it is oneness with the mind of God.

Now these two healings are not to be confounded and mixed up together. We are not to have both the *knowing* and the *looking*, for in truth they are but one thing, the looking being the type of the knowing. In the bodily healing, we have a *material* type of the salvation of the gospel, and so a *material* looking is required for the cure; whereas in the soul-healing, we have no type but the very salvation of the gospel, only shadowy and dim, and knowledge of God's character manifested in the appointment of the serpent is all that is required for the cure; and *it* is required, because the truth could not otherwise enter the mind.

In these two healings there is, however, a perfect harmony, according to the different natures of the subject to be cured, viz., the body and the soul. For as soon as the bodily eye of the Israelite came in contact with the actually existing circumstances of the camp; that is to say, as soon as it rested on that brazen serpent, which was there whether it was looked at or not, the bodily life was healed. In the same way, as soon as the mental eye, which is faith or understanding, came in contact with the meaning of the serpent, or the character of God revealed in it, the life of the soul was healed.

The *thing sovereignly appointed* as an ordinance of healing to the body, was an object addressed simply to the bodily senses, through which alone the body acts or perceives. The *thing given* for the healing of the soul and fitted for it, not by any sovereign appointment, but by the eternal constitution of things, was a manifestation of the true character of God, a truth addressed to the understanding and the feelings through which alone the soul acts or perceives.

In both cases the cure was effected by the diseased subject's becoming apprised of a thing which *already existed;* the diseased body, by being apprised through its senses of the presence of the brazen serpent; and the diseased soul, by becoming apprised through its understanding of that sin-hating, and sin-punishing, and yet forgiving love of God, which was manifested in the brazen serpent.

As the bodies of the bitten Israelites who looked on the serpent were healed in a supernatural way, so the souls of those distrustful murmurers who understood the truth revealed in the serpent were also healed in a supernatural way; that is to say, neither the bodies nor the souls were healed according to the operation of those natural laws with which we are acquainted. But in the case of the bodily healing, the departure from the laws of nature was within a sphere wherein these laws are constantly seen to operate: whereas, in the case of the soul-healing, it is truer to say that the whole matter belongs to the sphere of a higher nature, with the laws of which we are unacquainted, than to say that there was any departure from the laws of nature.

The bodies were healed by the supernatural acting of a sovereign omnipotence, such as that which created the heavens and the earth; the souls were healed by the entrance into them of a supernatural but intelligible truth concerning the character of God, and the character of his love to sinful men, namely, that this love manifests itself in a way of healing their souls by making them know the bitterness of sin; and although it is a love which has forgiven them, yet that it condemns and hates their sin, and will allow them no peace nor rest except in unity and fellowship with God. Ever since the fall, the gospel has consisted in various developments of this great truth, and the souls into which it has entered have been healed by it, or have received the eternal life in it, "for this is life eternal, to know thee, the only true God, and Jesus Christ whom thou hast sent."

And it is because this healing or quickening of the soul is only effected by the knowledge of the truth concerning God's love, that the healing of the soul is always a *salvation by faith.*

The bodies of the bitten Israelites were not healed by faith; they were not healed by a knowledge of the true character of God, but by a sovereign omnipotence, which acted in the way of healing towards all those who looked on the brazen serpent. Those Israelites who knew the miraculous virtue of the serpent would look to it in the faith of being healed by the acting of that sovereign omnipotence; but they were not healed by faith, nor by that which they believed; they were not healed by a truth concerning God's character entering their minds, but by the sovereign omnipotence of God acting towards them according to that promise, "It shall come to pass, that every one that beholdeth the serpent of brass shall live." They believed the promise—looked—and in consequence were healed. When the discovery of a truth heals a soul, there we see an example of salvation by faith; but when the discovery of a truth sets a man to *do* something which will heal him, there we see an example of salvation by works. The discovery that there was a brazen serpent which healed those who looked on it, did not heal the Israelites, but only *set* them *to do* something, namely, to look at the serpent, in order to be healed. The knowledge of the true character of God revealed in it healed the murmuring souls at once; it did *not* set them *to do* anything in order to be healed.

It is the *faith* or *belief* that God rewards penances and pilgrimages with salvation that induces Papists and Hindus to undergo them; yet that does not bring them into the sphere of salvation by faith, for their faith does not heal them, but *only sets them to do something in order to be healed*. And if our faith be, that God forgives those who believe that Christ died for sinners, our faith will not heal us, but just *set us to do this thing in order to be healed*, and, therefore, however we may delude ourselves with words, it is a salvation not by faith, but by works.

The bodily healing effected by beholding the brazen serpent was only a *material type* of salvation by faith, it was *not an example* of it. Whereas the healing of the murmuring souls by the knowledge of God's love was not a type, but an actual example of salvation by faith.

Herein lies the great difference between a salvation by faith and a salvation by works. And this difference is lost sight of by mixing up together the body-healing and the soul-healing, in the type of the brazen serpent. And therefore it is that I am so urgent in warning you against the mixing up of these two healings.

My dear reader, do you fully understand what I mean by warning you against mixing up the body-healing with the soul-healing in this history of the brazen serpent? You think that there can be no danger of that. But there is great danger of it; and when you can, without detecting the fallacy of it, hear or read such a sentence as this, "You must not only know that the Son of Man was lifted up on the cross, but you must also look at him; in the same way, as an Israelite had not merely to know that the serpent was lifted up, but he had also to look on it,"—I say, when you can hear or read such a sentence as this, without detecting the fallacy in it, it proves that you do not understand the danger of mixing up the body-healing with the soul-healing. Knowing a thing as truth is *believing* in it, and this is the only way in which the soul can *look* on anything.

Looking in this case is just the material type of *knowing* or *believing* a thing; this particular information only being given by the nature of the type, concerning the thing believed, that it is a thing which has a direct reference to myself, and can only be known to me by my apprehending it in its direct reference to myself. The type is *seeing*: Now, I only see by the rays of light which strike on my *own eye*, and I only become acquainted with the general character of light through its direct reference to myself individually; and at the same time it is true that I get my own special share in the light out of the general fund, and because it is general. This is just personal assurance founded on the general forgiving love, and which is absolutely necessary to the understanding of that general love. Tasting, hearing, eating, drinking, are all typical of the same truth. They all imply that the thing to be believed can only be known by personal experience, like light, and sound, and taste; that is to say, they imply that the gospel of God's forgiving love in Jesus to the world comes with a special and direct and individual reference to each person of the world, and therefore is not understood nor believed except where that special reference is apprehended, just as the sun is not seen by me except through that ray of him which strikes on my own eye. And the reason is evident,—the purpose of the gospel is to purge the conscience from dead works to serve the living God, and most assuredly no message of forgiveness can purge my conscience except a message of forgiveness *to myself*. The law burdens my conscience only in consequence of its personal reference to myself, and the gospel can only purge my conscience by a reference to myself equally personal.

Fleeing into the city of refuge is another material type of believing in Christ, which has been confounded and mixed up with its antitype. Thus it is said, "You must not only believe in Christ, but you must also flee into him, as it was necessary for an Israelite, not only to believe that there was a city of refuge, but also to flee into it, in order to be protected."

Oh, I know that there is a perplexity and a misery, and a self-righteous working, produced by this error, which cannot be reckoned up. Mark the simple explanation: We are in God's hand—living and moving and having our being in his hand—whilst we think him a stern Judge, or a severe task-master, his hand appears a prison to us, and in very truth it *is* a prison, for we are kept in it to meet the judgment to come; but as soon as we discover that this is our Father's hand, as soon as we discover the print of the nail in his hand; then that which had been a terror or a wilderness to us, that which we before had felt to be a prison, we find to be in fact a city of securest and sweetest refuge. We have not to *move* to get into the refuge, we are in it. All that is needful is just to know *where* we are; to know the God to whom the hand appertains; to know the things that are freely given us of God. Fleeing into the city of refuge and *going* into the ark are just material types of *believing* in Jesus. And as soon as we know the meaning of that word, "He that hath seen me hath seen the Father," we know that the hand of the infinite and omnipotent God, away from which we cannot go, is the hand of our brother, "who loved us and gave himself for us, and tasted death for every man."

The parable of the prodigal son is interpreted in the same way, and it is said, "You must not only believe in the love of God, but you must also arise and go to your Father." Now, in truth, unbelief is the far country: we never move out of our Father's hand; and as soon as we know him as he is revealed in Jesus, we know ourselves to be in our Father's house.

Well, but this history of the brazen serpent is merely used as an illustration of the way in which alone men can obtain the life from above, the eternal life. "As Moses lifted up the serpent in the wilderness, so must the Son of man be lifted up, that whosoever believeth in him might not perish, but have everlasting life. For God so loved the world, that he gave his only begotten Son, that whosoever believeth in him should not perish, but have everlasting life."

I have shown that the Gospel—or the word of life (for nothing is gospel to sinners doomed to *die*, except a word of *life*)—is shadowed out by the serpent lifted up, in two different ways; first, in the body-healing; secondly, in the soul-healing. And I have shown how the material type, namely, the bodily healing, by the mere beholding of the serpent, subserved the purpose of the soul-healing, and was a basis to it; first, by proving the fact of a general forgiveness, seeing no one died after the lifting up of the serpent by the sentence of God, but by his own choice; secondly, by showing that their sufferings did not proceed from any lack of love in God, for that the very infliction itself by which sin was punished, was in the purpose of God to become the source of *new life*. These two truths were the gospel or word of life preached to the Israelites *doomed to die* in the wilderness. And nothing can be a gospel to creatures in our circumstances which does not contain these two truths. There is no provision for spiritual life where these two truths are wanting, for the knowledge of them is absolutely necessary in order to confidence before God; and life rises out of the confidence in the true character of God. But if the shadows and dawning of the gospel contained these truths, much more does the substantial gospel, which is Christ Jesus, the fulness of the Godhead in a body, and which hath come to us that we might have life *more abundantly.*

In him who is the Sun of Righteousness, all the rays of light scattered over the former dispensations are gathered up, as they in truth proceeded originally from him, for he is the "Lamb of God slain from the foundation of the world." And in him they appear *with advantage;* for these former dispensations, glorious as they were, had no glory by reason of the glory which excelleth in the Christ. Whatever, then, we have of love or forgiveness or hope set before us in these former dispensations, we are to consider but as the distant whisperings of that full voice with which the Lamb, who came from the bosom of the Father's love to take away the sin of the world, and to unite man to God, proclaimed the love of God, the forgiveness of sin, and the hope of glory, when he said, "*It is finished.*"

It must then be evident to the reader, that unless he discovers in the Son of man lifted up, all that he has seen to be contained in the serpent lifted up, namely, a past forgiveness to all, and a love working life through affliction and death to those offenders who believe in the love, he really does not understand the truth declared in the Son of man lifted up, for thus the antitype would be inferior to the type, and the substance to the shadow, which cannot be true. We ought surely to find *more*, and much more, in the thing typified than in the type. We ought to find in it the principle in the mind of God from which the good things revealed in the type proceed. For in Christ the way into the holiest is laid open, and the serpent belonged to a dispensation which had no glory, by reason of the glory which excelleth in that dispensation of which the Son of man lifted up is the grand and characteristic feature.

In the former dispensations it was the *spoken word* that gave the light, but *now* it is the substantial word, the word *made flesh*. But our knowledge of the power of the light, and of its intensity, and of its extension, is intimately connected with, or arises mainly out of, the word being made flesh. Actions are our only measures of mind and feeling. And therefore, whilst the word continued to be only a *spoken word*, we could not rightly enter into the mind and feelings of God towards us. But God did not content himself with uttering sounds or sending messages to us. He came himself—Jehovah the word became flesh, and in the history of the word made flesh, we have a concentrated history of God's actions towards our nature, our flesh;

and thus we have a standard by which we may at all times measure the mind of God towards ourselves and every individual of the nature. For that which the divine nature did to the human nature in Christ, was done to him in character of head and representative of the human nature; and, therefore, is to be considered as indicating the mind of God to every man.

Now mark how the true principle of the serpent lifted up is contained with unutterable advantage in the Son of man lifted up.

A forgiving love condemning sin—yet bestowing blessing through penal affliction, and life through penal death—is the true principle of the serpent lifted up. Well, look at the cross. What do we see there? A man suffering a most agonising and shameful death between two thieves, to signify that his death is specially penal. Now, why does that man suffer? Is it because God hates him that he has thus bruised him? No. That man is the well-beloved, only begotten Son of God. He is himself God in flesh. And why does he thus torture and kill the flesh which he has assumed into so near and indissoluble connection with himself? Why, just that he may raise it to the throne of heaven, and make it capable of partaking of the glories of Godhead, and that he may fit it to become a fountain of eternal life for that whole nature, of which it is a part, and in which he personally dwells. But why was this suffering of our nature in the person of Jesus needful? It was a *fallen nature*; a nature which had fallen by sin, and which, in consequence of this, lay under condemnation. He came into it as a new head, that he might take it out of the fall, and redeem it from sin, and lift it up to God; and this could be effected only by his bearing the condemnation, and thus manifesting, through sorrow and death, the character of God, and the character of man's rebellion; manifesting God's abhorrence of sin, and the full sympathy of the new Head of the nature in that abhorrence, and thus eating out the taint of the fall, and making honourable way for the inpouring of the new life into the rebellious body. Because *thus* only there could be an open vindication given of the holiness and truth of God, against which the fall was an offence, and who were pledged to its punishment; and *thus* only could it become a righteous thing in God,—in consideration of this new Head of the nature, who had, in that nature, and in spite of its opposite tendencies, vindicated the character of God, and fulfilled all righteousness,—to declare the race partaking of that nature forgiven, and to lay up in him, their glorious Head, eternal life for them all, which should flow into each member, just as he believed in that holy love of God which was manifested in the gift and work of Christ.

So this spectacle of agony and ignominy is just an exhibition of a righteous love of God passing knowledge, manifesting itself to the human nature, in the only way by which that human nature, fallen as it is, can be delivered from the bondage of corruption, and fitted for communion with God, and for participation in his glorious blessedness,—namely, in a way of suffering.

But we must examine the nature and necessity of this suffering more closely.

When we contemplate the Son of man lifted up on the cross, and see in him the Son of God, in our very nature, suffering by his own will, and by the infliction of the Father, the whole curse denounced against sin —sorrow and death—that thus he might, as the head of our nature, become the righteous channel of divine favour and life to every individual of the nature, and be highly exalted, and receive a name above every name, even the name of King of kings and Lord of lords. When we see this, and when we know that this was the forthcoming of the eternal love of Father, Son, and Spirit, we see a glorious manifestation of that same truth, concerning the character of God's love, which was declared in the serpent lifted up by Moses. We see a glorious and blessed truth concerning our God, which may well be liberty and life to a soul lying bound and dead in the disbelief of God's love; and which may well be strength and joy to a weak and sorrowful heart, pressed down and overburdened by the afflictions of this wilderness.

But we must not content ourselves with the general aspect of this mighty work. There is life in every part of it. The whole word is *living* and powerful, and our God invites us to look into it, by the light of his own Spirit, that we may press on to know even as we are known.

CHAPTER II.

CHRIST THE HEAD.

When we ask, What is the meaning of the sufferings of Christ; or in what way did those sufferings tend to accomplish the purposes for which he left the bosom of the Father, and came to this world? we ask a question which, in its bearings, involves the whole character and purposes of God, and the whole character and prospects of man. If this question were put to many persons, we should probably get various answers. One answer that would be pretty generally given to this question is, "That he came to save sinners, and that he could accomplish this only by suffering in their stead the punishment due to their sin, because thus only their salvation could be reconciled with divine justice, and thus only could it become a righteous thing with God to remit the punishment of the real offenders. In this way both the justice of God and his love were magnified: his justice, in demanding the full penalty of the law; and his love, in providing a substitute to stand in the place of the real offenders, and bear that for them which would have overwhelmed them in everlasting perdition, if they had been obliged to bear it themselves." I believe that the Spirit of God has made this view of the atonement spirit and life to many souls; and yet I believe that, with some truth in it, it is a very defective view, to say the least of it.

This view of the atonement, which is generally known by the name of *the doctrine of Christ's substitution,* has, I know, been held by many living members of his body; and yet I believe that, with some truth in it, it contains much dangerous error. In the *first* place, I may observe that it would not be considered *justice* in an earthly judge were he to accept the offered sufferings of an innocent person as a satisfaction for the lawful punishment of a guilty person. And as the work of Christ was wrought to declare and make manifest the righteousness of God, not only to powers and principalities in heavenly places, but to men, to the minds and consciences of men, it is not credible that that work should contain a manifestation really opposed to their minds and consciences. Let me here entreat of my reader to be patient and not to misunderstand me, nor to suppose that, by using this language, I do at all mean to deny or bring into doubt the blessed truth, that Christ tasted death for every man; for verily and indeed I believe that Christ did taste death for every man, and that, too, in a far deeper and truer sense than is taught by the doctrine of substitution in its ordinary acceptation. The humanly devised doctrine of substitution has come in place of, and has cast out, the true doctrine of the headship of Christ, which is the large, and glorious, and true explanation of those passages of Scripture which are commonly interpreted as teaching substitution. Christ died for every man, as the head of every man, not by any fiction of law, not in a conventional way, but in reality as the head of the whole mass of the human nature, which, although composed of many members, is *one thing*—*one body*—in every part of which the head is *truly* present.

If my right hand had committed murder, and my left hand had committed theft, and my feet had been swift to shed blood; were I to suffer beheading for these offences, no one would say that my head had been the substitute for my hands and my feet. And although, in this case, it be true that the planning head is the real offender, and therefore is the proper sufferer, yet the force of the comparison is not thereby destroyed, for even if these members were capable of independent action, they would be punished in the punishment of the head, because they are all really contained in the head, in virtue of its being the root of that system of nerves which, by pervading them all, does in fact sustain them all. Now remember this word of Christ, "The earth and its inhabitants are dissolved, I bear up the pillars of it;" and recognise him as the sustaining head, to the power of whose pervading presence through all the members of the human nature the actual existence of every individual of the race is alone to be attributed. He was indeed the head of every man, and therefore when he died, he died for every man. The blood of bulls and goats could never take away sin, not only on account of their comparative worthlessness, but also because they were *substitutes;* their blood was not the blood of the offender, and therefore it could not fulfil the condemnation; for thus it is written, "And the land cannot be cleansed of the blood that is shed therein, but by the blood of him that shed it" (Numb. xxxv. 33). But when Christ offered his blood as an atonement, he offered the blood of the offender, for God "hath made of *one blood* all nations that dwell on all the face of the earth" (Acts xvii. 26); and Christ offered that one blood, and here was the mighty marvel, although it was the blood of the offender, yet it was blood untainted by sin. It was in virtue of his taking part of the one condemned flesh and blood that he could meet and fulfil the condemnation, and could by death overcome him that had the power of death, even the devil.[1] The whole nature is as one colossal man, of which Christ continues the head during the whole accepted time and day of salvation;[2] and according to this head is the whole at present dealt with. The doctrine of the human nature of Jesus Christ is not merely that he is of the *same nature, of the same flesh and blood* with every man; but that he has *part* of that *one nature,* that *one flesh and blood,* of which, as a great whole, all are partakers. Unless the first Adam had been truly the root and the head of the nature, his fall could not have involved and embraced all the rest; he could not have fallen for every man. Thus, if Cain

---

[1] Heb. ii. 14. [2] 1 Cor. xi. 3; Rom. v.; John xv.

only had fallen, his fall could only have involved his own posterity. And unless Christ had been truly the head and the root of the nature, he could not have tasted death for every man, and his resurrection could not necessarily have involved that of every other man. But he was truly the head of the offending nature, and in his suffering the offending nature suffered the righteous sentence of God. It was no fiction of law. He suffered as the condemned head, he rose as the righteous head.

And *secondly*, he did not suffer the punishment of sin, as the doctrine of substitution supposes, to dispense with our suffering it, but to change the character of our suffering, from an unsanctified and unsanctifying suffering, into a sanctified and sanctifying suffering. And thus, when our Lord himself speaks to the disciples about his cross and sufferings, he uniformly calls upon them to take up their cross and follow him by the same road of suffering. This connection is marked through all the evangelists, and must therefore be a designed connection.—See Matt. xvi. 21-25; Mark viii. 31-35; Luke ix. 22-24; John xii. 23-26. And Paul desires fellowship in Christ's sufferings, and conformity with his death. The substance of all these passages proves that the substitution of Christ did not consist in this, that he did or suffered something instead of men, so as to save them from doing or suffering it for themselves. And this agrees with the obvious fact that Christ's death does not save the believer from dying a natural death, nor does his sorrow save the believer from sorrowing. On the contrary, the believer dies; and moreover, dies daily, in consequence of and in proportion to his faith. What Christ did *for* us, was done for us in a sense and with a view very different from that of saving us from doing it ourselves. He fulfilled the law, for instance, certainly not with the view of saving us from fulfilling it, but, on the contrary, with the very view of enabling us to fulfil it. For the salvation of Christ consists mainly in " writing the law upon our hearts," and he made himself a sin-offering, " that the righteousness of the law might be fulfilled *in* us, who walk not after the flesh, but after the spirit."

When, therefore, it is said that Christ did or does things for us, it is not meant that he did or does them as our substitute, but as our head. He does them for us as a root does things for the branches, or as a head or heart does things for the body. He is given as a *Leader* as well as a Commander to the people; he leads them the way, he does not call on them to do things which he does not himself do; nor does he himself do things which he does not call on them to do. He is the "Forerunner who is for us entered," not to dispense with our entering, but to open the way for us, and keep it open. Suppose a man dead and buried, and life coming again to him into his head, that living head might force a way for the body up from the grave, but it would not do this to dispense with the rising of the body, but as the leader and commander of the body. So also is the work of Christ.

But further, the common doctrine of substitution is inconsistent with the true nature of the punishment of sin. For it supposes that punishment is an arbitrary or conventional thing, appointed merely to maintain the dignity of the Lawgiver, but which may be dispensed with, without the sinner's suffering thereby any loss, if that dignity is otherwise secured. But the punishment of sin is the manifestation of the holy God in relation to a creature that has left the Fountain of life; it is a manifestation of God just suited to the creature in these circumstances, and surely the creature that loses it, loses a blessing, for it loses so much of God. All the Bible is full of proof that punishment in this present dispensation is sent as a blessing: "Blessed is the man whom thou chastenest, O Lord, and teachest out of thy law, *that* thou mayest give him rest from the days of adversity."[1] "Blessed is the man that endureth temptation, for when he is tried, he shall receive the crown of life."[2] "Whom the Lord loveth he chasteneth;" "if ye be without chastisement, then are ye bastards and not sons."[3] And it is the Father of the spirits of all flesh, in speaking of his own dealings with his children, who says, "He that spareth the rod hateth the child."

There is something to be done by penal suffering which cannot be done without it. It is not a ceremony, it belongs to the eternal constitution of things. It is the refiner's fire, without which the refining cannot take place. Our holy head " was made perfect

---

[1] Ps. xciv. 12.　　[2] James i. 12.　　[3] Heb. xii. 6, 8.

through sufferings;" "though he were a Son, yet learned he obedience by the things which he suffered;" and "God chasteneth us for our profit, that we might be partakers of his holiness. Now no chastening for the present seemeth to be joyous, but grievous; nevertheless, afterward, it yieldeth the peaceable fruit of righteousness to them that are exercised thereby."[1] Now, as it would be an unspeakable loss to us to be partakers of holiness and the fruit of righteousness only by substitute and not in reality, so it must be a loss to partake of the chastening which yieldeth these fruits only by substitute and not in reality. Christ said, "The cup that my Father hath given me, shall I not drink it?" and he asks the disciples whose mother prayed for them that they might sit on his right and left hand in his kingdom, "Can ye drink of the cup which I drink of?" thereby intimating that he did not drink it to dispense with their drinking it, but, on the contrary, that those who drink deepest of it after his example should sit nearest to him in his kingdom. This also is the evident meaning of that passage in the Epistle to the Romans, where our joint inheritance with Christ is described, "If so be that we suffer with him, that we may also be glorified together." Reader, would you wish a substitute in holiness, or in blessedness, or in glory? I know you would not; and therefore I say, dream not of a substitute in suffering, for these good things rise out of the suffering. A sick man might as well have a friend to take his medicine for

---

[1] Heb. ii. 10; v. 8; xii. 11.

him, as a sinner have a Saviour to take his suffering for him.

But if Jesus did not suffer punishment to dispense with our suffering it, what has he accomplished for us by suffering for us? Take this answer in the meantime. Sin can only be burned out of our nature by our sense of its misery, and by our acquiescence in the righteousness of that misery, which acquiescence we can never truly give until we see the holy love of God resting upon us, and manifesting itself in the law against which we have sinned, and in the misery which is inflicted upon us through our sin, and on account of our sin. But holy love is a thing which our natural life is incapable of seeing; for our natural life is consciously under the condemnation of sin, and is bearing its punishment, and it cannot draw near to God, or look on God; for its condemnation implies and contains a separation from God; it therefore cannot know love, or see love, because God is love; the natural life, in truth, is the carnal mind, which is *enmity* against God. And thus, while we continue to live in this natural life, and to see things in its light, we can see nothing in the punishment of sin but what increases our fear, and enmity, and opposedness to God. And thus punishment acts as a poison until we see it by the light of another life—an uncondemned life—which has freedom of access to God, and which can see his love. Now this is the great thing which Christ has accomplished by suffering for us; he has become a head of new and uncondemned life to every man, in the light of which we may see God's love in the law and in the punishment, and may thus suffer to the glory of God, and draw out from the suffering that blessing which is contained in it. For "this is the record, that *God hath given* to us eternal life, and this life is in his Son." The flesh or natural life, which lies under a condemnation, never will condemn itself, it never will acquiesce in God's condemnation on it. We cannot condemn the natural life, except in the power of the eternal life. It was in the light of this eternal, this uncondemned life, even the light of his Father's approving love, that Jesus himself suffered the punishment of sin, acquiescing in its righteousness, and it was by suffering it in this way that he was "made perfect through sufferings;" that is, by sufferings thus endured, his human nature became capable of containing the glory of Godhead, and was made a Fountain-head of eternal life to all the rest of that nature. This eternal life was never under condemnation; it had always access to God, and fellowship with him. And thus being itself uncondemned, but coming into the condemned human nature, it takes part with God in his condemnation of the flesh. It was in the power of this uncondemned life that Jesus always condemned the flesh or natural life which was under God's condemnation; and in him, as the righteous head, eternal life is given to all, in which they also may appear before God, and take part with him in his condemnation of their natural life.

Let us here shortly consider the purpose of punishment. With regard to the governor or lawgiver who inflicts it, it testifies to his abhorrence of the offence, and to his sense of the importance of the law, and to his zeal in maintaining it. And with regard to others, it serves as a warning to them, and a manifestation of the law and the lawgiver. But as it regards the offender, what is the purpose of punishment? Is it not that, by sufferings felt to flow from the breach of the law, he should be taught the intrinsic excellence and value, as well as the authority, of the law, and should thus learn to estimate it more highly, and cleave to it more, and love it, and hate what opposes it? No man can ever be benefited by punishment, except in so far as it works in this way; and unless he sees that the law contains love for him, and that it is a good thing—not in virtue of an arbitrary appointment, but in itself—punishment never can work in this way with him. He must see love in the law before he can see love in the punishment. For unless he sees love in the law, he never can understand punishment to be a voice of love, telling him that it was indeed an evil thing in him to depart from what was good and from what was loving, and warning him that this sin in him is the enemy of his own soul as well as the enemy of God, and calling him to join with God in hating it and destroying it. But as soon as he knows and feels that the law is good and loving, then he will hate his offence against it, and even though there were no actual infliction, he would punish sin in himself, by the *painful hatred* with which he contemplates its actings in himself. And yet he will have an enjoyment in this *painful hatred*, not only because he recognises it to be right that he should so suffer, but also, and chiefly, because he will feel that this very painful hatred is separating him more and more thoroughly from the sin. And seeing there is actual infliction appointed by the law, he will receive it as a fresh proof of the love of the law, for he will receive it as an urgency to the work of condemning and hating sin, in sympathy with the law; he will receive it as God's seal to the unrighteousness of sin, and, in pressing it to his heart, he will put his seal to God's righteousness in its appointment. In this way every sorrow will be an increased separation between him and sin, and a binding between him and the law. Now it is quite manifest that the provision, in the strength of which alone such a work as this could be done, is the knowledge of a love of God in the law. This knowledge of his love is the new and uncondemned life, and, until it is known, punishment can do nothing but increase enmity. The man broke the law originally because he thought he could make a better provision for his happiness than the law had made; and the punishment that follows does only this, it lets him know that he is in an evil case, being in the hand of an enemy that is stronger than himself. The sorrow of a man, in these circumstances, is the sorrow of the world that worketh death; it is not a sorrow for sin, but for the painful effects of sin; it is not a condemnation of sin nor a hatred of sin; it is a condemnation of the law and a hatred of the law; such feelings can never separate a man from sin, they can only separate him farther from the law.

Christ saw the law to be the character of his Father, to be the character of that God who is love; he saw that the law was holy love; he saw God in every feature of it; he could see God in it, because he himself was born of the Spirit,[1] and lived solely by the new life, and therefore he loved the law, and he condemned with a *painful hatred* everything that was against it; and as the whole human nature was pressing on him, as belonging to himself, and as it was all an unclean thing, as it was altogether sinful, with the exception of that part which the Spirit had sanctified as his own personal body, he was burdened with it exceedingly, yea he roared for the very disquietude of his heart, and yet he suffered the whole of it in the spirit of holy love; he embraced every pang, every infliction, as the righteous desert of sin, and put his seal to the righteousness of God. He thus bore our sins and carried our sorrows. Thus, he was wounded for our transgressions, and bruised for our iniquities. And thus, in the very root of the nature, he put the mark of hatred and condemnation on every form of human sin, as a corrosive and a blight upon it, and as a purifying salt infused into the source of life. And this he did whilst he was manifesting the law to us, as he himself saw it, even as the character of the God of love, who had put away the imputation

[1] To say that the law is spiritual, is the same thing as to say that God is in it; and because it is spiritual, it can be only obeyed, and even rightly discerned, by a person born of the Spirit. See the footnote at page 6.

of sin from man by the sufferings through which God in the flesh had condemned sin. And those who understand this manifestation do indeed become partakers of the same spirit, even the eternal life, in the strength of which they also join in God's condemnation of their natural life; for this is life eternal, to know the only true God, as he is manifested in Jesus Christ. The sinful fallen nature could only be restored through penal sufferings received in the spirit of holy love, which is just the eternal uncondemned life of God. That life was in the *word*, and the *word* was made flesh; and thus it came to pass that, on the one side, God saw that in the flesh on which his approving love could rest, and the flesh had that in it which could look on God, and approach him with confidence, and enter into his condemnation against sin in the flesh.

There is a remarkable promise to Israel connected with this very subject, which doubtless we shall soon see accomplished. It is a promise of restoration when they see God in their calamities: "If in their enemies' land, their uncircumcised hearts be humbled, and *they accept of the punishment of their iniquity*, then will I remember my covenant with Jacob, and my covenant with Isaac, and my covenant with Abraham will I remember; and I will remember the land" (Lev. xxvi. 41). As soon as they get such a sight of God's holy love in punishing as will lead them to say, "Righteous art thou, O God, that judgest thus," then they will be in their right place, then they will be restored; then they will also say, "The cup that my Father hath given me, shall

I not drink it?"—for the sight of that love is the very spirit of Jesus, and will, in those who see it, work even as it did in Jesus. *Accepting our punishment* is just being of one mind with God in hating and condemning sin, and longing for its destruction. It is submitting ourselves to the process of its destruction, and setting our seals to the righteousness of God in the process. *It is the death-pang of the crucified head thrilling through the member, and accomplishing in it what it did in the head.* This is a mighty thing, a mighty truth, reader, which may the Lord make life to us. This pang was in the heart of Jesus through the whole of his life on earth, though it only had its consummation on the cross. It was this pang which was continually condemning and crucifying the flesh in him. It was this pang, willingly endured, which was continually witnessing in him that God's judgment on the flesh was a righteous judgment. And it was on account of this pang that he was highly exalted; for it is written, "Therefore also God hath highly exalted him." And as it is only by the thrill of this pang through a member that it can be a partaker of the holiness of the head, and along with him justify God's judgment against sin, giving him the glory that is due to him, so it is only thus that it can be a partaker of the exaltation of its head. This is no substitution. It is a great substance, a great reality. No creature that has sinned against God can have fellowship with him again, except by *accepting the punishment of sin.* The thrill of this pang is the sin-consuming power of the Spirit, and until it passes through the creature, the power of sin remains in it, and must exclude it from God. To dispense therefore with this would not be merely a departure from righteousness, it would be a departure from the eternal constitution and necessity of things. Throughout the whole course of his life on earth, Christ was just accepting his punishment as the head of the sinful nature; and that eternal life which his believing members receive out of him, is continually doing in them what it did in him. Christ suffered then for a purpose directly opposed to the purpose which is implied in the doctrine of substitution; he suffered not to dispense with our suffering, but to enable us to suffer, *as* he did, to the glory of God, and to the purification of our natures. And here then is the simple connection between the atonement of Christ and the sanctification of his members. The atonement consisted in Christ's accepting the punishment of sin as the head of the nature; and the sanctification of his members consists in their accepting it also in the power of his spirit dwelling in them.

I believe that there is much instruction on this subject contained in that ordinance of the Mosaic law which declared any man who touched a dead body to be *unclean*, and inadmissible into the sanctuary as a worshipper until he had passed through the appointed process of purifying by the water of separation. The water of separation was water strained from the ashes of a red heifer, which had been consumed by fire. The person to be purified was sprinkled with this water on the third day, but continued unclean until the seventh day, when he was again sprinkled, and then he became admissible into the tabernacle. The red heifer must mean the Church, for a female never could typify the Lord himself. It must typify the bride or body of Christ; and the appointment of draining the water of separation from her ashes teaches that her own purification is to be by passing through the furnace; she is to be made perfect through suffering just as her head was. His sufferings are not instead of hers, but to lead hers.

Now what is the meaning of the law which excluded from the tabernacle, as unclean, any person who had touched a dead body? It was just a declaration that it is impossible to worship God in the flesh, or natural life. *The flesh or natural life is the dead body.* And he who attempts to worship God in it commits sin. For the whole flesh of man is under the sentence of death, and death is in it already, it is a polluted thing; and whenever we think or act under its impulse, we are polluted and incapable of worshipping God.

And what is taught in the appointed process of removing the uncleanness by sprinkling the unclean person with the water of separation on the third day; and then, again, on the seventh day, on which day, if he has undergone this process, he is declared clean and admissible into the sanctuary? It is the purifying power of a hope which passes over the present life, and looks for blessedness only to a life which is to arise out of death that is here taught. Observe, there is something gained by the sprinkling on the third day, but the accomplishment of the purification, and the free admission of the person, do not take place till the seventh day. Now mark, on the third day Jesus rose from the dead, possessed, as the head of the human nature, of eternal life, the life of God, thus declaring the condemnation which barred man from the presence and fellowship of God, evidently removed; for here was a man (and that man the head and representative of the whole nature) who was a partaker of the natural life, and had died under the condemnation which rested on that life—here he was, risen from the dead, having passed through the condemnation in the strength of another life, over which death had manifestly no power; here he was risen—and let me repeat it, not as a mere individual, but as the head of every man, and having that life in which he himself passed through the condemnation laid up in him for every man; and, therefore, every individual of the race who knows Christ's headship will, in his resurrection, see the pledge of his own resurrection, and the full assurance that now there exists in the nature an uncondemned life, in virtue of which the condemnation which had separated the nature from God is righteously taken out of the way; and he will also see that it is the will of God, by the construction of this wondrous channel, to restore and to glorify the fallen nature by filling it with his own spirit, his own eternal life, in order that the work which has been accomplished in the head may also be accomplished in the body. He who sees this in the resurrection of Christ is " begotten to a living hope by it,"[1] " which hope

[1] 1 Peter i. 3.

he has as an anchor of the soul, sure and steadfast, and which entereth into that within the veil, whither the forerunner is for us entered;"[1] "and he that hath this hope in him, *purifieth* himself, even as Christ is pure."[2] He will see that it is only through the actual death of the flesh that he can be personally fitted for the presence of God, and that at present he can have fellowship with God in the spirit only in so far as he is separated from the flesh; he will therefore hate the garment spotted with the flesh, and he will enter into God's plan of crucifying it; he will see that the flesh is the bar between him and the enjoyment of God. Thus the sprinkling with the water of separation on the *third day*, consists in the knowledge of *Christ's resurrection* and in the *purifying hope* which arises out of it, and he who is thus sprinkled is sprinkled from an evil conscience, his conscience is purged from dead works to serve the living God; because he sees that God's will and God's glory are one thing with the blessedness of the creature, and because he sees that in his righteous head he has a righteous life, even God's own pure life, in which he may look on God's face with joy. Even now he has his conversation in heaven through the Spirit; and, on the seventh day, on the true Sabbath, the millennial rest, his body also will be sprinkled, and he will be raised an incorruptible and glorified member of the glorious Redeemer. But he who is not sprinkled on the third day, is not clean on the seventh day, and shall not be admitted into the sanctuary; for he who

---

[1] Heb. vi. 19.   [2] 1 John iii. 1-3.

knows not the resurrection glory of Jesus as his head cannot have hope of his own glorious resurrection, and it is hope only that purifies.

Those who are thus sprinkled on the third day "worship God in the spirit, rejoicing in Christ Jesus, and having no confidence in the flesh;"[1] they are the true circumcision. Their joy in Christ Jesus arises from their knowledge of his resurrection as their head, and this joy separates them from the flesh, for it looks forward to its own fulness only through the death of the flesh; and being thus separated from the flesh, they worship God in the spirit, they rise up through their living head into the living God. Their life is hid with Christ in God, and their joy in Christ draws them up thither, being indeed the natural movement of that eternal life through which they have fellowship with God.

The water of separation was drained from the ashes of the heifer; this declares that the purification lies in the knowledge of a love which, though it hath forgiven the sinner, yet hateth iniquity; a love which is a consuming fire, and which purifies a sinner only by consuming his sin. The knowledge of that love is eternal life[2] (as the sight of the sun is a participation in his light), and that eternal life, which is the spirit, is the only life in which we can approach God acceptably. To worship God in the spirit, then, is just to worship him in the knowledge of that righteous love which gave Jesus to die for our sins, and which raised

---

[1] Phil. iii. 3. [2] John xvii. 3.

him from the dead, and gave him glory, as the righteous head of the human race.

The flesh in its present state, the natural life, cannot worship God, for it always regards him as a taskmaster, and his service as a task. It never accepts its punishment; it never says, "Thou art righteous, O God, that judgest thus," and therefore it is excluded from the sanctuary. And the forgiveness of sin does not mean that the condemnation on the flesh is taken away, but that a new and uncondemned life is given in Jesus, the righteous head, to sinners who had corrupted their natural life so as to be righteously incapable of approaching God in it. The condemnation remains on the flesh until it has accomplished its purpose of burning out sin from the flesh; at which time, but not before, it will be taken off, and the purified flesh will be welcomed into the presence of the holy God. The body will then live by the eternal life, it will be raised a spiritual body, and the whole man will be uncondemned and righteous before God. And thus, in the forgiveness of our sinful race, God has not departed from his just condemnation of sin; but he has bestowed a righteous life, even eternal life, in Christ, in which we may approach him without polluting his sanctuary. And thus the record that God hath given us eternal life, is also the record that God hath forgiven our sins. Reader, this is no light thing for the glory of God. Think of it.

In the meantime, that is, during the present dispensation, all of us stand under the righteous head, as members of the one colossal man, who, in the person of Christ the head, has accepted his punishment to the glory of God, and has become partaker of the uncondemned life; and thus, whilst this dispensation lasts, we are all free from that condemnation on sin which would bar the sinful creature from the enjoyment of God's love; because we have a righteous head, and in him a righteous life, in which we may appear before God uncondemned. The oneness of the flesh unites all men with the head, whether they are believers or unbelievers, just as the continuous texture of the vine unites the branches with the root, whether they be living branches or dead. The oneness of substance in the root and the branch, puts the branch in the condition of receiving the sap from the root; if this oneness did not exist, the branch could not receive the sap of the root, and could not be justly blamed for being sapless. The condemnation of the dead branch lies in its oneness of substance and texture with the root. So it is the oneness of the flesh that puts the member in the condition of receiving the life from the head; and it is this same oneness which is its condemnation, if it is found without life. It is clear from the parable of the vine in John xv., that there are barren, withered branches on the vine; and if there be one, there can be no limit short of the whole human race. Judas was a branch of that vine, but he abode not in the vine, therefore he was cast out as a branch, being withered.

Christ, the head of the body, is now saying to us,

Be ye witnesses for me upon the earth *until* I come again ; cut off *now* the offending right hand, pluck out *now* the offending right eye, whilst the day of grace lasts, and by thus doing bear witness to that which I shall do when I return to judge all flesh ; for *then* I shall cut off the offending right hand, and pluck out the offending right eye ; I shall cut off from me all the partakers of my flesh who are not also the partakers of my spirit. "Judge therefore yourselves, brethren, that you be not judged of the Lord." The precepts of Christ are declarations of what he himself does or will do. They are calls on his members to show forth his light unto the world—to be like their head.

Let me not be misunderstood when I say that the furnace is necessary to purge away sin, as if I said that the atonement of Christ was incomplete, and that any affliction on our part is necessary to complete it. No, " He hath finished transgression, and made an end of sin, and made reconciliation for iniquity, and brought in an everlasting righteousness."[1] "Now where remission of sin is, there is no more offering for sin."[2] I am not speaking of atonement, but of the purifying of the nature which is produced by sorrow received in a godly sort. And even with regard to this need of suffering, I do not mean to say that any amount of suffering is necessary to salvation. It is the suffering spirit of Jesus in us that is necessary. Now every one who really knows Christ does, according to the measure

[1] Daniel ix. 24. [2] Heb. x. 18.

of his faith, receive that spirit of Christ which suffered in Christ, and which in Christ accepted the punishment of sin, and gave God glory as its punisher; and he by that same spirit accepts his punishment, giving God glory therein, and this is true although he have no apparent afflictions. The entrance of that Holy Spirit into the heart of the sinful creature is the entrance of the purifying fire which withers and consumes the flesh: "All flesh is grass, and all the glory of man as the flower of grass; the grass withereth, the flower fadeth, that is, the natural life withereth, *because the spirit of the Lord breatheth upon it.*"[1] *The punishment is always in our flesh*, and the entrance of the spirit of Christ at once discovers to us the presence of the punishment, and teaches us to accept it. Every pain that we suffer arises from sin, for nature is a suffering nature, simply because it is a fallen nature. This is true whether the suffering be mental or bodily. But above all, our personal exclusion in the flesh, or natural life, from the presence of God, is a continual punishment, though a punishment which is not felt until the manifestation of the Holy Spirit in the heart of the sinful creature. As soon as that manifestation takes place, the punishment is not only felt, but acknowledged to be righteous. Punishment, lovingly received, is the process by which we are sanctified. This process began in our Head, and must descend into every member. Christ's sufferings made the atonement, because through them the life was let

[1] Isaiah xl. 6.

into the body; through them Christ became the head of life to the body, and it is only by that life in us that we can lovingly receive our punishment, putting to our seal that God is righteous in it. Any sinful creature that accepts his punishment is necessarily saved, because, in fact, such acquiescence is salvation, one-mindedness with God; but no sinful creature can acquiesce in this thing, except in the power of an uncondemned life. And here was the mighty effect of the atonement, to open a righteous way for the inpouring of the uncondemned life, even the eternal life, into the condemned nature. And as it is in that life only that we can condemn sin and accept our punishment, so it is only in that life that we can look on God or approach him. The work of Christ is thus the source of life. It was a work which no *creature* could have done; a work which none but he could have done; a work without which no man could have been saved; a work, to attempt to do which, or to add to which, is to crucify the Son of God afresh, and without which no man ever did or ever could have done any of those things which his leader and head and God calls on him to do, or indeed ever could reasonably have been called on to do them. It was the great work of atonement, on the credit of which, before it was accomplished, and through the channel of which, since it has been accomplished, the love of God, in the form of favour and forgiveness and the gift of the Spirit enabling man to glorify God, has been given to every human being. And thus every one who is endeavouring to win the forgiveness of God, and the Spirit of God, as gifts not already bestowed in Christ, is sinning against the work of Christ and the headship of Christ, and denying that he has made atonement. This he accomplished in virtue of his personal Godhead, which always upheld him in union with the Father's love. In this lay the exclusive character of Christ's work. And thus to attempt to make atonement is to attempt to be God.

Before the fall, God and man were united by the law of love. This was the bond; this was the medium of communion, and the bond was both of God and of man, because love is God's nature, and whilst man continued faithful, it was his nature. And through this medium God communicated and man received all blessings, and all these blessings were but different forms of love. But when man fell this bond of love was broken, and there was no longer a medium of communion between God and man. Then it was that God promised the seed of the woman who was to destroy the works of the devil: that is, who was to renew the broken bond, and restore the interrupted communion, by becoming himself the medium or mediator of communion—himself, who was the *living law of love.* And thus he did it. He was himself Jehovah, and he assumed to himself the nature which had fallen, and thus within his own person he united the two natures. On the one side he was one with the Godhead, on the other side he was one with the fallen manhood.

This was the plan of that living bond by which man was to be again united to God, and to be put in a condition of receiving out of his fulness. But this bond had to be made perfect through sufferings. " It became him for whom are all things, and by whom are all things, in bringing many sons to glory, to make the captain of their salvation perfect through sufferings." And why through sufferings? What pleasure could the Father take in the sufferings of his holy child Jesus? for it is written that he did take pleasure in them. " It *pleased* the Lord to bruise him." Now, compare this with that other word, " I have no pleasure in the death of (the wicked) him that dieth, saith the Lord." Reader, do you understand the agreement of these two passages? God has no pleasure in the mere suffering of any creature, even although that suffering be the merited infliction of a righteous law, much less in the sufferings of a righteous person. If God had pleasure in the execution of a just sentence, he would have pleasure in the death of the wicked; but he says that he has none. It is not then in suffering, as suffering, or as the execution of a sentence, that God takes pleasure. It is not because the Godhead of Jesus gave a character of infinity to his sufferings, so as to make them infinitely exceed in weight the deserved sufferings of all the individuals of the human race, that God takes pleasure in them; for if God has no pleasure in the merited punishment of one sinner, he can have no pleasure in the punishment of millions. The Father's pleasure in the sufferings of Jesus then did not arise from their being a just satisfaction to the law, *in the sense of their meeting the law in its demand of so much punishment to answer so much sin.* Wherein then did their value consist in the Father's eyes?

There was something in the character of those sufferings which glorified God, with the incommunicable glory which is due to him, on the ground of which it became him righteously to surround the sinful fallen race, of which he had become the head, with the light of his reconciled countenance.

In the first place, there was infinite glory given to Jehovah by the coming forth of the Word, the second person in the Godhead, to declare the character of the Godhead. When we consider what love is, and that God is love, and that the glory of God is love, and that there is no love but of God, we see that none could rightly and fully declare this glory except God himself, and that therefore there is an exceeding excellence and fitness in the manifestation of the Godhead by the Word made flesh, and that the complacency of the Father in this work of the Son must be infinite.

The Father's heart was yearning over the works of his hands that had destroyed themselves just by disbelieving in his love. The calumny had been uttered against him by the devil, that he did not love man, that he grudged man a happiness, and man had believed it and was ruined by the belief of it. Now, how was this to be answered? God was the Omnipotent God, and he might have sat on the throne of heaven, and commanded things to be as he would have them. But omnipotence is not love, and love alone could answer this devil's lie. Therefore the Son answered it in love. This was a thing, let me say it with deepest reverence, that God could not do by a messenger or a proxy. And therefore it was Jehovah himself that did it. God loved every man, even in the loathsomeness of his pollution, even in his state of bitterest enmity, with a love that made him willing to taste death for every man. This love was to be declared to answer the devil's calumny. But how was it to be declared? God might have sent a messenger who would have been highly honoured by the commission of declaring his love to the guilty, and by suffering death in the execution of his commission, but this would *not* have declared *God's* willingness to die for every man. This love could not have been declared except by a personal sacrifice on the part of God. It could not have been declared except by God actually becoming man, and dying for every man. It could not avail itself of omnipotence, and God's love did not draw back from the proof. Jesus was God, and he declared this love by descending and condescending into the human nature, and in that nature tasting death for every man. The Father's love rejoiced in its full manifestation. He was well pleased in the only begotten Son. He saw his own perfect image, and he saw it in that very nature which had revolted; he saw it, and was well pleased. Thus only could God's love have been truly declared.

The world has various imaginations about God's love, but in this act the true love is declared. Some think that it is mere approbation, so that those only can be loved who deserve it. And some think that it is connivance, under the shelter of which they may sin without danger. Whilst others, more versed in the divine character, think it a holy benevolence in the spirit of which God grieves over sin, and desires the righteousness and happiness of men, and would find his own full satisfaction in seeing them thus restored. But this is not love. God is all this; he is holy and he desires the holiness of his creatures. But he is something more than this. God is love, and love desires to be loved; love demands fellowship, a communion of happiness, and can be satisfied with nothing short of it.

A holy benevolence could have been declared through a proxy, *love* could not. God has a personal tender affection for every man, so that he desires union and fellowship with every man. Now the Son declared this love of the Father, by coming into the *root* of the nature, that part which Adam occupied, and thus coming into every man, and thus testifying to the Father's loving desire of union with every man, and thus fulfilling that word, "I have drawn thee with cords of a man and with bands of love." Being as the head and root of the race, he is in every man as the root of a tree is by its fibres in every branch and twig that grows from it. The fibre of that root in every man is the cord of a man and the band of love wherewith God draws him. This is the meaning of Christ being called "the second Adam." And this is the meaning of the word also, " The head of every man is Christ." And this is that gospel which Paul was commissioned to preach amongst the Gentiles, " Christ in you (yea in every man), the hope of glory."[1] Reader, do you understand this? It is eternal life. Well, it is this movement of the Son, to declare the love of God in the fallen nature, and to the fallen children of men, and through them to all the creation, which must be recognised in every action and suffering of Christ, before we can understand what that element in them is which gave them, and gives them, their infinitely meritorious value in the Father's eyes. I may add that this same movement must be recognised by us in every event of providence before we can fully understand the blessedness of the mediatorial dispensation. Every event comes to us in the spirit of that first movement. For everything comes to us from the hand of Jesus, and that movement was the origin of His mediatorship.

Thus was there a great glory given to the character of God, by the condescending of the Son into the fallen nature of man, a glory which none but God in the flesh could have given to it. Because love questioned cannot be justified by any form of words, or any messenger, it can only be justified by the personal act of him who loves. And therefore it required the personal act of him who was God to justify the questioned love of God. And behold how he justified it!

[1] 1 Cor. xi. 3 ; xv. ; Rom. v. ; Col. i. 27.

But further, in thus justifying the love of God, Jesus also justified the righteousness of God in giving the law. The law which God had given to men was *love:* " Thou shalt love the Lord thy God with all thy heart, and thy neighbour as thyself ;" this was the law of God to man, and man, by disobeying it, had denied its righteousness, not only because every disobedience to a law is a denial of its righteousness, but also because his disobedience to this law had arisen from his disbelief in God's love to him. Whilst he continued to believe in God's love he himself continued to love and consequently to obey, but the moment he disbelieved God's love, that moment he fell; for that very moment his heart shut against God's love, and thus had no more love in it wherewith it might love, for love is of God, and of God alone. The disobedience of man then contained this charge against the righteousness of God,—that God had given a law to his creatures, which he did not keep himself; that he had commanded them to love, whilst he himself did not love. To justify God from this charge, the Word who was God voluntarily put himself under the law; and though he was truly the giver of the law, yea the living fountain of it, he became the willing subject of it, and as such he fulfilled the righteousness of it. He thus doubly justified the challenged righteousness of God,—first by the manifestation of the love which brought him from the bosom of the Father, and secondly, by fulfilling the law as a subject of it.

And it was in the power of this righteous love that

he justified God as the punisher of sin. Having become partaker of that *one blood* which had sinned against God, he became in consequence excluded as a man from the presence of his Father's glory, and subject to death. The tainted life which was in that blood was not permitted to appear in the presence of the holy God; and thus he was shut out from his presence, until that tainted life was poured out in death; and he accepted the punishment, the exclusion, and the death, saying, "Thou art righteous, O God, that judgest thus." He had always access to his Father in the Spirit, that is, in the eternal life, because that life was not under the condemnation; but whilst he bore about with him the natural life, the man Christ Jesus could not appear in the holy of holies. In all this the holiness of God was unspeakably declared and glorified. The Holy One of God become flesh could not stand in the pure presence of God, because the flesh was tainted. And that Holy One, by accepting this punishment of sin, testified to the righteousness of the punisher. And he knew what he testified, for he was God, and he was man.

He saw the Father's love in its fulness; he saw it in the beauty of its holiness, and he loved it in its own spirit; he saw it and knew it as the only fountain of life, and he knew its unutterable and exclusive worthiness to be the fountain of life, and thus he could truly know the sinfulness of that rebellious and blasphemous lie which had denied this, and which had persuaded men to forsake the fountain of living waters,

and to hew out to themselves broken cisterns which
could hold no water ; he knew the awful guilt of
yielding to that lie, for he saw in it the deliberate
rejection of all good, and the choice of all evil ; and
as he knew its guilt, so he knew its misery, the
tremendous misery of a soul which had lost its God,
and which had put from it everything of God, except
that creature-existence which it could not put away,
and which in itself is nothing else than a craving
desire, which must ever agonise in its own unsatisfied
cravings, until it is filled with God. He knew the
sin and the misery, and the righteousness of the misery ;
and when he came into the nature which had by this
sin fallen into this misery, he accepted the misery,
and thus he condemned the sin, and set his seal to the
righteousness of the misery ; he set his seal to the
righteousness of that word, "The soul (or life) that
sinneth shall die ;" he partook of that tainted life, and
he accepted death as its righteous due. The word of
God went forth upon him, and did not return void,
but accomplished that whereto it was sent ; the condemned life which he took was a life of sorrow until it
was poured out in death ; it was a veil between him
and the brightness of his Father's face, which, whilst
it lasted, kept him from the glory of God. Against
that life the sword of the Lord had been bared, and
when the Son became flesh and partook of that life, the
sword pursued it thither, and this voice was heard,
"Awake, O sword, against my shepherd, against the
man that is my fellow ;" and his answer still was,

"Righteous art thou, O God, and true are thy judgments." Thus no word of God fell to the ground, his justice was declared to be loving, and his love was declared to be just. The love gave the new life, the justice consumed the condemned life. The God of holy love was thus mightily glorified.

But besides the direct inflictions which he thus lovingly endured as the head of the sinful nature, he suffered also from the actings of holy love within him, in contact with, and in opposition to unholiness and hatred. He loved the Father, and he loved the truth, and he loved man, and wherever he was he saw God dishonoured, the truth despised, and man destroying himself. He saw nothing in the world but sin and misery and a headlong rushing to ruin, and his love mourned over these things, and his holy nature was revolted by them, and so he says, " Horror hath taken hold of me, because men keep not thy law ;" and thus he was a man of sorrows and acquainted with griefs, and every grief and every sorrow was an acting of holy love, well pleasing and glorifying to God. Even had he been merely a dumb spectator of the world's course, he could not have escaped being a man of sorrows and of griefs; but he was not a dumb spectator,—he was the faithful witness; he could not keep silence; the fire of holy love burned within him, and he spake with his tongue, he testified for God and the truth, and he testified against the world that its deeds were evil. He testified against the rebellion of man, and claimed for God that which was due to him. And he spoke not with his tongue only, he was the *life* of God made manifest in the flesh; he was the *life* made *light*, and he walked up and down in that living light; and as it was in a world of spiritual death and darkness that he thus walked, the life in him continually condemned the death, and the light the darkness. And though this living light was love, and a love to every man, for it was the light that lighteth every man that cometh into the world; and though he went about doing good and healing all that were oppressed of the devil, yet he drew upon himself the hatred of all men, and this just because he was the very character of God, and he was shining and acting among the poisoned posterity of that fool who had first said in his heart, "No God." At last they cast him out of the vineyard and slew him, they crucified him who had come from the throne of glory and the bosom of the Father to save them, by lovingly submitting to all this for them. They killed him, but they could not kill his love; that was stronger than death, and stronger than hatred. Blessed be his name; his love conquered. Every action of his being was a part of that warfare of love against hatred, and of righteousness against unrighteousness, which he with perfect success, but with uninterrupted sorrow, waged through his life. That warfare could not be carried on without sorrow; it was a continual grieving over sin and ruin, and a continual condemnation of those whom he loved unto the death; for he was every man's brother, and his condemnation was not the condemnation of a stranger, but of a brother.

He thus glorified the Father by his sorrow unto death, and the Father was well pleased. He manifested the glorious brightness of God's love in the face of man's hatred and pollution, and he did this in the flesh, in that nature by which God had been dishonoured. He did it too in the root of the flesh which had in the person of its first root said, "No God." And thus out of that very field in which Satan had appeared to have gained a victory over God, he brought forth much glory to God, by showing, not only that his love was stronger than hatred, and his good stronger than evil, and that where sin had abounded, there grace had much more abounded; but by showing that God could force the wrath of man and devils to praise him, and that he could make hatred subserve the purposes of his love, and evil subserve the purposes of his good. And thus he gave the Father to see something in the human nature in which he could be well pleased, and over which he could rejoice. And he did it in all respects to the exceeding glory of the Father, for he waged this hard and successful warfare under all the disadvantages of the fall, not in the power of his own personal Godhead, but in the power of the Holy Spirit communicated by the Father in continual answer to the continual actings of his faith, as the faith of a dependent creature. This is clear from the Psalms as well as the New Testament, especially from the whole history of our Lord's temptation in the wilderness. See Luke iv. 1, 14.

He thus in every thought and word and deed condemned the thought of that first man who had said in his heart, "No God." For he lived to the glory of God, and he lived by faith in the love of God. He condemned the natural man by being just the opposite of the natural man, and, therefore, as Cain slew Abel, so did the natural man slay Jesus. There was a wonderful meeting of opposites in the cross of Christ. There we see Jesus bruised. Who bruised him? God bruised him. It pleased Jehovah to bruise him. And wherefore bruised he him? Because he loved with a holy love the nature which he thus bruised. So God's love crucified Jesus, the beloved one. But it is also charged upon the Jews by Peter, that "*they* killed the Prince of Life," and our Lord himself said that he should be delivered into the hands of *men*, and that they should crucify him; and, accordingly, he was delivered into the hands of men, and they slew him. And wherefore slew they him? Because their works were evil, and his were righteous. And who were the men that slew him? Were these Jews and Romans sinners above all men because they did such things? Nay, they were the representatives of *the flesh* in their act, as Jesus was in his. They showed the flesh as it was and is. He showed the flesh inhabited by the Spirit. *It was our flesh that crucified Jesus, as it was our flesh that was crucified in Jesus.* We must see this oneness of the flesh before we can understand fully our connection with the cross.

It was God's love that bruised Jesus, even the same love which in Jesus submitted to be bruised; but it was not man's love but man's hatred that co-operated. So we here see the love of God and the hatred of man, as it were, combining to do one thing. But what was the purpose of God's love in crucifying Jesus? It was that man might be delivered from the bondage of sin and death, and be made partaker of the life and joy of God. And what was man's purpose in that act? It was to kill God if he could. Men hated Jesus because he was the image of God, and testified for God, and declared God's character in all that he said and did. And so this act of theirs was just in accordance with that word of the fool, "No God." We'll have none. O reader, His thoughts are not our thoughts, neither are His ways our ways.

Now what was the meaning or purpose of this extraordinary meeting of opposites in the cross? It was that the light and the darkness might be contrasted in their full intensity, and that the whole excellence of love, and the whole malignant evil of sin, might be manifested in that act, which was at once the execution of the sentence pronounced against sin in the flesh, and the perfecting of the new righteous head of the flesh,—in that act which was at once the record of God's abhorrence of sin and of God's love and forgiveness of the sinner. And so it was, that at the moment that Christ, by dying as Head of the *flesh*, put his seal to the righteousness of the sentence of death which God had pronounced on the flesh of which he was a partaker, that *flesh* did, in the Jewish people and rulers, justify God in his judgment upon it, by the highest act of rebellion of which the creature is capable. The first head of the flesh, in his act of rebellion, had said in his heart, "No God;" and now the flesh had brought this *thought* to the utmost intensity of *action*,—it tried to kill God,—it killed Christ. And oh, the unfathomed mystery of love! that act was the execution of the sentence, on account of which sin was forgiven. For he who was killed was the head of the flesh. The *flesh* was taken in the fact of attempting to annihilate God,—and God, in the flesh, suffered the sentence, and so at once condemned and expiated the sin of the flesh. The sentence of death was inflicted in a spirit which proved the justice of it,—and suffered in a spirit which proved the love of the lawgiver and judge. Thus the love met the hatred face to face, and overcame it, whilst it condemned it and punished it.

Had the individuals who perpetrated the crime been called to suffer the punishment under the frown of God, they must have suffered it in the agony of fear and hatred against the punisher, and thus their sufferings, like their sins, could never have been other than hateful to God. But he who did suffer the punishment due to the sin of the flesh, of which he was one, yea the head, suffered it in the agony of holy love. He tasted death for every man at the moment that he was tasting death by the hand of every man. He felt the full sinfulness of the act by which he was dying, and he felt it as the head and representative, and most loving elder brother, of those who were doing the accursed deed. It was not what he suffered at their hands that hurt him most,—it was *their doing it.* He was bone of their bone, and flesh of their flesh; and they were trying to kill God,—that God who was holy love, and whom he loved with a love passing all understanding. It was *his* flesh (for there is but one flesh) that was doing this evil, and he felt and acknowledged that it was a righteous thing that the flesh which had so sinned should so suffer.

We are all of one flesh, but we are kept separate, and walled off, from each other, by our being individual persons. This individual personality gives us that feeling of distinct responsibility which, in a great measure, detaches us from the actions of others, as if we had nothing to do with them. But Jesus had no human personality, he had the human nature under the personality of the Son of God. And so his human nature was more open to the commonness of man; for the divine personality, whilst it separated him from sinners, in point of sin, united him to them in love. And thus the sins of other men were to Jesus what the affections and lusts of his own particular flesh are to each individual believer. Every man was a part of him and he felt the sins of every man,—just as the new nature in every believer feels the sins of the old nature with which it is connected,—not in sympathy, but in sorrow and abhorrence. This principle explains such passages as the following: "Mine iniquities have taken hold upon me, so that I am not able to look up; they are more than the hairs of my head, therefore my heart faileth me." And thus he bare our sins on his own body on the tree, acknowledging God's righteous judgment, that the flesh which had so sinned should so suffer. And therefore he suffered as a willing victim. "He was led as a lamb to the slaughter, and as a sheep before his shearers is dumb, so he opened not his mouth." God never was rightly glorified by the penal suffering of the fallen nature, until that suffering was undergone in the spirit of holy love, by one who partook of the fallen nature, and felt for all its sins as if they had been his own, and yet had not personally partaken of them. And here that thing was done, and done by God in man's nature; and thus God was glorified in man, and by man, and yet God had all the glory. Now this is the expiation, —this is that which put away sin. And thus it is that God's glory and the sinner's peace agree in one, according to that heavenly song on the birth of Jesus, "Glory to God in the highest, and on earth peace, good-will to men."

The crucified head was the head of the *whole body* —the whole flesh; so he was in every part of it, just as the natural head is by its nerves in every part of the body. And thus in every part of the flesh there was that recorded sentence and execution which justified the forgiveness of God.

The divine person of Jesus, pervading the whole of this work, gives it an infinite glory,—not merely as giving a weight to suffering, but as giving its only true and equal declaration to the love and holiness of God, and to the sinfulness of sin. So that in fact God is only giving its proper glory to love and holiness, when he, through this transaction, proclaims himself as having reconciled the world to himself, not imputing their trespasses unto them. And the sinner who has confidence before God, through the knowledge of this transaction, even in the fullest sense of absolute unworthiness, is giving to God a glory that is dear to his heart, because, in that confidence, he avows that the manifestation of love in the gift of Christ, and of holiness in the sufferings of Christ, is enough for the gracious purpose for which God set it forth; because, in that confidence, he gives a demonstration, that man needs only to know God, in order to rejoice in him, and that he needs only to know God's holiness in order to give thanks at the remembrance of it; and because, in that confidence, he recognises the value of the work of Christ in which God is well pleased, and in which he has revealed his own character as an ever-present ground of confidence, and an overflowing fountain of life to the very chiefest sinner of Adam's race.

There is something very wonderful, to see the same flesh suffering in Jesus, according to the will of God, and sinning in the Jews against the will of God, and to see that the sin should be the direct cause of the suffering, and the suffering the divinely inflicted penalty on the sin by the endurance of which the sin is expiated; and yet that the sufferer should be without sin, and that his sufferings should be most glorifying to God, whilst the inflictors of the punishment were dishonouring God, and sinning exceedingly against him. We must see the absolute oneness of the whole flesh before we can rightly enter into this thing.[1]

[1] We also see in this that the *will of God* is quite distinct from the *purposes* which may be accomplished by his controlling power, through the means of human actions. It was *against the will of God* that the Jews should murder Jesus; but he accomplished the purposes of his own love through that murder, for it was *according to his will* that Christ should die "a ransom for all."

[An additional note on the subject of this chapter will be found at page 279.]

CHAPTER III.

CHRIST THE RESURRECTION.

THERE were three things that took place in connection with the death of Christ, which are recorded, to the end we might believe that man was indeed forgiven in consequence of this sacrifice. First, the rending of the veil of the temple; indicating that the way into the presence of God, which sin had barred, was now opened. Second, the opening of the graves, and the saints rising; indicating that the prison of the grave was broken, and that death was overcome, and could not keep his hold, which could not have been unless sin were forgiven, for death was the sentence on sin. The third thing which I mention along with these occurred before them, but is evidently one with them in meaning. Jesus died that men might have life. Well, was there any man whose life was actually saved by the death of Jesus? Yes, there was one man, and that man was an insurgent, and a murderer, and a robber—that man was Barabbas. He was a prisoner waiting for execution in Jerusalem at that time, along with many others who had made insurrection with him; his life was saved by Pilate setting Jesus and him up together as the two out of whom the customary selection for liberation, granted to the people as a privilege at the time of the feast, was to be made. Now why was it that Pilate set up this man as the single alternative of Jesus? It was just because Pilate "sought to release Jesus," knowing his innocence, and knowing that the jealousy of the priests was the true reason of the charge brought against him, and therefore he did not give the people a choice of all the prisoners, for so they might have fixed on some less offensive or some less known criminal, but he put Barabbas, a notable leading malefactor, as the single alternative of Jesus ("whether of the *twain* shall I release unto you?"), that he might thus shut them in to save Jesus, conceiving doubtless that it was impossible that their feelings or consciences should be so poisoned and deadened as to prefer a man "notable" as a seditious murderous plunderer, to one whose whole life had been a continued action of benevolence, and against whom they could procure no witnesses whose witness agreed. But the people were themselves filled with the spirit of murder, and so they desired the murderer to be released, and they killed the Prince of Life; murderers themselves, they had pleasure in him who murdered. Thus the life of Barabbas was saved. Had there been a general selection allowed, *he* never could have been chosen. But he was set up by Pilate as the alternative of Jesus, in order to insure the release of Jesus. "Whether of the *twain* shall I release unto you?" He was the man supposed by Pilate to be the most hated, and the most justly hated individual of the nation. And for *this reason* he was set up along with Jesus; *and thus he was saved.* He, the chief of sinners, was saved from death by the death of Jesus. Surely this history has a solemn and important meaning in it, filling out the measure of the sin of the flesh, and, at the same time, typically shadowing forth the all-inclusiveness of the forgiveness declared through the Saviour's death. The holiest, it may be said, was laid open for those who would walk into it by the new and living way. The rising of the *saints* proves nothing with regard to *sinners*. But there is something for sinners, yea for the chief of sinners. Let this sign be connected with the conversion of the thief on the cross, and they will together illustrate that word, " God is the Saviour of all men, *specially* of those who believe."

Thus we have in these three things shadows of the effects produced by the sacrifice of Christ. In the rending of the veil we have the shadow of the removal of all barriers between God and man. In the rising of the saints we have the *proof* that the grip of death was relaxed, and the *shadow* of the first resurrection in the coming dispensation. And in the release of Barabbas we have the shadow of the non-imputation of sin to the chief of sinners, during this present dispensation. By these signs testimony was borne to the character and completeness of the work of Christ, by him whose mind that work declared—even by God, " who will have all men to be saved, and to come to the knowledge of the truth; for there is one God, and one Mediator between God and men, the man Christ Jesus; who gave himself a ransom for all, to be testified in due time" (1 Tim. ii. 4). "And his blood cleanseth from all sin" (1 John i. 7). "And for this cause he is the mediator of the new covenant, that by means of death, for the redemption of the transgressions that were under the first covenant, they which are called might receive the promise of eternal inheritance" (Heb. ix. 15).

But the great proof that Christ's death has indeed put away sin is his own resurrection. The grave is God's prison. Into that prison he was put as *our* Head and representative.

We pass a prison and see a man put in by an officer. I ask you, Why is he put in? You directly answer me, Because he is an offender. We pass the prison again on another day, and we see this same prisoner liberated by the officer. I ask you, Why is he let out? You as directly answer me, Because he has suffered his sentence. That is the only reason why an offender is let out of prison. The offences for which he was put in have been punished, and so the law discharges him.

Now it is written of Christ, that "he tasted death for every man," and that "the Lord hath laid on him the iniquities of us all," and that he is "the Lamb of God that taketh away the sin of the world." He was put into the prison of the grave for the offences of the flesh of which he was the head. And why was he liberated? Because those offences, the offences of the flesh, of the world, of every man, were punished and cancelled. He died as the condemned head of the race. He rose as the justified or righteous head of the race. He died because of our offences (*not* that we might offend, but because we had offended), and he rose again because of our justification (*not* that we might be justified, but because we were justified).[1]

[1] Rom. iv. 17-25. This translation has been much objected to; and I don't wonder at it, for the whole theology of man is opposed to it. To those who have any knowledge of the language, and who oppose this translation, I can confidently say, that they must have some other ground of objection to it than any which they can discover in the form of the expression; for this is certainly the natural and obvious translation of the passage. But for the sake of those who, from ignorance of the language, are obliged, in some degree, to lean upon names, I may mention that this is the translation given of the passage by Bishop Horsley, a name certainly amongst the first of England's many scholars, and actually the first of her modern biblical critics. The passage is the text of the second of five sermons bound up in a volume, entitled Nine Sermons on the Nature of the Evidence by which the fact of our Lord's Resurrection is established, and on various other subjects, by Bishop Horsley. I shall transcribe two or three sentences, which prove that the Bishop would not have dissented from the subsequent part of this note. "The original words are without ambiguity, and clearly represent our Lord's resurrection as an event which took place *in consequence of* man's justification, in the same manner as his death took place *in consequence of* man's sins. It follows therefore that our justification is a thing totally distinct from the final salvation of the godly," pages 262-3. Our justification is the grace "in which we now stand," page 265.

Much error has originated from confounding two words, which, though related to each other, are yet quite distinct: these are δικαίωσις and δικαιοσύνη,—the first (viz. δικαίωσις) being the *judicial act* by which God has removed the imputation of sin, during this accepted time, in virtue of the sacrifice of Jesus Christ for the sins of the world,—and the second (viz. δικαιοσύνη) being the righteousness or character of God manifested in that act. The δικαίωσις is never said to be ἐκ πίστεως (by faith)—that is to

Now if this remission of sins had only regarded the sins which had been committed before the death of Jesus, his sacrifice would have been nothing to us who have lived since that event. Or if it regarded original sin only, and had not taken away the condemnation of our personal transgressions, it would in like manner say, it is independent of man's faith, and rests upon man during this life, whether he believes it or not. The δικαιοσύνη is said to be ἐκ πίστεως (by faith), not that God's character depends upon man's faith, but that this righteousness cannot enter into the man's heart, so as to become his character, except by his believing it, which he does in believing the act in which it is manifested. So it is by faith alone in the δικαίωσις that a man becomes righteous, or the subject of δικαιοσύνη; but it is simply in virtue of Christ's work, and independently of faith altogether, that the man is delivered from the imputation of sin, as becomes the subject of δικαίωσις. As our translators uniformly translate δικαίωσις *justification*, and δικαιοσύνη *righteousness*, they ought to have known that, although righteousness by faith is a Scripture doctrine, there is not the smallest shadow of such a doctrine in Scripture as justification by faith; taking justification to signify the judicial act which is expressed by δικαίωσις.

This confusion may, in some measure, have originated from there being but one verb answering to these two nouns, viz. δικαιοῦμαι, which verb may either signify "I am the subject of δικαίωσις," *i.e.* I am freed from the imputation of sin; or "I am the subject of δικαιοσύνη," *i.e.* I am made righteous. It was a great offence against grammar, as it has been an immense sin against the truth, on the part of our translators, to connect this verb exclusively with δικαίωσις by translating it *to justify*, or *to be justified*. They knew that there was no such thing as δικαίωσις ἐκ πίστεως, and that there was such a thing as δικαιοσύνη ἐκ πίστεως, and therefore they ought to have known that when δικαιοῦμαι appeared in connection with ἐκ πίστεως, it did not contain δικαίωσις but δικαιοσύνη. The context, if considered, will determine which of these nouns it does contain; but we may be sure, that wherever it is connected with ἐκ πίστεως it must mean "I am made righteous." This is the end and object of the whole matter, and for the accomplishment of have been nothing to us, for there is no other sacrifice, no other deliverance from condemnation revealed.

But it is evident from the argument in the beginning of the 10th chapter of the Epistle to the Hebrews, that the remission of sins is just as efficient prospectively as it is retrospectively. For there the proof given of the complete inefficiency of the legal sacrifice rests on the necessity of their yearly repetition. If these sacrifices really took away sin, the apostle reasons, would they not have ceased to be offered, because the worshipper, once purged, would have had no more conscience of sins? And the proof of the efficiency of Christ's sacrifice is that it was done *once for all*. "But now where remission of these is, there is no more offering for sin," *no more is required*.

And that personal sins are expressly included in the sacrifice is clear from Rom. v. 16. "For the judgment

this, the δικαίωσις has been ordained. The δικαίωσις answers to the universal atonement,—the δικαιοσύνη ἐκ πίστεως to the purging of the conscience, or the personal assurance; the one declares God the Saviour of all men—the other declares him the Saviour specially of those who believe. The sprinkling of the blood on the people, and the sprinkling of the water of separation, and the laying of the hands on the head of the victim, were all types of the purging of the conscience by faith; they did not refer to the δικαίωσις, but to the δικαιοσύνη ἐκ πίστεως; they did not add to the sacrifice, they only taught that no man could truly worship God until he was righteous, or had his conscience purged, by knowing that he was forgiven. Compare on this point especially Numbers xix. with Hebrews ix. and x., from the comparison of which passages it appears that the *cleansing* in Numbers does not refer to the putting away of a condemnation, but is simply the type of the purging of the conscience, by the belief of a bypast atonement. I beg my reader to weigh this note.

was by one (or after one offence) to condemnation, but the free gift is after *many* offences unto justification." These *many* offences must be personal, for there is only *one* original sin.

But all perplexity on this matter arises from not seeing, that as Christ died as the head of the race, so he rose as the head of the race. He rose as the justified head of the race, with the mark of the cross upon him, showing that the penalty had been sustained by the *race* in the person of their head. Had the first man risen again after his death, his resurrection would naturally have been considered by all his posterity as the pledge of their own resurrection, because their own liability to death arose from their connection with him and his offence. And as death was the condemnation of his offence, his resurrection would necessarily have been regarded as a declaration and a proof that the condemnation on the race was taken away. And thus the intelligence, "Adam is risen," proclaimed amongst the families of his children, would have been received as an entire equivalent to the news that "sin was forgiven." Jesus rose as the *second Adam*, and this is the good news to every creature, "Him hath God raised from the dead;" and "through him forgiveness is proclaimed." And it is not a forgiveness that requires a continual renewal. That would not have suited us. What we needed was something very different from an occasional clearing away of accounts and charges against us. We needed *a dispensation of forgiveness*, a dispensation the character of which might be, that there should be no condemnation in it, no imputation of sin in it. For we were dead in sins, and there is life in God's forgiving favour *alone;* there is no other atmosphere in which the soul can live. There is no other dispensation which can be a dispensation of life to us, than a dispensation of the forgiving favour of God resting upon us, altogether independent of our deservings or undeservings. A man may doubtless be enclosed in the favour of God, and yet remain dead, in consequence of his ignorance and blindness to that favour; but unless that favour is actually resting upon him, it is impossible that he can have life, for life consists in that favour being received into his heart, and he cannot receive it unless it is there. A man may be surrounded with light and yet be in darkness, by shutting his eyes; but the opening of his eyes cannot give him sight, unless there be light actually upon him, unless the light be there.

It is not an occasional wiping off the scores that lie against us, that will suit our need; we must have a settled unwavering dispensation of forgiving favour, in which our souls may live and breathe as our bodies breathe in the wholesome atmosphere which surrounds us. And this we could only have through a Head— a righteous Head in whom we are represented and contained,—a righteous Head on whom the approving smile and favour of God ever rests, and from whom that oil of joy descends even to the skirts of his clothing—the meanest of the race, independently of all their undeservings.

The object was that we should be made partakers of the life of God, of the holy, righteous, spiritual life of God; but we could not have this life unless the holy righteous love of God rested on us in the form of favour, and that could not be whilst we were dealt with according to our own deserts. And therefore God planned the dispensation of the righteous Head, during which his favour should rest on men, not according to their own deserts, but according to the deserts of Jesus Christ.

"For God sent not his Son into the world to condemn (judge) the world, but that the world through him should be saved." The time is coming and is at hand, when Jesus will come *to judge* and reign, but as yet he is only manifested as the *Saviour* or righteous Head. This dispensation of the righteous Head is preparatory to the dispensation of judgment, the dispensation of the kingdom. It is the same thing as "the accepted time and day of salvation." It is preparatory to the dispensation of the kingdom, when men will be judged according to the use that they have made of the righteous Head—according to the use which they have made of the light which has been resting on them so long.

It is of great importance to understand the nature of this "accepted time and day of salvation." It is a time when sinners are not treated as sinners; it is a time when men are not treated as individuals, but as members of the righteous Head. It is as it were a space walled off from the regular and direct action of the principles of God's government, not for the purpose of evading them, but for the purpose of putting a race of creatures, who by sin had become incapable of anything but enmity and wretchedness under their regular and direct action, into the condition of again loving them and rejoicing in them, which is the same thing as loving God and rejoicing in him.

This appointment has been made for a very different end than that of evading the moral principles of God's government. Indeed there has been a manifestation of these principles in the work on which the appointment is founded, more striking and more glorious than ever has been made in the universe before, and it is the object of the appointment, that through this manifestation, the very life and character of God should be infused into men. During this accepted time Christ says to all prisoners, "Go forth;"[1] to all who are in darkness, "Show yourselves." He proclaims "liberty to the captive, and the opening of the prison to them that are bound." This is "the acceptable year of the Lord" (Isaiah xlix. 8; lx. 1). But when this "accepted time" is ended, every man shall be judged according to his own actual character.

It is as if a violent and malicious man were placed in a society of gentle and loving persons, with this

[1] A man is not a prisoner merely by being in a prison, but because he is in it by the restraint of law. The condemnation lies in this restraint; when the restraint is removed, the condemnation no longer exists. And therefore when it is said to a prisoner by a rightful authority, "Go forth," in truth it is said to him, "Thy sins are forgiven; thou art no longer under condemnation."

intimation, "You are placed here for a year, and during that time nothing that you have hitherto been shall ever be remembered, and every act of violence which you may commit shall be met with love, and every offence shall be met with forgiveness. At the end of the period you shall be tried, and if you shall be found to have acquired the life of love, you shall remain always as a member of that gentle society in an increasing happiness, but if you shall be found still to be possessed by the spirit of malice, you shall be cast into outer darkness."

And so Paul gives this as the reason of his great urgency in preaching the gospel: "We must all appear before the judgment-seat of Christ, that every one may receive the things done in the body, whether they be good or bad. Knowing therefore the terror of the Lord, we persuade men." Then he declares the gospel, viz., "that God was in Christ" (the righteous head) "reconciling the world unto himself, not imputing unto them their trespasses;" and then he beseeches men not to receive it in vain, "*for now is the accepted time, now is the day of salvation.*" You are now within the walled city; hear and your soul shall live; but beware, the night cometh when no man can work. The time is at hand when you must appear before the judgment-seat of Christ, to be judged according to the things done in the body, and this is the great work of God, that ye believe on him whom he hath sent (2 Cor. v. 10, 11, 19; vi. 1, 2). This is the same thing as that which our Lord says, "Strive to enter in at the strait gate; for many shall seek to enter in and shall not be able, when once the master of the house is risen up, and hath shut-to the door."

When forgiveness is spoken of in the Bible as a future thing, it will be generally found that the reference is to the announcement of the sentence of acquittal or condemnation on that day when we shall all appear before the judgment-seat of Christ.

We are placed in these present favourable circumstances, to the end that we may have *life* by the knowledge of the only true God, and Jesus Christ whom he has sent. And if this purpose is accomplished in us, we are so made meet for the inheritance of the saints in light, when the kingdom comes. But if this purpose is not accomplished in us during this period, then when that kingdom which is a kingdom *of life* shall appear, we being spiritually dead shall be treated as strangers to it, and enemies to it. "As for those mine enemies that would not that I should reign over them, bring them hither and slay them before me."

Now it was by the sufferings unto death, which he endured as the Head of the race, that Jesus merited and gained the high glory of being raised from the dead as the righteous Head of the race, in honour of whom and in virtue of their connection with whom, sin is forgiven to men, and is not imputed to them, during the whole dispensation of "the accepted time and day of salvation," which lasts till the time of judgment, or the removal of each man by death. We have seen that Christ is of the one lump, of the one mass;

that he is the root of the tree, and that in virtue of this oneness with all men, he felt with and in every man,—that he felt for every man's sin, and bare it on his own body on the tree. We have seen also that every suffering which he thus endured as the head contained in it an acting of holy love, and an acting of hatred against sin,—*a protest against sin*, the sin of that flesh which was *his own*, and of which he was the head. And so he says of himself, "I was also upright before him, and I kept myself from mine iniquity" (Psalm xviii. 23). And the Father approved and rewarded, for it is said, "Therefore hath the Lord recompensed me according to my *righteousness*, according to the cleanness of my hands in his eyesight." And what was that reward? "Therefore as by the *offence* of one, judgment came upon *all men* to *condemnation*, even so by the *righteousness* of one, the free gift came upon *all men* unto *justification of life* (Rom. v. 18). This is the constitution of the righteous head. It is, in fact, the kingly priesthood. Thus again, "Who shall ascend into the hill of the Lord? who shall stand in his holy place?" That is, who shall be king and priest? "He that hath clean hands, and a pure heart, and hath not lifted up his soul unto vanity, nor sworn deceitfully. *He* shall receive the *blessing* from the Lord, even *righteousness* from the God of his salvation." That is, he shall be the *righteous* head. The meaning of this is clearly, that the condemnation is taken away from the race of which he is the head. For he is here implicitly opposed to the first head and king, namely,

Adam, through whom the *curse* came, even *condemnation*, and now through *him* the second head and king the *blessing* comes, even *righteousness*. What can that mean, at the very least, but a deliverance from the curse, a deliverance from the condemnation? This king already had clean hands and a pure heart, so he had righteousness *personally*, and therefore the *blessing* of *righteousness* spoken of in the passage must refer to something else; and what else can it refer to but to that very fact declared in the passage quoted from the Epistle to the Romans, "As by the offence of one, judgment came upon all men to condemnation, even so by the righteousness of one the free gift came upon all men to justification of life"? Compare this with 2 Cor. iii. 7-9, where the gospel is called the ministration of *righteousness*, in opposition to the law, which is called the ministration of *condemnation*. This can signify nothing else but that the distinguishing feature of the gospel dispensation is *condemnation removed*. And this is the very thing which makes it a dispensation of *life*, in opposition to the law which was a dispensation of *death*, just from the want of a righteousness; for it is written (Gal. iii. 21), "If there had been a law given capable of giving life, verily there would have been a righteousness provided in it." And this is the thing done in the establishment of the righteous head. Now these passages do not mean that, because all men are under the dispensation of the gospel, therefore they are all saved,—they only mean that all men, during this dispensation, are treated as the members of the righteous head; that is, that from all men, during this *dispensation*, the condemnation, which their character deserves, is withdrawn, and that on all men the light of God's forgiving love is shining; and as that light is life, every one whose eye is opened to the light receives life, and becomes a living and an abiding member of Jesus Christ; whilst those who continue blind to it shut out the life, and remain dead, and exposed to condemnation, when the time of judgment comes.

The light can only enter into my eye by being first on my eye; and as the light of life is just *God's favour*, in which alone there is life, that favour must first be *upon* a man, before it can be *in* him, as life. And it is written, that this light lighteth or shineth on *every man;* and now the condemnation is, that, though the light hath come into the world, yet men have loved darkness rather than light. This light of God's forgiveness, then upon the race, shining in the righteous head, is the *blessing* in opposition to the *condemnation*,—"the blessing in which all the families of the earth are blessed."

But, my dear reader, you would see that this must be so, if you rightly apprehend the oneness of the nature, and its perfect representation in the person of its head. The Bible speaks of the human nature as being the unfolding of Adam, just as an oak is the unfolding of an acorn. And it speaks of Adam as the type of Christ; it speaks of Adam as the *first* man, and then of Christ as the *second* man. Now, he could be the *second* man in no other sense than as the second representative, the second root. And that this is the literal meaning of these expressions is abundantly proved from the Scripture generally, but especially from Rom. v.; 1 Cor. xv.; Heb. ii.; and the Epistles to the Ephesians and Colossians. Now, what is or was the condemnation? There can be no condemnation on me personally for belonging to a fallen nature. I could not help it. No one could; and, therefore, it is no one's personal sin, except Adam's. But even the absence of personal sin could not, and did not, deliver from the condemnation. Adam sinned, and was condemned; and we are unfoldings of Adam, and in him we were condemned. He was "*the one man* through whose offence the judgment came upon all men to condemnation." He was the unrighteous head,—the froward head, with whom God showed himself froward. Christ came into Adam's place; and he was the righteous head whom God recompensed according to his righteousness. He was "the one man through whose righteousness the judgment came upon all men unto justification of life."

Now mark, as in the dispensation of the fall, the condemnation was upon all men irrespective of their personal sinfulness or sinlessness, just because they were under the *unrighteous* head; so in the dispensation of the gospel, the forgiveness is upon all men irrespective of their personal characters, just because they are under the *righteous* head. And this constitution has been made by the love which passeth knowledge, to the end that the righteousness of the head might enter into the members, and become their life, as it is the life of the head, yea the life of God. For this light of forgiving love and favour, which shines upon the sinful fallen nature on account of Christ, and in the character of Christ's work, is nothing else than the very character, the very life of God, made intelligible and visible. The life became light; and, as light, it shines on every man; and thus the life of God is really given *to* every man. But it is not life *in* the man until he sees the light. Then the light returns into its original character, and becomes *life* again in his soul; and he becomes a habitation of God through the Spirit; he has fellowship with the Father and the Son.

This light of favour is upon every man, whether he sees it or not, just as the light of God's favour was upon Adam before his fall. Adam stood and lived as long as he looked at that light, and he fell into spiritual death just in shutting his eyes upon it. His sin consisted in shutting his eyes on that light. Had the light been withdrawn, his spiritual life must have ceased, but he would not have had any guilt, because he could not have helped it. His life depended on his beholding that light, and his guilt lay in his refusing or neglecting to behold it, when he might. Now observe, when he sinned he fell out of his dispensation; the light of God's favour was withdrawn, because that favour had respect to himself *personally*, and so when he personally offended, the favour was withdrawn. He had shut his eyes against the light, and the light was withdrawn, and therefore although he had immediately opened them again, he would still have found himself in darkness, for the light of God's favour is that love which rejoiceth in the truth, and when the truth had left man, God's love could no longer rejoice with him. It frowned.

But where sin abounded, grace hath much more abounded. The love of God, although it could not rejoice with man in his iniquity, did not cease to be love, and did not cease to desire that it might again rejoice over man, and that man might again have that truth in him over which and with which love might rejoice; and this was the work of love. God's love put the truth into man's nature; for he who was the truth, and who was God, and in whom and over whom the love of Jehovah continually rejoiceth, became the head of the human nature, and *in that character* he earned and obtained the favour of God. He became the righteous head on whom the favour of God ever rests, and from him that favour descends to every individual of the race, during the continuance of the dispensation, without respect to any deserving or undeserving, except only the deserving of the head.

So we are in a much better condition than Adam; for, first, the favour of redemption-love is much higher in its manifestation than the favour of creation-love, and therefore also the life received in the belief of it is proportionably higher; and then we cannot fall out of our dispensation whilst it lasts or we live; for the favour has not respect to ourselves personally, in which case we should be sure to lose it, but to our head, who is the Holy One. We are *always under forgiveness* for his sake. Before the fall, God only dwelt in man by his Spirit received through faith, and so whenever faith failed, the Spirit was shut out, and man fell. But now Christ is God permanently united to the flesh; we cannot shut him out of the flesh by unbelief, and thus whilst we continue in this dispensation we cannot fall, for falling is being cut off from God, which we cannot be, seeing Christ is in our flesh.

But as the love is of greater manifestation than that to Adam, so our sin in despising it is proportionally greater, and God cannot look upon it without grief and displeasure; but yet during the continuance of this dispensation, it is a sin which does not, any more than other sins, interrupt the forgiving favour, which never ceases to flow from the righteous head. If persevered in till the end of life, it will then be our condemnation. Light rejected is the condemnation. My guilt does not lie in being a fallen creature, I was born so, and *now* if there were no favour upon me, I could have no more guilt in being spiritually dead than I should in being physically dead, were I in a place destitute of vital air; my guilt, like Adam's, lies in wilfully shutting out life, by disbelieving the truth of God's love, when I might do otherwise. This is man's sin during the present dispensation. And it is the same sin, only of a deeper dye, than that by which Adam fell. We are too much in the habit of thinking that Adam's sin must have had something very peculiar in it, because it had such consequences; but his sin just lay in disbelieving the love of his dispensation, and therefore going out of it to look for a happiness, as our sin consists in disbelieving the love of our dispensation, and therefore going out of it to look for a happiness.

It was a great glory to God that the unfallen man needed nothing more in order to rejoice in him, and to remain conformed to his image, than just to know and remember the circumstances in which he actually was, even that creation-love of God which was his origin, and his provision, and his element. But it is a far higher glory to God, that the sinful fallen man needs only to know and remember the actual circumstances in which he always is, even the redemption-love which continually embraces him, in order to rejoice in God, and to become a partaker of his holiness, and of that very life which is in the Father and the Son, yea, to be a habitation of God through the Spirit.

It was a great glory to Joseph that his brethren needed only to know who it was before whom they were standing, full of sorrow and anxious foreboding, and what was in his heart, in order to be at once delivered from all their sorrows and all their anxieties. And what a glory it is to our elder brother that we, who are by nature alienated from God, and have been enemies to him by wicked works, and have therefore been regarding him with dark suspicion and fear, and have been cherishing in our own hearts the principle of sorrow which worketh death,—that we have just to know who Jesus is, and what he hath done, that he is Jehovah in our nature, that he hath put away sin by the sacrifice of himself, and that he hath risen again in the character of our righteous Head, having the Holy Spirit for us,—in order to be at peace with God, and to be delivered from the bondage of corruption into the glorious liberty of the sons of God.

They who believe this enter into *rest;* they cease from their own works, as God did from his (Heb. iv. 3, 10). This is the keeping of God's Sabbath. Adam broke the first Sabbath, by endeavouring to make for himself a happiness and an advancement independent of that creation-love which was given him as his provision. He thus broke the *rest,* he ceased not from his own works. He endeavoured to provide for himself, and thus he ceased to be the receiver and the enjoyer of a provision already provided.

Man was never called on to make a provision for himself; he was called on to live by a provision of God's providing; and his sin has always been, a refusing to live by God's provision, and a persisting to make a provision for himself.

This was Adam's sin, and this is just the sin of unbelief under our dispensation. The man who is seeking to obtain a pardon, or the favour of God, or an interest in the atonement of Christ, as if these blessings were not already bestowed, is not ceasing from his own works, nor keeping within God's provision, nor keeping God's rest; he is denying the constitution of the righteous Head, in which all these things have been freely given him richly to enjoy, and thus he is polluting God's Sabbath, and he is making God a liar by disbelieving the record, that God hath given to us eternal life in his Son.

They who believe not this record shut out the *life*, and so they belong not to that house which is composed of *living* stones, which "house are we, *if we hold fast the confidence and rejoicing of the hope unto the end.*"

Understand this. Adam was not called to make for himself a provision by dressing the garden and keeping it; no, but he was called on to do this work in the strength of the provision which God had made for him. Even so we are not called on to make to ourselves a provision, by dressing and keeping our own hearts, the gardens which God has committed to our care; but we are called on to do this work in the strength of the provision which God has made for us. Adam's provision was creation-love, our provision is redemption-love.

And mark. The claim of work is always founded on the provision, in the strength of which it is to be done. And the condemnation arises simply out of the contempt of that provision. And thus the claim of the law is now founded on the provision of the gospel. Men mistake, and think that they are called on to *make* the provision, instead of *living* and *working* by it.

Dear reader, let us give glory to God by rejoicing in his provision; we do not need anything which he has not given us. Let us join in with our Head when he says, "What shall I render unto the Lord for all his benefits towards me? I will *receive the cup of salvation,* and call on the name of the Lord." He has given us the Holy Spirit in Jesus; let us be filled with the Spirit, let us give place to the Spirit, and not grieve him.

Those who believe not, and therefore enter not into rest, but continue to "make haste," are those "who err in their hearts, and know not God's ways." Now what are God's ways? After the rebellion in the matter of the golden calf, Moses said to the Lord, " I beseech thee show me now thy *way;*" and the Lord answered him, " My presence shall go with thee, and I will give thee *rest*." And from what occurs afterwards it appears that the *presence*, and the *way*, and the *glory*, and the *goodness* and the *name* of God, are all one thing, and that is his *living character;* "The Lord God, merciful and gracious, forgiving iniquity, transgression, and sin, without clearing the guilty." So it was their ignorance of this *way* of God that kept them from rest. They erred in their hearts, not knowing this way (Exod. xxxiii. and xxxiv.; Psalm xcv.; Heb. iii.)

In the 55th of Isaiah the gospel is proclaimed, and men are called on by it, not to do anything, nor to provide anything, but to enjoy a provision already made, even that rich provision which is set forth in the two preceding chapters. "Ho, every one that thirsteth, come ye to these waters." The *wicked*—who are addressed in the seventh verse, "let the wicked forsake his way"—are described in the second verse to be just those who will not enjoy God's provision, and who persist in going out of it in search of happiness. This is their *way*, and they are urged to forsake this way, and instead of it to take God's way, which is not as their way, a barren wilderness, but is in truth the full fountain of love, whose waters satisfy. Let them turn to this fountain, to this way of God, and they will find it a way of mercy and of abundant pardon; its waters fail not. The wicked, then, are those who believe not that the Lord hath laid their iniquities on Jesus, and who, therefore, drink not at that fountain; they are those who know not the way or name of God, and who are therefore spending money for that which is not bread (verse 2). They cease not from their own works. And whilst they continue to do so, they are like the troubled sea that cannot *rest*, whose waters cast up mire and dirt. In the following chapter there is an urgent exhortation to keep the *Sabbath* from polluting it, which appears to be just an exhortation to enjoy the gospel provision, and to enter into God's rest by ceasing from our own works. The sixth verse of this 56th chapter gives confirmation to this view, for in it loving the name of the Lord, keeping the Sabbath from polluting it, and taking hold of God's covenant, are spoken of as if they were the *same things*.

Yes, we need only to know and to remember the circumstances in which the love of God has placed us, in order to have life, and peace, and holiness; and so it is said, "This is life eternal, *to know thee* the only true God, and Jesus Christ whom thou hast sent;" and it is also said, "He that lacketh godliness, brotherly kindness, and charity, lacketh them because he is blind, shutting his eyes against the light, *having forgotten* that he was purged from his old sins." Now, as it is the *beginning* of our confidence which we are called on to hold fast unto the end, this purging from sin, or the atonement, as including ourselves personally, must be *the first thing to be believed by every one*, and to be believed as a past truth, true to every one. It is not a personal experience of the believer which is the foundation of his confidence, although it be only through that personal experience that he knows it; it is the atonement,—the righteous Head; it is a thing done for all. And thus it is, and thus only, that the salvation of the gospel is a salvation by faith. A man is saved by coming *to the knowledge of the truth*—of what is and has been always true. If a man's circumstances were such, that the knowledge of them would not be life and joy to him, he never could be saved by faith, because he never could be saved by coming to the knowledge of the truth concerning them; he would need to make *a change*, and that would destroy it as a salvation by faith. But the work is completed; nothing can be added or need be added to it; and now it is only "through the ignorance that is in us, that we are alienated from the life of God;" for he hath created the fruit of the lips, that is, he hath given cause for thanksgiving, by giving to every man Jesus, who is the peace— peace to him that is far off, and to him that is nigh, even a healing peace (Isaiah lvii. 19).

Jesus has taken our flesh, and become one flesh with us, in order that we might be one spirit with him. These are the two bonds. All men are necessarily connected with him by the first bond, namely, the flesh; and all who believe in the love which produced that first bond become connected with him by the second, namely, the Spirit, and these only. And the gospel consists in explaining what the manner of love is, which connected every man with Jesus, by the first bond, namely, the flesh, and what it did for each man, when it established that connection.

Now the manner of the love we have seen to be this—that God so loved every man, that, in order to destroy the work of the devil in him, he was willing to die for him, and that he so loved every man, that he desired fellowship and union with him, in the spirit of holiness.

And that which the love did for each man, when it established the connection of the first bond, namely, of the flesh, between him and Christ, is, that during this present dispensation of "the accepted time and day of salvation," sin is not imputed to him, and Christ is truly given to him as his head (for "the head of every man is Christ"), in whom he has a standing in the favour of God, and the Spirit, or eternal life, which he will receive according to his faith.

And the man has not to make anything in the matter; he has just to acknowledge or believe what God has done. And this belief will open his heart to let in the life, the spirit. And thus he becomes connected with Christ by the bond of the Spirit; he becomes a living member of the righteous head—an heir of the righteousness which is by faith; he is reckoned righteous—not in virtue of something put *upon* him, as in the bond of the flesh, but of something *within* him, even the life of God, and that life is righteousness.

And as the belief of what God has given us in the flesh of Christ lets in this blessed life, so the unbelief of it shuts out the life and the righteousness, and the man remains unconnected with Christ by the Spirit; he remains dead in his sins and in his unrighteousness.

And here is a remarkable thing. Those who are connected with Christ by the Spirit are living members, and they shall be raised to the resurrection of life, which is the first resurrection *by the Spirit that dwelleth in them*, see Rom. viii. 11, Rev. xx. 6. And those who are not connected with Christ by the Spirit shall be raised also, but not to the resurrection of life, nor by the Spirit, for they have it not, but, it would seem, simply by their connection with his flesh, to be judged for their contempt of all that was contained in that connection.

And as the connection with Christ by the second bond, namely, of the Spirit, is just the same thing as being born of the Spirit, or having the life from above, the everlasting life,—so those who are thus connected with the Head see the kingdom of God, and shall enter into it when it comes, whilst those who are not thus connected with him cannot see that kingdom, and cannot enter into it. But yet so long as they continue living in this dispensation, they do not fall out of the forgiving love of God, which rests upon the righteous Head, and descends from him, on all the body, quite irrespective of the character of the individuals; and, although of a truth God's eye sees and condemns every form of sin, in every heart, and especially condemns the unbelief which rejects his love, and thus shuts out the life, yet this condemnation is not the imputation of sin, it is the displeasure of a Father because his children will not believe that he loves and forgives them.

Had an Israelite, after he had been bitten, refused to look *immediately* at the serpent, he certainly would not have been cured *immediately*. But his delaying to do so did not destroy the virtue of the serpent; and did not disqualify him from looking afterwards at it so long as life lasted. No doubt God condemned him for not looking at it, but this condemnation was the disapproving love of a friend, and not the sentence of a judge removing him from the serpent, or withdrawing its healing virtue with respect to him. The interval between the bite and the death, or the removal of the serpent, was the accepted time and day of salvation, during which he might look and be healed. Whilst life lasted, his not looking would prevent a cure, but it would not throw him out of the dispensation of forgiveness.

The first bond, namely, that of the flesh, is the provision which God has made for every man, and it lasts during this life or this dispensation, with all that is contained in it. And we have seen that the favour of God flowing from the righteous Head, and the non-imputation of sin, are specially contained in it, as coming on all, whether believers or unbelievers, just in virtue of this oneness with Christ in the flesh. And we have further seen that the knowledge of this bond produces the second bond, namely, that of the Spirit, which is life everlasting. The preaching, therefore, of this first bond of the flesh is, in fact, the preaching of the gospel; it is the preaching of that provision, by the knowledge of which the creature becomes the habitation of God through the Spirit, and it is in the knowledge of this provision that the only true knowledge of God consists, for we can only know God aright when we know him who came in our flesh to declare the Father.

Every spirit that confesseth that Jesus Christ is come *in the flesh* is of God (1 John iv. 2). What is the meaning of this?

The view of the bond of the flesh which has been given throws a strong light on this remarkable word. For compare it with a passage in the first chapter of the Epistle to the Colossians. We may begin at verse 19th: "It pleased the Father, that in him should all fulness dwell: and having made peace through the blood of his cross, by him to reconcile all things unto himself; by him, I say, whether they be things in earth, or things in heaven. And you [Colossians] that were sometime alienated, and enemies in your mind by wicked works, yet now hath he reconciled in the body of his flesh through death [that is, he hath brought you into the first bond], to present you holy and unblamable and unreprovable in his sight [that is, in order to bring you into the bond of the Spirit which will take place and will hold] ; if ye continue in the faith grounded and settled, and be not moved away from the hope of the gospel, which ye have heard, and which was preached to every creature which is under heaven, whereof I Paul am made a minister,[1] according to the dispensation of God which is given to me for you, fully to preach the word of God, even the mystery which hath been hid from ages and from generations, but now is made manifest to his saints: whom God would have to make known amongst the Gentiles what are the riches of the glory of this mystery, which is, *Christ in you the hope of glory;* whom we preach, warning every man, and teaching every man in all wisdom, that we may present every man perfect in Christ Jesus."

Now it seems to me that there must be a denial of the obvious meaning of this passage, unless it be admitted that the gospel which Paul was intrusted to preach amongst the Gentiles, and which he did declare to every individual who heard him, whatever his character might be, was just this: " Christ is in thee the

---

[1] I have omitted the 24th verse, which is evidently parenthetic, in order to preserve the continuity of the passage. And I have made a slight alteration on the 27th verse, which is justified by the original, and is a clearing of the sense. The reader who understands Greek will see that the relative pronoun in the beginning of the verse is put in the dative, instead of the accusative, according to that common Grecism, by which the relative, instead of being put in the case governed by the verb, is put in that which agrees with the antecedent. Unless this is admitted, an evident tautology in the text must be admitted. I have also given the marginal reading of the 25th verse, instead of that in the text.

hope of glory." This, he tells us, is the gospel which was preached *to every creature* under heaven, or in the whole creation under heaven. This must then be the true description of God's unspeakable gift to every creature, of his gift actually bestowed upon each one individual. For it never could be gospel or good news to one man to tell him that Christ was in another man, or in another class of men. It never could have been good news to other Gentiles to have told them that Christ was in the Colossian converts. This could not have done them any good. No; it was a message to themselves that Paul brought them—a message to each man—a Christ to each man—a Christ in each man, the hope of glory. Behold the riches of the glory of the gospel of Jesus —of that mystery which had been hid by the counsel of God from ages and from generations, before the manifestation of God in the flesh—and which since that manifestation has been much hid by unbelief—but which nevertheless remains true, the great truth, the mighty secret, proclaimed from the house-tops, and yet a secret.

But reader, you start at this, as if it were rather to be desired or wondered at, than to be believed as an actual fact. Yet only consider, we are assured, in the fifth chapter of the Romans, and fifteenth of 1st Corinthians that Jesus Christ came into Adam's place—actually into that place which Adam held in relation to us— into the root of the nature. Well, is Adam in you or not? Yes, most assuredly he is. Adam is in every man, just because every man is a mere unfolding of Adam, as the branch of a tree is a mere unfolding of the seed out of which the tree sprung. Adam is in you. Well, Christ is in you also, for he came into Adam's place. And as the condemnation which came by Adam, even sorrow and death, is upon you, so also is the blessing which came by Christ upon you, even the favour of God, and the non-imputation of sin, which, if believed, are life eternal.

But perhaps you will say, If a man does not hope in Christ, how can Christ be in him as the hope of glory? But this is a common use of the word Hope. God is called the hope of Israel even when Israel did not hope in him, and the hope of all the ends of the earth, although they had never heard of him. The hope of glory means the future glorious deliverer. If you see a child of remarkable promise in a decayed family, although the rest of the family do not appreciate him, you will say of him, There is the hope of the family. He is a reason of hope, though they do not see it. Even so Christ is in our decayed fallen family the hope of glory, though little appreciated, and he is in each one of the family, though unknown and unnoticed. Yes, reader, Christ is in you, the hope of glory, and you shall be presented holy and unblamable and unreprovable in the sight of the Father, if you continue in this *faith*, grounded and settled, and be not moved away from this *hope* of the gospel which ye have heard.

This is the gospel. This is that provision in the strength of which we are called on to be holy as God is holy, to be perfect in love as God is perfect, to be habitations of God through the Spirit. Consider this call, this commandment of God, and think whether it could be possible to answer it on any lower provision than this, "Christ in you the hope of glory." We are called on to have the same mind in us as was in Christ Jesus, and yet the Spirit witnesses of the carnal mind, which is the natural mind of every man, that it is enmity against God. Now God's service is a reasonable service. Yet how is this reasonable? How is it reasonable to ask love from enmity? The reasonableness of the call lies in this, "Christ in us the hope of glory." And the Scripture tells us that we have all things that pertain unto life and godliness, in the knowledge of him who hath called us to glory and virtue. It is in the knowledge then of Jesus himself *in us* that we have the mind of Jesus, which is life and godliness, and glory and virtue.

The preaching then of "Christ in you the hope of glory," is just the preaching of that *first* bond by which all men are united to Christ, namely, the bond of the flesh. It is preaching God tabernacled in the flesh of every man. For what is true of the whole race is true of every individual in the race. Each man is a microcosm, a miniature of the world and of the race, and therefore when we hear of Christ coming into the flesh of our race, we in fact hear of his coming into the flesh of every man. When we hear of God *so* loving the world, we hear of his *so* loving each man of the world. It is just the root of the vine being in every one of its branches, in virtue of its fibres pervading all the branches, the withered as well as the living. Remember, Christ came into Adam's place. This is the real substitution.

The power of the gospel lies in the union between God and the fallen nature of man revealed in it, and this union is called the *mystery*. "Great is the *mystery* of godliness, God manifest in the flesh" (1 Tim. iii. 16). The same apostle in his Epistle to the Romans says of himself, that he was "separated unto the gospel of God concerning his Son, Jesus Christ our Lord, who was made of the seed of David according to the flesh, and declared to be the Son of God with power, according to the spirit of holiness, by the resurrection from the dead, for the obedience of faith among all nations" (Rom. i. 3, 4, 5). And at the conclusion of the Epistle he calls this same truth "the revelation of the *mystery* which was kept secret since the world began, but now is made known to all nations for the obedience of faith" (xvi. 25, 26). This is just the *mystery* he speaks of to the Colossians in the expression, "Christ in you the hope of glory;" and to the Ephesians (iii. 6), when he tells them "that God by revelation made known to me the *mystery* which in other ages was not made known unto the sons of men, as it is now revealed unto the holy apostles and prophets by the Spirit, that the Gentiles *are* (εἶναι not *should be*) fellow-heirs and of the *same body* (σύσσωμα), and partakers of his promise in Christ." "And unto me is this grace given, that I should preach among the Gentiles the unsearchable riches of Christ and to make all men see what is the commonness (fellowship) of the mystery." Now the mystery is, Christ in the flesh; and the apostle here says, that he was commissioned to instruct all men in the *commonness* of this mystery, that is, to show them *that they were all sharers in it,* that it was no partial gift having relation to one man, and not to another. If you read these passages in the light of the love which gave Christ to the world, and if you carry along with you the fact that Christ came into the place of Adam, and that Christ's relation to the whole race is really his relation to each individual of the race, you will see in them, what will put your feet in a large place, you will see what will give you an assured confidence before God and good hope of glory. You will understand by them that God is saying to each of us as he said to Moses, "My presence shall go with you, and I will give you rest." You will see what will make you come with all boldness and child-like confidence unto God your Father, praying him that he would glorify his Son in you, by filling you with the Spirit and the life of his Son. For it is but a fibre of Christ that is in you until you have his spirit, and you cannot have his spirit until you know the love that gave him into your flesh, and unto death for you.

Read over the third chapter of the Epistle to the Ephesians carefully, and observe how Paul, after having said that the great matter which God had commissioned him to preach was the *fellowship of the mystery*, or that Christ was in the flesh of every man, yet goes on to say, that the great subject of his prayers for them was "that Christ might dwell in their hearts by faith," that so they might comprehend the love of God, and be filled with the fulness of God." Christ was in their flesh whether they believed it or not; but until they knew it, they could not comprehend the height and depth of the love of God, in the knowledge of which is eternal life, and therefore he desired for them that they should know it, that thus they might be filled with all the fulness of God. He desired for them that God would do in them what he had done in himself, even that he would reveal his Son in them (Gal. i. 16), and thus show them the things which were freely given them of God; *not that he would put his Son into them, but reveal him in them.* This is the connection of every man with the unsearchable riches of Christ, and it is by showing this connection that the Spirit gives us the conscious participation in these riches.

Reader, do you see this mighty thing? Until you *know* this gift of love, although Christ be in you, yet you are without Christ; and though the hope of glory be in you, yet you are without hope. But mark this awful thing: although by unbelief you may shut out the life and the blessing, you cannot shut out the responsibility. Christ is in you, and remains in you, during the accepted time and day of salvation; and if, through all this day of grace, you shut out the life, you shall be judged as one who has put from him eternal life, and who has trodden under foot the Son of God. You shall be judged not merely as one who is dead in sin, but as one who is wilfully dead, when he had life given him. "Christ in us" is the pound given to every man, and he who wraps it in a napkin shall, when the time of judgment comes, be condemned for having done so. It was this in him which put it in his power to be no longer under the dominion of sin; and he has made the pound of none effect by his unbelief. And this therefore is the condemnation. The light, which is the Lamb of God that taketh away the sin of the world, has come into the world, and has shone on every man; and men have loved darkness rather than light, because their deeds were evil. If Christ, in whom alone there is life, had not been given to us, we should most assuredly have continued dead in trespasses and sins; but we should have been so by the necessity of our condition, independently of our own evil choice,—we should not have had this heavy weight of personal responsibility; but now that God hath come in our nature—now that Christ is in us, the hope of glory; now that in him, as our Head, all fulness dwells for us, are we not verily without excuse? Yea, if we be found without life, it will then be said, "Take from him the pound"—"thou oughtest to have given my money to the exchangers." " God *hath given* to us eternal life." And the question in the judgment will be, What have you done with it? If you have it not, where is it? God saith that he hath given it to you. Have you trod it under foot? have you wrapped it in a napkin? have you put it from you?

The Psalms are just the cry of the Christ, crying out of the human nature. " Out of the depths have I cried unto thee." They are his cry to the Father to take his part, and to subdue all his enemies in that corrupt mass of the flesh to which he had in holy love united himself.

They are the cry of his holy soul, broken with the reproach thrown upon God, and with the longing which he had to God's judgments and precepts at all times. Now, remember the precious principle, that what is true of the nature is true of each individual. These cries of Christ are his cries out of each of us; they are the cries of the Christ in us—our hope of glory. And it ought to be our one business, and our one honour, to take part with these cries, and in the faith of the Christ given to us, to open our mouths wide that we may receive the Spirit which is given to us in him. "Send forth thy light and thy truth, quicken me with thy free Spirit." "Open thou mine eyes, that I may see wonderful things in thy law." "My flesh trembleth for fear of thee, and I am afraid of thy judgments;" "build thou the walls of Jerusalem." "O that men would praise the Lord for his goodness!" These are the strong cryings of the Christ in us. And it ought to be our one longing that Jesus may be satisfied by seeing of the travail of his soul in ourselves and our race, and that thus the Father may be glorified, and his will done in us. And this will be, when it is no more we that live, but Christ living in us; when the flesh falls off as crucified and dead, and Christ within us appears in his beauty, and we be clothed on with our house which is from heaven.

The process by which this is accomplished is a continual fellowship with the sufferings of Christ; a continual rejection of evil, or grieving over its power; a continual protest for God against the devil, and the world, and the flesh. This, I say, is the *process* by which it is accomplished. But the *power* by which the process is carried on, and the work is accomplished, is "Christ in you the hope of glory." This is the supply—this is the provision of life and strength. It is neither life nor strength to the man who disbelieves it, as the sun is not light to the man who shuts his eyes; but yet it is life and strength given to him, and which he may use if he will, and for the use of which he will be judged.

"Christ in you the hope of glory," then, is the gospel to every man, for it is the description of the first bond, namely, that of the flesh, by which every individual of the race is united to Christ. "Christ dwelling in your hearts by faith" is the second bond, namely, that of the Spirit, by which those only who believe in the truth are united to him; and without which the other bond will at last bring against unbelievers the charge of love, and power, and bliss rejected—when the time of judgment comes.

This union of God with the whole fallen nature in the person of Christ is the great matter in God's dealings with men. It is the foundation of the constitution of the *righteous Head*, and so it appears as the title or epigraph to the Epistle to the Romans, which chiefly refers to that constitution. And it is also the foundation of the priesthood of Christ, and therefore it stands at the front of the Epistle to the Hebrews, which treats of the priesthood. The priest was necessarily *of one, i.e.* of the same blood and family and relationship with those for whom he acted. And, therefore it was on this account further necessary, that the true Melchisedek—the King of righteousness—or righteous head, who was also the High Priest over the household of God, should be every man's brother. See Heb. ii. 11-15, "For both he that sanctifieth, and they who are sanctified, *are all of one;*" " forasmuch then as the children are partakers of flesh and blood, he also himself likewise took *part of the same,* that through death he might destroy him that had the power of death, that is, the devil, and deliver them who through fear of death were all their lifetime subject to bondage." It appears from this, that Christ came to deliver those who were liable to Satan's power and to the fear of death. Now, does this description apply to any particular class of persons? No, it is applicable to every human being. All are subject to the assaults of that subtle and powerful foe; and all who know not the better resurrection are subject to the fear of death, that is, all men naturally. So Christ came into the nature of all men, as the deliverer of all men. This proves the extent of that word a little above, " he tasted death for every man ;" and he is now in the flesh of every man as the High Priest for every man. He is *of one* with them all. They are all connected with him by the common bond of the flesh, to the end that they may be connected with him by the bond of the Spirit. This is the manner of love which the Father hath bestowed on us, in order that we should be called or become the sons of God. The *manner* of love is declared in the first bond—the *purpose* of that love is declared in the second, that we should become the sons of God—born of the Spirit.

The spirit or teacher, then, *that confesseth that Jesus*

Christ is come in the flesh, is one who teaches that, by the incarnation of the Son of God, every man is connected with Christ by the bond of the flesh, and, in virtue of that connection, is embraced by the favour of God, and is freed from the imputation of guilt during this dispensation; and that in the knowledge of the love which constituted this bond, and which hath accomplished the atonement through it, there is everlasting life. The doctrine of the human nature of Jesus Christ is just an exposition of the *manner* of God's love to every man. God *so* loved the world, as to give His only begotten Son; and the object of that love is, that men should, by the belief of this great gift, receive everlasting life, and become the sons of God. And thus "God is the Saviour of all men, especially of those who believe" (1 Tim. iv. 10).

"And every spirit that confesseth not that Jesus Christ is come in the flesh, is not of God; and this is that spirit of antichrist whereof ye have heard that it should come, and even now already is in the world." Brethren, beware, and know where you are treading, and pull off your shoes from your feet, for it is holy ground.

CHAPTER IV.

CHRIST THE CONQUEROR.

Let us now look back, and gather up what we have seen in the sufferings of Christ, and consider how the principle of the brazen serpent is contained and explained in them.

The murmuring and rebellious Israelites had their souls healed as soon as they understood that the sufferings of the wilderness—although the consequences of disobedience, and therefore penal—were yet sent by a God who not only loved them, but who actually had forgiven them, and who, through the sorrows and death to which they were doomed, would train them in a meetness for a higher blessedness in another age or dispensation. The hope inspired in the Israelites by the serpent lifted up must have been the hope of a better resurrection—it could have been no other; for they knew that they were to die in the wilderness: God had said it. And therefore the life which was indicated to them in the serpent, as to arise out of their vanquished enemy, was necessarily a life that was to arise out of, or at least to be perfected by, death.

It was a life which was to be enjoyed not in that wilderness, and yet they were to die in that wilderness; so it must have been a resurrection-life—a life after death.

The material type indicates the same thing. The hurtful serpents were not removed, but the healing serpent was raised. Thus God's forgiveness in this present dispensation does not consist in the removal of a penalty.[1]

[1] And I may be allowed here just to observe, that there is something very monstrous and absurd in the supposition that the early revelations of God did not contain the doctrine of a future state, or rather of a resurrection. The Bible commences with an account of the entrance of death into the world, as an unnatural thing, as a work of the devil, as a penalty on rebellion; and the whole of the after-contents of the Bible relate to the way in which God was to overcome this evil, and destroy this work of the devil. Man was created immortal, that is, with the assurance of life, unless he sinned; he sinned, and became mortal. Then there was a *deliverer* and *restorer* promised, who should *destroy* the work of the devil. What was he to deliver man from? Certainly, that evil thing which man had brought upon himself by listening to the devil—namely, death. And what was he to restore man to? Certainly that good thing which man had lost—namely, immortality, resurrection. Death was the palpable form in which the evil of man, and the work of the devil appeared. The seed of the woman was to destroy the evil. Wherever, therefore, the idea of a Deliverer or Saviour was suggested, there also was necessarily suggested the idea of a resurrection. And the Jews from the first knew the promise of the seed, and therefore they knew the resurrection. The Sadducees were infidels—they were theological philosophers; but the Jews in general regarded the Messiah, and the kingdom, and the resurrection, all as one thing. This is evident from the words of the thief on the cross, "Lord, remember me when thou comest into thy *kingdom*," and from the answer of Martha to Jesus. He had said, "I am the resurrection and the life; believest thou this?" She answered, "Yea, Lord, I believe that thou art the Christ;" as if she had said, Of course I believe that thou art the resurrection, for I know that thou art the Messiah.

I know that this is a great difficulty in the way of many. They ask, what is the meaning of pardon, if the penalty remains? Yet they would find an answer very near, if they would only consider a little. Sorrow and death are penal, and no man is freed from them in this state, be he a believer or an unbeliever. Yet there can be no doubt, and there is no doubt nor difference of opinion amongst those who receive the Bible as the word of God, as to the fact that *believers* are forgiven. So we have here, in the case of every believer, a proof that a penalty may, yea does, lie on a forgiven man during this dispensation. It is a characteristic feature of the "accepted time and day of salvation," which is only a preparatory dispensation, and God's dealings in it will not be fully cleared up until that which is perfect is come, when the mystery of God will be finished.

Those Israelites who, in the serpent lifted up, saw the assurance that the forgiving love of God, against which they had offended, and which seemed to have deservedly changed into an unforgiving displeasure, had not abandoned them, but was still upon them, and was watching over every step of that rough way, and was actually adapting every sorrow to the accomplishment of a gracious purpose towards them, which was no other than to make them meet for the resurrection blessedness; those who saw this saw the light of life, —they saw and lived—their souls were healed. They saw God's love, and that love entered into them and became their life, and then all things worked together for good to them as lovers of God. They did not wait till the resurrection to get the new life, they got it then; and it was that life in them which extracted the blessing from the afflictions of the wilderness. I believe that one of the physiological definitions of *life* is, "The power in a thing of appropriating extraneous or foreign matter and converting it into its own substance." And so, when the love of God is believed, and through the door of faith enters into the heart as a life, it converts all matter, however foreign to it, into its own substance. And thus by the strength of this living principle the believing Israelites would not only be sustained under present trials, but grow by them all in a meetness for the resurrection blessedness.

And those Israelites who did not see this forgiving love of God would remain without true life, and the carnal principle of selfish fear and enmity being their only life, would convert all events into its own substance, and thus they would be growing and strengthening in evil by those very afflictions which gave nourishment to the spiritual life of the others.

Thus, in the serpent lifted up, we see that the only supply of spiritual life for creatures under the sentence of sorrow and death in the wilderness, is the forgiving love of God, the favour of God, working in us, through sorrow and death, a meetness for resurrection blessedness, and that we can only draw out of that supply by believing in it. And we also see in it the assurance that such in very deed is the manner of God's love towards men,—that he has this forgiving love towards them. But this is all. It is a great deal, to be sure, but it is nothing in comparison of what we have in the Son of Man lifted up. In the type we have got a declaration of forgiving love, but it has to be taken upon *trust;* there is no opening up of God's heart to let us *see* the fountain out of which that stream of forgiving love flows. There is no explanation of that difficulty so burdensome to the awakened conscience: How can the forgiving love of the Holy God rest on and seek fellowship with an unholy man? We have, to be sure, the promise of the resurrection; and in the bodily cure of the bitten Israelites there was a sign given of it, but for many a long day after there was no actual specimen of a resurrection life.

And so, in the serpent lifted up, we have only got the earthly things, which Nicodemus ought to have known. It was only a shadow, but the body is Christ. It indicated the stream flowing upon the earth—upon the sons of men; but it did not show the heavenly things, it did not show the fountain, it did not lay open the heart of God. It told that there was a love, and a love which had forgiven sin, and which was using the afflictions which man had brought upon himself as the instruments of fitting him for a better state, a resurrection life. But it could tell nothing about that love; it could tell nothing of the breadth and length and depth and height.

Until the coming of Christ, the love of God had in a great measure to be taken upon credit. God had to be taken upon his spoken word merely. And so long as this was the case, God could not be fully known by men; they knew what he had said about this love, but they had not seen it, and they could only know it by seeing it. But now, in the Incarnation, in the Word made flesh, our eyes have seen and our hands have handled the Word of life. It is like trusting the friendship of a man who has already sacrificed health and life and fortune for us, in comparison of trusting the friendship of one who says that he is *ready to do* these things.

Again, in the serpent lifted up, we see a promise that death should die, and that he who had the power of death should be overcome and cast out; but the manner of the victory over the old serpent and over death is not explained to us. And so also we have the announcement of a past forgiveness; but the ground of it and the character of it are not explained. We thus have only *effects* declared to us in the symbol of the serpent, we are not admitted into the *causes*. It is still the *stream* only, the earthly things; not the fountain, the heavenly things.

In Christ we see the fountain, the heart of God, the heavenly things—the first cause. The Son of Man lifted up is a step higher than the serpent lifted up; it is a step within the veil. In the cross we not only have the old serpent overcome, and death overcome, but we have also their *overcomer*, and the strength in which he overcame, and the manner in which he overcame. The serpent is not the type of Christ. The serpent had poisoned the people, Christ had not. The type consists in this, that the death of the serpent was the triumph of the Saviour. But the serpent is not the Saviour. And thus, in the serpent lifted up, we have the triumph of the Saviour, but not the Saviour himself. No; he was the bruiser of the serpent's head—he trode upon the dragon. Through death he overcame him who had the power of death, even the devil. Nevertheless the serpent was truly upon the cross, for he was the chief of those "powers and principalities, of which Jesus made an open show, triumphing over them in the cross" (Col. ii. 15). Satan fell as lightning from heaven, and death received that wound which can never be healed.

In the serpent lifted up we have the lords of the Philistines overwhelmed; but in the Son of man lifted up we have not only our cruel oppressors vanquished and dead, but we have the mighty Nazarite also, who slew them at his own death, himself revealed to us, with the secret of his seven locks. In the serpent lifted up we have Goliah slain, but in the Son of man lifted up we have David also, who slew him, after having put off and refused to wear the armour of Saul, *the first king, the old man.* Jesus put off the fallen flesh of the first Adam, the *armour which he had not proved,* and having done so, he destroyed the destroyer and led the captivity captive.[1] In the serpent lifted up,

[1] This appears to be the meaning of that word ἀπεκδυσάμενος in Col. ii. 15. The fallen flesh has been taken possession of by the powers and principalities of evil: it is the armour in which they have made themselves strong; and, therefore, when Jesus overcame them, he put off that flesh. the armour in which they had intrenched

we have only the head of the serpent bruised; but in the Son of man lifted up we have also the seed of the woman who bruised him.

The truth concerning God's forgiving love, and the manner of that love, namely, to make men meet for the better resurrection through sorrow, was the fountain opened to the Israelites in the serpent lifted up. This was their *provision of life.* And those who believed the truth possessed the life. And it was God's life, for the truth was God's own character; and in the power of that life they resisted the devil, the world, and the flesh; and though they were continually moving from one spot of the desert to another, yet they could say to God, "Thou hast been our dwelling-place in all generations;" they were strangers and pilgrims on the earth, but they were strangers with God, they were no strangers to him; they knew God and he knew them; He knew their souls in adversity; he had said, "I will never leave you, nor forsake you;" and they knew that he was a faithful God, and they took this word as their heritage for ever; it was the joy of their heart.

themselves. "*Having unclothed himself,* he made an open show of the powers and principalities, triumphing over them in the cross." This translation has not only a more pointed meaning, but is much more according both to the grammar and the letter of the original than the common version. Compare this passage with 2 Cor. v. 4: "We who are in this tabernacle (in the flesh, which is the armour of the old man) do groan, being burdened: not for that we would be *unclothed* (merely separated from this mortal body), but clothed upon (with our resurrection body), that mortality may be swallowed up of life." Compare it also with Col. ii. 11 and Eph. vi. 22.

We thus see the extent of the provision which was contained in the serpent lifted up. But our provision is much fuller and larger in the Son of man lifted up. As the *life* is just God's own character, the fulness of the life must be in proportion to the fulness of the manifestation of the character of God. That is to say, were the faith in the two cases equally strong and unfeigned, this proportion would hold perfectly. But the fullest provision is nothing to an unbelieving soul. And even where there is some faith, the weakness of it, or the mixtures with it, may neutralise the fulness of the provision. If we compare the saints of the Old Testament with the Christians of the present time, we shall see the fullest life drawn out of the slenderest provision. Many of them walked with God in a nearness to aspire to which even would be considered presumption and fanaticism in these dark and dead days. And yet our provision is the fulness of God, and our dispensation is the dispensation of the Spirit. Alas! brethren, God is dishonoured amongst us and by us. It is a crying evil. The light has been hid, and the Spirit has been quenched; yea, his power has been questioned and scoffed at. The truth hath fallen in the street. It is no question between different statements of doctrines; the question is between the living God and a metaphysical abstraction. Now, let those who see these things lift up their testimony against the evil, and let them join the sigh and the cry of the spirit, and let them give God no rest until he make Jerusalem a praise in the earth. The signs of the times are fast running out, and the hour of the judgments is coming on.

Well, this was the provision of life for the Israelites in the brazen serpent. And our provision, however it may be neglected or misused or denied, is far greater. The very heart of God has been laid open to us, and the love hath come forth from it, and hath come even to us—*into us*—into our enmity—into our loathsomeness—into our death—that we might be partakers of God's love and purity and life.

The serpent lifted up declared the victory gained, or to be gained, over the arch-deceiver and death; it declared the earthly things, or the manifestation of that victory in its effects upon the earth, namely, Satan and death cast out, and a new life rising out of their defeat. But the Son of man lifted up declares the conqueror as well as his triumph; it declares the heavenly things, because it lays open that power and principle in the heart of God by which the victory was gained; it lays open the fountain of everlasting life in the everlasting love of God; it reveals him who revealed the Father; it reveals him, and it reveals his work and conflict by which he achieved and obtained the righteous headship, in which man's redemption consists; and, to crown all, it reveals this conqueror as being in our flesh, in our nature—in the flesh and nature of every man, holding the Spirit for every man—ready to do in each member what he had done in the head. And thus in the Son of man lifted up is contained and revealed that *provision*, in the strength of which we also are called on to take up our cross and follow him, and to fight and overcome, even as he suffered and fought and overcame, that we may sit down with him on his throne, even as he sat down with the Father on his throne.

I have already observed that the Son of man lifted up is a step above the serpent lifted up, and a step within the veil, because it connects the conquest with the conqueror. Even so, although the conqueror calls on us to take up our cross and follow him in the very path which he trod, yet his conflict is, in fact, a step above our conflict. For, observe, the provision in the strength of which we are called on to fight rose out of his victory; it had no previous existence except in the anticipation of his victory; so he himself must have waged the war in the strength of another provision, a provision which he had independently of his victory. This is what I mean by saying that his conflict was a step higher than that to which we are called. The conflict is the same conflict,[1] but it was on a higher field, and in the strength of a higher provision. It was a higher, not a fuller provision. His provision lay in the known and believed love and favour of the invisible, unmanifested God. Our provision lies in the known and believed love and favour of God made visible and manifest in the flesh.

---

[1] His conflict differed from ours in this respect, that he was the Leader and the Breaker-up of the way. We have to contend against the same enemies, but they are now, in comparison, vanquished enemies. No *creature* could have done what he did.

He commenced his work in the known and conscious possession of the favour of God to himself personally: he was not called on to earn this possession; it was his inheritance. As the second person in the Godhead, he was the object of the unutterable complacency and favour of Jehovah. He knew from the beginning that he was the beloved one, and that he should see of the travail of his soul and be satisfied; he knew that by his work the whole earth should be filled with the glory of God, and that he himself should be the Lord of the glory: and thus the favour of God, as his known personal possession, and the Holy Spirit given without measure to him, and the hope set before him that his work should be rewarded, constituted his provision of life and strength, out of which he continually drew by faith.

The work of Christ is the first link of the chain which is to bind creation to the throne of God. By that work it was effected that the provision which Christ possessed personally in the favour of the invisible God, and in the strength of which he had overcome, should henceforth be lodged in himself, the incarnate God, the head of the fallen flesh, as the property of every individual of the flesh, and the provision in the strength of which every individual is called to fight and to overcome.

We begin where he left off; his victory is our provision. We take hold of him as he took hold of the unlimited Godhead. "For as the Father hath life in himself, so hath he given to the Son to have life in himself" (John v. 26). Then, again, "As the living Father hath sent me, and I live by the Father, so he that eateth me, even he shall live by me." Eating Christ is believing in the love which constituted, and in the privileges contained in, that bond of the flesh whereby Christ is united to every man. It is believing in all that Jesus did in the flesh for us. It is believing that Christ is in us the hope of glory. Now this is just the provision which we need. Christ overcame in the strength of his provision; his victory is set before us on the cross and in the resurrection, to assure us that his provision was certainly sufficient; and then he is himself given to us along with his provision, to be our provision. He that believeth that Christ is in him—the Christ who hath condemned sin in the flesh and made reconciliation for the transgressors—the Christ who is anointed with the Holy Ghost and with power—who is the well-beloved of the Father, and who came from the bosom of the Father to live and die and revive in our flesh, and in our flesh reign gloriously for ever, that he might declare God's holy love to every man, that we might become one spirit with him, and be partakers in his glory—he that believeth that this Christ is in him, he eateth Christ and he liveth by him. He liveth in the strength of Christ; yea, it is no more he that liveth, but Christ that liveth in him. This is our provision, whether we live by it or not, whether we believe in it or not. And it is simply because this provision has been actually given to us that Christ says, Follow me. This is a command which never could have been given unless the provision of Christ had first been given. And it is also simply on the ground of this provision being actually given in Christ to every man, that Christ is appointed the judge of all men. *He* is to judge every man who is every man's brother, who died for every man, and who had life for every man. There is something very solemn in having such a judge. "As the Father hath life in himself, so hath he given to the Son to have life in himself; and hath given him authority to execute judgment also, because he is the Son of man." Compare this with Acts x. 40-42, where the same reason is given for his being appointed Judge. The judgment is on the ground of a provision of life having been made for every man.

We have been hitherto considering the provision chiefly as it consists in the character of God already manifested; but we must also consider it as it consists in the accomplishment of the purposes of God. For our provision consists of two parts—a present possession and a hope of good things to come. The present possession is the forgiving love of God, which ever embraceth us and Christ given to us as the head of our flesh, who hath loved us and made atonement for us with his own blood, and in whom we have the fulness of the Spirit. And the hope of good things to come is the hope of the glorious appearing of our great God and Saviour, even of him who was despised and rejected of men, to reign on the earth in righteousness, and "to purge out of his kingdom all things that offend," "taking vengeance on them that know not God and obey not the gospel."

Now it is manifest that the glorious appearing of Christ to render recompence can be no provision of life or of strength except to those who know that Christ is their friend. My dear reader, "behold, he cometh" —"he cometh in clouds." But how will you abide the day of his coming? I am sure that nothing but the knowledge of the love of God to yourself—nothing but the knowledge that Christ is your Saviour, who hath loved you, and given himself for you,—can enable you to regard that day without terror. But the prospect of that day can only be a provision of life and strength to those who desire its coming; it can only be *a hope of glory* to those who see in its coming the accomplishment of all their longings. It cannot be a provision of life to those who regard it with fears or misgivings. It can be a provision of life only to those who know that the cause of Christ is their own cause, and who know that all blessedness is summed up in that word, "The glory of the Lord shall cover the earth as the waters cover the seas." And none can know this who do not know themselves to be loved and forgiven and accepted in the beloved. Thus it is that we can only enter into the provision of hope through faith in the present forgiving love. Christ entered into his provision of hope, even the assured hope that he should never be ashamed, but that he should see of the travail of his soul and be satisfied, through faith in the ever-present and ever-faithful unbought love of his Father.

There can be no greater delusion than to regard the forgiving love as a future thing, as an object of hope; for thus the key to our whole provision of life and strength is thrown away. Faith in the forgiving love of God as already bestowed on us in Christ Jesus is the only key to our provision. And if this love is not ours now, how are we to get it? The Bible does not tell us how; the whole Bible rests on the ground of a love already bestowed. It was forgiving love that gave the Bible.

Christ, the gift of God's present forgiving love to every man, is the door through which alone we can enter into our provision of hope. Until we know the love of our Father's heart to us as manifested in Christ, the future must always be to us at best a dark and doubtful wilderness. It cannot be a strength, it cannot be a fountain of living waters. But when we know that all that we have conceived of our Father's love is as nothing to the reality; that he is indeed love itself —a love passing knowledge—a shoreless, boundless, bottomless ocean-fountain of love, of holy, sin-hating, sin-destroying love, which longeth over us that we should be filled with itself, and be by it delivered from the power of evil, then, indeed, we are saved by hope, for we know that that love must triumph and fulfil all its counsel. Then are we prepared to welcome the treader of the wine-press of the wrath of Almighty God, as knowing that he is coming to finish the fearful controversy which the creature has so long maintained against the Creator; that he is coming to destroy everything which opposeth holy love; that he is coming to establish that kingdom which is righteousness and peace and joy in the Holy Ghost.

A promise of a future blessedness, conditional on placing confidence in God, but which does not involve the assurance of a present forgiving love, can never be gospel to a sinner, for the condition can only be fulfilled in him by the belief of the love. And thus it is that although "Behold, he cometh in clouds" is really the blessed gospel to those who know Christ in them as their righteous Head, it is not the gospel to those who are ignorant of this mighty truth. The sin-condemning and yet peace-speaking blood must be known before there can be any joyful hope. Forgiveness of sin through that blood is the characteristic of our dispensation, and therefore is the object of present faith; and there can be no Christian hope at all without this present faith. Dear reader, consider this.

Faith embraces everything which God hath revealed; hope is the earnest outstretching expectation with which the renewed soul waits and longs for the coming of Christ in glory. Hope is the natural feeling of a soul which has entered into God's plan. The Spirit of God is grieving over this sinful, miserable world, and longing for the coming of that king who is to reign in righteousness; and the soul that is born of the Spirit will have the same grievings and longings—it will hope according to the will of God. And therefore, also, it is that "love hopeth all things," because love is just the spirit of God, and so longs for the things which God desires.

And so the hope of the gospel is not the hope of anything merely personal, or of any gift of God as separate from God himself; it is just the confident expectation that that character of God which is revealed in Christ shall be no longer hidden as it now is, and trampled upon by sinful men and shut out from the world, but shall come forth and dispel the darkness, and triumph gloriously, and vindicate itself before the powers and principalities of heaven and hell, by unfolding and destroying the mystery of iniquity, and by unfolding and mightily glorifying the mystery of godliness, and then reign for ever and ever : Amen. And therefore it is that we can only understand and enter into the hope by understanding and entering into the present mind of God, for the future is just an unfolding of the present.

This principle is strikingly set forth in the sixth chapter of Isaiah. The prophet finds himself in the temple standing before the throne of Jehovah, a throne high and lifted up, and he hears the seraphim crying one to another, " Holy, holy, holy is the Jehovah of hosts : the whole earth is [*or rather*, shall be] filled with his glory." This voice was just the foretelling of that consummation of all things concerning which the spirit of Christ in all the prophets has witnessed; it was the foretelling of the coming kingdom of the bruiser of the serpent, of the destroyer of evil, who should root out of the earth all things that offend. And the voice came to him as a message which he was to carry forth and deliver to every man. It was not spoken to him as an individual merely; it was spoken to him as the Lord's messenger. And it ought to have been a welcome message. It ought to have been glad tidings to a world trodden down by violence that a day was coming when God would right what was wrong, and his glory should cover the earth. And yet the prophet did not welcome it. He remembered his own sin and the sin of the people, and he remembered that the glory of the holy God must be a holy glory; he remembered these things and was afraid. He was afraid himself of the coming glory, and he was afraid to deliver an unwelcome message to a rebellious people who stoned those that were sent unto them. He was afraid, because he felt that the glory of God was not one with the blessedness of man; and he said, "Woe is me! for I am undone; because I am a man of unclean lips, and I dwell amongst a people of unclean lips: for mine eyes have seen the King, the Jehovah of hosts." In this state of mind he could not rejoice in hope of the coming glory of God, and he could not be a fit messenger to declare it to others. Now, how did God fit him to be a messenger? "Then flew one of the seraphim unto me, having a live coal in his hand, which he had taken with the tongs from off the altar: and he laid it upon my mouth, and said, Lo, this hath touched thy lips; and thine iniquity is taken away, and thy sin is purged." As soon as he heard this word he rejoiced in the glory, for he saw it to be the glory of a forgiving king,—and he was ready to carry the tidings of it, as tidings of joy, to his fellow-sinners. For this word was not spoken to him as an individual merely, any more than the other; it was spoken to him as the Lord's messenger; and therefore it was a word which he was entitled and bound to declare to every man as the truth of God to every man. The altar from which the coal was taken was the altar on which was offered up the Lamb, slain from the foundation of the world, whose blood cleanseth from all sin,—and the coal from off the altar, which touched his *mouth*, was a word concerning that sacrifice; and as soon as that word was believed he knew the power of the prayer, "Thy kingdom come. Thy will be done on earth, as it is in heaven." He was of one mind with God, and therefore he rejoiced in hope of the glory of God; he could now rejoice in anything that God could do. And he was willing to be the Lord's messenger now, for he knew that he had a message to every man, which, if believed, would necessarily make the coming glory of God a joyful hope to every man. He thought that that second message could not fail of being thankfully received by every man, but the Searcher of hearts knew otherwise, and warned him that it would be rejected. And why is this? Just because the forgiveness is the forgiveness of a holy God; it is not a forgiveness which passes by sin, but which destroys sin. Therefore it is unwelcome to an unholy heart just as the glory is.

The message which he was commissioned to declare was twofold: First, that the Messiah's glorious king-

K

dom was coming, even the kingdom of him who was to judge the world in righteousness; and secondly, that there was a sacrifice which had put away all sin, through the knowledge of which the chief of sinners would be fitted to rejoice in their king. He was also instructed to foretell the rejection of this message by the Jews, and the desolation, and wasting, and forsaking that should come on the land in consequence of it, until the time of the ingathering.

The gospel has always consisted of these two parts, the coming kingdom, and the sacrifice for sin. Now it is manifest that the approach of that kingdom can only be good news to those who know the power of the sacrifice, and through the knowledge of it have been taught that God indeed loves them, and has forgiven them, and that he is their hiding-place, and that all his ways are mercy and truth to them; for thus alone can a sinful creature, that is conscious of having merited punishment, have confidence when God arises to judgment; and that kingdom is a kingdom of judgment; it is to dash in pieces everything that is not of God, it is the stone cut out without hands, which is to strike against the plans, and the policies, and the counsels, and the kingdoms of this world, and they shall become before it as chaff on the summer threshing-floor. The establishing of that kingdom shall be introduced by the great and terrible day of the Lord,— the day of vengeance of our God,—the day of the treading of the wine-press of the wrath of Almighty God. And who are they that can find a joy and rejoicing in

the prospect of the coming of that day? nay, who can
abide the thought of it, but those who know that God
is their loving Father, and Christ their loving brother
and friend, and Saviour, who hath redeemed them by
his own precious blood; and who know that the
vengeance of Christ is the destruction of hatred, and
pollution, and misery, and every evil, and that the
reign of Christ is the reign of righteousness, and peace,
and joy in the Holy Ghost; who can abide it but those
who know that the establishment of that kingdom is
the accomplishment of the purpose of him whose name is
Holy Love, and whose thoughts have been thoughts of
love from everlasting, who has taken man's nature that
man might be a partaker of the divine nature, who has
died for man, that man might have the life of God, who
has tabernacled in our flesh, that we might become
habitations of God through the Spirit? And therefore,
when the beloved John declares to the church the
glorious visions of the terrible appearing of Jesus
Christ which had been given to him, he prefaces them
with a salutation, and an ascription, which converts all
the terror into joy, for those who know the truth of
them in reference to themselves: "*Grace* be unto you,
and *peace*, from him which is, and which was, and which
is to come; and from the seven spirits which are before
his throne; and from Jesus Christ, who is the faithful
witness, and the first begotten of the dead, and the
prince of the kings of the earth. Unto him that loved
us, and washed us from our sins in his own blood, and
hath made us kings and priests unto his God and

Father; to him be glory and dominion for ever and ever. Amen." Those who know the truth of this salutation and ascription are prepared to welcome the opening of the seals, and the blowing of the trumpets, and the pouring out of the vials; for they take part with God, and rejoice that he is to arise and plead his own cause, and to put away out of his kingdom everything that offends.

The great truth then with regard to the sacrifice, and the only truth which can enable a sinner, in the full knowledge of all his evil deserts, to welcome the coming of him who is to tread the wine-press of the wrath of Almighty God, is that Christ is in the flesh of every man, and that the blood of Christ hath been shed for every man, and that by its shedding every man's sin has been condemned and put away, so that sin is not imputed to him, and he is looked on by God as a member of Christ's flesh, with that love which ever rests on the well-beloved Son. The man who believes this,—who believes that Christ as his head died because he had offended, and as his head has risen because his penalty was exhausted,—is brought into his right place before God; he is made righteous by faith, and rejoices in hope of the glory to be revealed.

In the beginning of the 5th chapter of the Epistle to the Romans, it is written, "Being justified by faith," or, having the righteousness of God which is by faith, "we have peace with God, and rejoice in hope of his glory." The great questions then are, What is the righteousness of God? and, How is it to be had?

These questions, which in fact are the same as those answered by our Lord in his conversation with Nicodemus about the *birth* or *life from above*, are treated in the preceding chapters of the Epistle; from which it appears, that the righteousness of God is just the name or character or life of God as revealed in Jesus Christ, viz. *Holy love forgiving sin without clearing it*, and that a man becomes a partaker of it by believing in it. "Abraham believed God, and it was reckoned to him for righteousness." "He believed God, and became heir of the righteousness which is by faith."

The Epistle begins with a statement of the gospel; of that gospel which gives present peace, and prepares for the coming kingdom. And what is the statement? The union of the two natures in Christ, the union of Jehovah with our fallen flesh. "The gospel of God concerning his Son, who was made of the seed of David according to the flesh, and declared to be the Son of God with power according to the spirit of holiness by the resurrection from the dead, even Jesus Christ our Lord." This is the gospel; this is that great truth of the fallen humanity of Jesus, the truth that he who was Jehovah should have consented to be made of that one blood of which God has made all nations on the face of the earth, in order that he might shed that one blood, and thus make atonement for the sins of every man,[1]— the truth that he should have become one flesh with us, that we might become one spirit with him; this is

[1] See Acts xvii. 26; Heb. ii. 14; 1 John ii. 2.

that gospel, the belief of which must fill with joyful and glorious hope, in the prospect of the coming kingdom of him who hath thus loved us and given himself for us.

I do not wonder that Christianity withered away when this glorious truth was let slip. It contains all— the universal love of God, and the atonement for every man, as the ground of personal assurance, and the indwelling of the Spirit; and it contains also the personal glorious advent and reign of Jesus Christ upon this earth, because it connects him by an eternal bond, with the very substance of this earth. Blessed be God for having again revived it before the end come. O may he put his own mighty voice into those mouths which he has opened to declare it, and make it a mighty instrument for the ingathering of the harvest!

It is just the same gospel as "Christ in you, the hope of glory." And when we understand that "*Christ is the power of God unto salvation* to every one that believeth, because *in him* is revealed the righteousness of God which enters by faith into those who believe"[1] (Rom. i. 16, 17), then we shall understand the value of that gospel, which tells us, on the authority of God, that *this Christ is in us*, for we shall see in it that which will give us boldness to meet the day when

---

[1] The pronoun αὐτῷ applies more naturally to *Christ* than to the *gospel*. It is Christ himself who is the *power* of God and the *righteousness* of God (see 1 Cor. i. 24, 30). "I am not ashamed of the good news I bear concerning Christ, for he is the power of God unto salvation, to every one who believeth, for in him is revealed the righteousness of God," etc.

the wrath of God shall be revealed from heaven against all ungodliness and unrighteousness of men, who oppose the truth by unrighteousness.

The righteousness of God is now preached—his righteousness in forgiving and bearing long with a race for which Jesus died, and of which he is now the risen and glorified Head,—in order to prepare men to meet the judgment. It is now preached, just as it was preached by Noah during the hundred and twenty years before the flood; it is preached during the accepted time and day of salvation, but when this time is past, and the day of wrath is come, "God shall render to every man according to his deeds."[1]

As the preaching of righteousness is always connected with the announcement of a coming judgment, in which strict justice will be rendered to every man, according to his actual character, it is evident that the righteousness thus preached must, in order to fit a man for meeting that day of reckoning, be something which will enter into his character, and make him such as the Judge on that day may justly acquit and approve. It is not something merely on the *outside* of the man, like a pardon, which will fit him to meet that day; it must be something *inside*, something which enters into his inmost heart, and produces there a character conformed to the will of God. The apostle charges all men with being wanting in this character, and therefore, being unprepared for the judgment. He, as it were, summons the whole world before him, and in

[1] Rom. ii. 6.

order to explain to them the reason of their being in this awful condition, he singles one from the crowd, and in his case describes the case of all in these words: "Despisest thou the riches of God's goodness, and forbearance, and long-suffering; not knowing that the goodness of God leadeth thee to repentance?"[1] or is even now urging thee to turn to him. This is the reason why men go on in sin. There is a goodness, and forbearance, and long-suffering of God, pressing upon them, and striving to enter into them, but, through the ignorance that is in them, they despise *these riches;* and thus it is that they treasure up for themselves another kind of riches, even wrath against the day of wrath, and of the revelation of the righteous judgment of God.

Now the righteousness of God is just these riches of his goodness and holiness, as manifested in the work of Christ; and whilst this righteousness is unknown to a man, it is an outside thing to him merely, it rests on him as a forbearance and a goodness urging him to turn and live; but it does not fit him to meet the wrath, because it does not make him righteous. But as soon as it is known, it enters into him, and becomes a life, and thus, by making him righteous, prepares him to welcome the coming of the Judge.

The righteousness is the very character of God, as revealed in Christ, namely, *Holy Love* forgiving sin without clearing it. This character is the only fulfilment of the law, and therefore until it enters into a man, he can never be prepared to meet the judgment. And

[1] Rom. ii. 4.

it can only enter into a man by being believed, and no man has a right to believe it unless it be actually resting on him. And as it is the only preparation for the judgment, so the only ground of condemnation against a man for being unprepared on that day must be that he might have had this righteousness and would not, that is, that he despised the riches of God's goodness, which was pressing on him and urging him to turn.

This righteousness of God's holy love, forgiving sin without clearing it, was not contained in the law; for the necessity of the yearly repetition of the atoning sacrifice proved that sin was not taken away; and thus "by the law is the knowledge of sin," as remaining on man, yet was it borne witness to by the law and the prophets, and now it is manifested, even the righteousness of God, through faith in Jesus Christ, which is *into* all (as well as *upon* all, which last is truth both of unbelievers and believers) them that believe, for there is no difference; for all have sinned and come short of the glory of God; being justified freely by his grace through the redemption that is in Christ Jesus, whom God set forth (as witnessed by the law) under the figure of the mercy-seat, in his own blood, in order to explain the nature of his righteousness, in consistency with the remission of sins, by the forbearance of God,[1]

---

[1] This is evidently the meaning of the 25th verse of the 3d chapter. The fact that men were committing sin and were yet suffered to live, required explanation. In the day thou sinnest thou shalt die. That explanation was contained in the blood sprinkled on the mercy-seat. The blood of Jesus was the reason why the earth

until the manifestation of his righteousness, which has been made in the present time, that God might be declared righteous, when reckoning righteous the believer in Jesus.[1] The righteousness of God then is revealed and contained in Christ crucified, in the Son of man lifted up. And how is man made a partaker of it? He who believeth in Jesus hath the righteousness, hath the everlasting life.[2]

And is there no other way of getting the righteousness but by faith? "What! shall we say that Abraham our father acquired righteousness, in the way of the flesh, *i.e.* by his own working?" This is the commencement of the 4th chapter, in which we are instructed by the case of Abraham as to the way of becoming heirs of the righteousness which is by faith. I may say that we are instructed by the case of David

and its rebel inhabitants were not swept from the face of the creation. "The earth is dissolved, and the inhabitants thereof: I bear up the pillars of it." Reader, the only reason why you or any child of Adam is now in existence is, that Christ's blood has been shed. The voice of our brother's blood speaketh better things than the blood of Abel; but the day is coming when this blood also shall cry for vengeance—the day is coming when God will make requisition for this blood.

For the sake of the unlearned reader, I may observe that the word translated "propitiation" in the 25th verse is the name commonly given by the LXX. to the covering of the ark, that is, the mercy-seat, and that the words "through faith" are omitted by some of the most authoritative MSS.

[1] Rom. iii. 20-26.
[2] Rom. iv. 5-25; Gal. ii. 16; John vi. 47; 1 John v. 1-13. This oneness of the *righteousness* and the *life* is the key to the connection between the Gospel and Epistles of John, and the Epistle to the Romans.

as well as of Abraham; for though David himself is not personally introduced here by the apostle, as Abraham is, yet inasmuch as the psalm[1] from which the quotation is made certainly embraces and describes David's own personal experience, we may consider him as here really brought forward along with Abraham, to fill up the pattern of righteousness by faith. It is worthy of remark, that although the apostle begins with the case of Abraham, yet he has no sooner entered on it, than he leaves it and goes to the psalm which contains the case of David. Now, why does he do this, but just because, in the case of David, that point which is the key and entrance to the whole righteousness, namely, the non-imputation of sin, is most strongly brought out? And so the Spirit joins the two cases together, and out of them thus joined draws one example of the righteousness which is by faith. There is no explicit and direct mention made to Abraham of the forgiveness of sins in all the recorded communications of God to him, and it is to supply this part of the gospel that the case of David is introduced. David's conscience had become burdened with a sense of unpardoned sin in the matter of Uriah, and his love for his sin had kept him from looking to that holy love of God, which, whilst it forgives sin, condemns it, and insists on a separation from it. Whilst he continued in this state, we may be assured that all the blessed promises concerning his seed (recorded in 2 Samuel vii.) were quite powerless and joyless to him, and thus that the provision of hope

[1] Ps. xxxii.

was to him a sealed fountain. Whilst his conscience remained unpurged, he could not enter into God's purposes. He had not confidence before God, and, therefore, he could have no joy in the prospect of God's glory covering the earth; he was not righteous, and, therefore, he could not rejoice at the coming of the righteous judge, who shall cast out from the kingdom everything which offends, even although that judge was to be his own Son. But, as soon as that word, "the Lord hath put away thy sin," entered into his heart, that heart which had been so long like the nether millstone became a heart of flesh; he had confidence before God,—he became righteous,—he was sprinkled from an evil conscience. He then saw God as his loving and reconciled Father, and immediately the promise became life to him, and his long-closed mouth was opened to say, "Thou shalt compass me about with songs of deliverance: Be glad in the Lord, and rejoice, ye righteous, and shout for joy, all ye upright in heart." The faith in forgiveness of sin through the blood which has condemned sin is the only thing which can fit a man to yield himself with confidence to all God's purposes declared in his promises, and so it is the only thing which makes a man righteous; it puts him in his right place towards God, because it puts him in the condition of rejoicing that God's will must be done, and that though he now seems to be shut out of the world, yet that he will reign and will cast out from the kingdom everything that is evil. David says, " Blessed are they whose iniquities are forgiven, and whose sins are covered: Blessed is the man to whom the Lord will not impute sin." This *blessedness* is just the same thing as the *life* and the *righteousness*, and like them also it is *by faith*. The man is blessed *by believing* that his iniquities are forgiven and his sins covered, and not otherwise. "God *is* the hope of the ends of the earth;" and the man *is blessed* who knows this, for it is written, "Blessed is the man whose hope the Lord is."

After the forgiveness of sins, which is the first part of the gospel, and the key to all the rest, has been illustrated by the case of David, the apostle comes back to Abraham. By turning aside to the case of David, he did not mean us to suppose that one gospel was preached to David, and another to Abraham; or that David became righteous by believing one thing, and Abraham by believing another. He meant to teach us that the forgiveness of sin, which was explicitly and pointedly declared to David, and by the belief of which alone he became righteous, was truly implied in the promise made to Abraham of that Seed in which all the families of the earth were to be blessed. That Seed was the same that was promised to Adam as the bruiser of the serpent's head; that is, the destroyer of the works of the devil. That Seed was the righteous Head, on whom the Lord hath laid the iniquities of us all, and on account of whom, therefore, sin is not imputed unto men, and through whom "God is the Saviour of all men, specially of those who believe." Abraham's faith, therefore, might well see a present forgiveness in the promise of this Seed; and he did see it, and embraced it, and had confidence before God; his heart opened and received into it the righteousness or the life of God; and thus he became righteous— God reckoned him righteous.[1]

But though the word spoken to Abraham included and implied in it the assurance of a present favour and forgiveness, yet its direct and distinguishing feature was the promise of that glory which was to be revealed. "Thy seed shall be as the stars," in number and bright-

[1] He did not become righteous in consequence of God reckoning him righteous, but God reckoned him righteous because he was righteous. He that believeth hath *life*—he that believeth is *righteous;* they are the same things. The same truth is asserted when it is said that Christ is the living Head, and when it is said that he is the righteous Head. He is the righteous and the living Head, on account of whom all men are, during this dispensation, freed from the imputation of sin, and preserved in life; which is the bond of the flesh,—and from whom flows righteousness or spiritual life into every soul that believes in the holy love which has been manifested in this appointment; which is the bond of the Spirit. The blessing which Christ obtained by his obedience unto death is called *righteousness* in the 24th Psalm, "He shall receive the *blessing* from the Lord, even *righteousness* from the God of his salvation;" and it is called *life* in the 133d Psalm, "There the Lord commanded the *blessing,* even *life* for evermore;" and in the 21st Psalm, "He asked *life* of thee, and thou gavest it him." The righteousness is the character of God revealed in Christ, and which rests *on* every man during this dispensation, as a love not imputing sin through the atonement of Christ, to those who are partakers of his flesh. And this righteousness enters *into* those who believe in it, and becomes their life; and so they have it not only *on* them, but *in* them. They have in them the spirit of Christ the promised Seed—they have not only the general blessing which is to all, but the special blessing which is to those who believe. This was the Seed, and this was the blessing spoken of to Abraham, when it was said, "In thy seed shall all the families of the earth be blessed." Abraham believed God, and became heir of this righteousness.

ness. This promise is the same thing as the word which Isaiah heard, "The earth shall be full of the glory of the Lord, as the waters cover the sea." It had only a partial fulfilment, a beginning of fulfilment, in the first coming of the Messiah in humiliation: its full accomplishment is reserved for his glorious return; it relates to the *day* of Christ—the day of his power—in opposition to the *day* of man—the day of man's rebellion, which began with the fall, and will continue till the reappearance of the Deliverer without sin unto salvation. The day of Christ, or the day of the Lord, which now hasteth greatly, is that day which is to be ushered in by the treading of the wine-press of the wrath of Almighty God, and by the casting out from the kingdom of everything that offends, in order to make full room for the establishment of righteousness, and peace, and joy in the Holy Ghost. That was the day which Abraham desired to see, and he saw it and was glad; he looked for the city which hath foundations, whose builder and maker is God, and the sight of it made him a stranger and pilgrim on the earth. The promise was the prediction of the future day of glory; and as Isaiah was fitted to rejoice in that prospect by the knowledge of the atonement alone, so Abraham's gladness in the sight of it could have arisen from no other source. He was prepared to welcome the coming glory by the knowledge of that love of God which even then embraced him, and put away his sins,—just as David was prepared for it as soon as he heard Nathan's message, "The Lord hath put away thy sin."

But look again at the word which was spoken to Abraham. God bade him lift up his eyes to the stars, and said, "So shall thy seed be." This promise of a numerous and *glorious* posterity derived its whole value from its containing in its meaning the promise of having in his line that Saviour in whom all the families of the earth should be blessed. That promise had been before made to him, and this was a renewal and confirmation of it. Now, my dear reader, examine this promise attentively. It deserves all our attention; for Abraham is the *pattern* of believers, and whatever is said to him is said to us. Consider it, and see if it be not just that very gospel which has been so often urged upon you in this treatise, " Christ *in* thee the hope of glory." As Levi paid tithes *in* Abraham, so was Christ verily at that time *in* Abraham; and thus that very gospel which Paul was commissioned to preach to the Gentiles was then preached by God's own mouth to Abraham—that gospel which declares the common bond of the one flesh, by which Jehovah has connected himself with every man. When the race had ruined itself, God laid help for it on one that was mighty; he gave it and put *into* it this mighty one, as a restorer and a glorious hope; and whenever he has comforted any of the children of this race, it has been by telling them of this hope of glory—the hope of Israel, and the hope of the ends of the earth—being *their own* hope also. And so this hope himself said in the time of fear—"It is I, be not afraid." When the poor ignorant disciples were in the ship with him, and saw the waves rise and him asleep, they came to him and said, "Lord save us, we perish." That ship could not have perished; heaven might have passed as a scroll, but that ship was safe: its freight insured it; and if the disciples had really known that this was the incarnate Jehovah in the ship with them, they would have known that their safety and God's omnipotence were one thing. Well, our flesh is the ship, our world is the ship. Christ hath come into the frail bark of our flesh, and he hath become a partaker of it; he hath come into our world, and he is now clothed in its substance; this is the hope of the ends of the earth. For he is coming again into this world, to manifest in power and glory that holy love which he has already manifested in weakness and contempt.

This was the gospel to Adam, and Noah, and David, and all the patriarchs. A word of peace and of power to every one who believed it; a word that shall never pass away; a word that is the salvation of God, and it is of that magnitude, that the very mention of it destroys the possibility of conceiving of it but as an absolute free gift of God, to be received as a truth simply by faith. Man could do nothing here; he is lost in the infinity of it. "The earth is dissolved and all the inhabitants of it: *I* bear up the pillars of it."[1] Christ, the glorious hope of the world, is even now sustaining it, and all its inhabitants, by being indeed in the flesh of every man; yea, the only reason that

[1] Ps. lxxv. 3.

can at this moment be justly given in heaven or earth or hell, for the present existence of this earth or one of its inhabitants, is, that the great kinsman Redeemer has bought back the forfeited inheritance, and all his brethren who had sold themselves for nought.

It has already been said that Abraham was a pattern of believers. This forbids us to suppose that he was placed in more favourable circumstances than others, or that he had greater facilities or inducements to confide in God than others. Had this been the case, he could not have been a pattern for others. In fact his case had a particular aspect of unfavourableness, and it was for this very reason that his faith was held up as a pattern. Sarah was barren, and he above a hundred years old, yet he received the word of God, and gave it the honour due to it. "He believed in God who quickeneth the dead, and calleth those things which be not as though they were; against hope, he believed in hope, that he should become the father of many nations, according to that which was spoken, So shall thy seed be. And not weak in faith, he considered not his own body now dead, when he was about an hundred years old, neither yet the deadness of Sarah's womb: he staggered not at the promise of God, through unbelief; but was strong in faith, giving glory to God; and fully persuaded that what he had promised, he was able also to perform. And therefore, it was reckoned to him for righteousness, or in this way he became righteous." And here follows a most important verse; most important, because it assures us, on the authority of eternal truth, that the word which was then spoken to Abraham, and by the belief of which he became righteous, is virtually the word spoken to each of us. "Now, it was not written for his sake only, that it was reckoned unto him, or that he in this manner became righteous, but for us also, to whom it shall be reckoned, or who shall also become righteous, if we believe on him who raised up Jesus our Lord from the dead, who was delivered because we had offended, and raised again because we were pardoned."

Reader, this is the message of God to every man, and a message it is which leaves every man without excuse, who is not reposing full confidence in God, and rejoicing in hope of the coming glory. This message contains all that was spoken to Abraham and all that was the foundation of his confidence before God, and of his gladness in the prospect of the day of the Messiah. Christ delivered to death for our sins is the pledge and proof to us of our Father's love, whilst we are yet sinners, as it is the seal of his abhorrence and condemnation of sin; Christ raised from the grave as our righteous Head is the pledge and proof of sin forgiven; and Christ raised to the right hand of the Father is our hope of glory. And this Christ is in the flesh of every man, as God's unspeakable gift. Abraham's word was less than ours, and why should his faith be stronger, or his communion with God nearer, or his hope of the Saviour's appearing more quickening and sustaining than ours?

Abraham had not to make the love of God, nor the forgiveness of his sins, nor his connection with the flesh of Christ, any more than we have. He could not have made them any more than we could. All that he did, and all that we have to do, is to believe what God has done. Everything in himself was against hope. But against hope he believed in hope. He considered not his own body now dead, neither the deadness of Sarah's womb. He knew that what God had said, God was able to perform. He believed that on this earth, which was even then a place of fraud, and of violence, and of misery, there should be established a kingdom of righteousness and peace and joy, that should never be removed, and that in the glorious King of that kingdom he should see one who was bone of his bone and flesh of his flesh—one who loved him with an everlasting love, and through whom God was even then saying unto him, Thy sins are forgiven thee. The belief of this lifted Abraham out of things present and seen and temporal, and placed him amidst things future and unseen and eternal, which he knew were not to be actually enjoyed till after his body had returned to the dust, and his spirit to God who gave it. This faith drew him out of the flesh, out of the carnal mind which is enmity against God, and thus it drew him out of the course of this world, and made him here a stranger in a strange land; but it was a peace-giving faith; the life which he was leading on earth was poisoned by sin, and also exposed to the continual wants and dangers of a wanderer's lot, but this faith gave him the foretaste and the assurance of another life, out of the reach of all evil, hid in the bosom of God.

My dear reader, has not this thought entered into your mind in reading this passage? It is no wonder that Abraham had confidence and good hope, when such gracious messages were addressed to him personally from God; but this is not my case. God never said any such thing to me personally. But observe the Spirit testifies that this history of Abraham's righteousness was not written for his sake only, but for us also, who in like manner shall become righteous, when we believe the message sent to us concerning the death and resurrection of Jesus on our behalf. Now, unless this message to us comes with as direct and special and personal an address to each one of us, and contains as full a declaration, both of the actual forgiveness of our sins, and of our interest in the coming glory, as Abraham's message did to him, it could never have been said that Abraham's case was written for our sakes as well as for his.

And although it be not true of us, as it was of Abraham, that the Christ is to be our *descendant* according to the flesh, yet it is true, that the common bond of the flesh, whereby Christ is the root of every man, and in every man, must be a bond as near and as close as the bond of actual descent, otherwise Abraham's case could never have been set forth as the common pattern of faith to all men, nor could his righteousness have been recorded for *our* sakes, as well as his.[1] We are called to be righteous as he was, and we cannot become righteous on lower grounds than he did. Unless we have equal grounds at least, the call would be unreasonable, and could not possibly be answered. But the call is a call from him whose service is a reasonable service. We have equal grounds with Abraham, yea superior, for the promise is now more unfolded. The seed hath appeared; he hath made reconciliation for the transgressors by his death; he hath risen from the dead; he hath ascended up on high, leading captivity captive, and hath sat down at the right hand of power. And to each one of us it is said, This very Christ, the glorious hope of the world, is in your flesh, and in him you have eternal life. Reader, however overlooked by God you may think yourself, and lost in the mass of mankind,—however excluded you may think yourself by sin from his mercy,—however polluted and defiled and corrupted you may know yourself to be,—however vain and futile you have hitherto found all your attempts to meet the demands of your own conscience,—this is the message of God to you. You have in your flesh him who is the righteous head, on whose account sin is not imputed to you, and who is the mighty God, in

---

[1] It is worthy of remark that the apostle, in the two last verses of this chapter, when he uses the pronoun "*us*" and "*ours*," evidently is not speaking of believers, but of those who are still unbelievers, and therefore still unrighteous; for he says of them, that they, like Abraham, *shall become righteous* when they believe the message. Yet he classes himself in with this body. Those who interpret everything in the Epistles as exclusively addressed to believers should consider this.

whose strength you may overcome all the evil that is in you. This may appear very improbable, but you have the word of God for it. When the promise came to Abraham, nothing could appear more improbable; he had nothing but God's bare word to trust to; his circumstances were all against it. But he did not look to his circumstances; the seed was not to arise out of his circumstances, but out of the power of God, and, therefore, he considered not his own body now dead, he considered the faithful word of God who was able to perform that which he had promised. Even so, we have not to look to our characters or to anything of ours, as reasons either of hope or despair; we have to look to the faithfulness of him who commissioned Paul to preach this gospel to the Gentiles, "Christ the hope of glory is in you," persuaded that what he hath promised, that he will assuredly perform. We have not to look to our own hearts either to make Christ or to make eternal life within us. It was not Abraham's dead body that made the seed; no, it was the free gift of God; "and this is the record, that God has given to us eternal life; and this life is in his Son."[1]

Though Abraham had not believed the promise, he might still have been the father of the Messiah according to the flesh, but he would have been, as probably many of the ancestors of the Messiah were, without righteousness and without hope, and therefore, without a capacity for welcoming or enjoying the glorious coming of his righteous Son, he would have been

[1] 1 John v. 11.

without the birth from above, and, therefore, he could not have *seen*, nor could he have *entered into* the kingdom of God.

Even so, we cannot by our unbelief annihilate that bond of the flesh by which God hath bound us to himself; but we may by our unbelief exclude ourselves from the blessing, for by unbelief we shall continue without righteousness, and without that life from above, which discovers to us, and fits us for entering into the kingdom of God.

When we believe in the death and resurrection of Christ as our Head, that is, in us, "we are begotten again to a lively hope" and desire of his coming kingdom and glory, knowing that we are members of him, and partakers with him. Our love remains a longing and unsatisfied love, till we see him.[1] And so the apostle, after declaring that the word of God to every one of us is just this, "Christ delivered because we had offended, and raised again because our sins were forgiven," proceeds thus in the 5th chapter: "Being made righteous by faith (in this word), we have peace with God through our Lord Jesus Christ, *and rejoice in hope of the glory of God.*" The belief of this word makes righteous, and he who is made righteous cannot but long for the coming of the king who is to reign in righteousness, and to destroy unrighteousness. The serpent, the prince of darkness, who was a murderer from the beginning, has long usurped this world, and filled it with sin and misery; but the bruiser of his

[1] 1 Peter i. 3, 8.

head is coming, the true King is coming, he who hath tasted death for every man is coming to avenge his cause and our cause; and shall not they who know his love, and who see the signs of his approach, rejoice in the hope of his glory?

Let me repeat here, because it is most important: The righteousness which is by faith is no imputed thing, in the ordinary sense given to imputation in man's theology. In that sense, namely, in the sense of being an outside thing, a non-imputation of sin, it belongs to every human being during "the accepted time;" but, in its true sense, it is an inside thing, being in fact the same thing as the *life*, even that good thing the possession of which prepares a man to meet that day of just judgment, when the wrath of God will be poured out on all unrighteousness of men. It is a partaking in the character of God, which can only have place in those who know his name or character. It is, in fact, a *trusting* in his character. And it is written, that "those who know his name," which means his character, and they only, "do trust in him." They know that he is well worthy, and alone worthy, of trust. And so they do not fear his coming, they long for it; and when he does come, this is a part of the song which shall be sung, "Open ye the gates, that the *righteous* nation, which keepeth the truth, may enter in. Thou wilt keep him in perfect peace, whose mind is stayed on thee, because he *trusteth* in thee."[1] And it is by this *trusting* that the righteous condemn

[1] Psalm ix. 10; Isaiah xxvi. 2, 3.

the world. And the world feels this, and says, What right have these people to have, or pretend to have, a greater trust in God than we have? This was their charge against the Righteous King himself: "*He* trusted in God, let him deliver him now, if he will have him" (Matt. xxvii. 43). And a servant of that righteous one says, "Therefore we suffer reproach because *we trust* in the living God, who is the Saviour of *all men*, specially of those who believe" (1 Tim. iv. 10). If God were not the Saviour of all men, it could be no just condemnation on any man that he did not trust in God, unless he had a particular revelation to himself; but seeing God has proclaimed Christ crucified and Christ risen, his unspeakable gift to every man, every man who has not confidence in God is condemned of making God a liar. It is striking that the *universal atonement* and the *personal assurance* should have been the reproach at all times.

Job's righteousness, which he so fearlessly maintained against the accusations of his friends, was just the same thing, namely, a confidence in God, founded on a knowledge of his forgiving love; and in the strength of this righteousness it was that he said, "Though he slay me, yet will I trust in him." And it was in the strength of this righteousness also that his hope sang that song, "I know that my Redeemer liveth, and that he shall stand at the latter day upon the earth: and though after my skin worms destroy this body, yet in my flesh shall I see God.[1]

[1] Job xiii. 15; xix. 25.

The righteous and those who *trust* in God are always spoken of in the Bible as identical characters; and they are always spoken of as persons who are outcasts in this world, and who are longing for and looking for the coming kingdom as their only rest, and consolation, and joy. They see the excellency of God's righteousness, and therefore they desire to see that righteousness dominant and glorified on the earth.

We have righteousness in us when we see God's righteousness, as we have light in us when we see the light of the sun. And thus God is glorified in us by being seen in us. Our right place is the place of receivers, "*submitting* ourselves to the righteousness of God"—"*receiving* the grace of God not in vain." And as soon as we have got into this right place, we shall feel that the world is in a wrong place, in an awful condition, denying God his glory, refusing Christ to be their King, worshipping the creature more than the Creator. Then it will be indeed good news to us that our King is coming, and that the glory of God shall yet cover the earth as the waters cover the sea. Then shall we be in the condition of her of whom it is written, "She that is a widow indeed and desolate, trusteth in God, and continueth in supplications and prayers night and day." That widow is the true church, "the importunate widow," and her daily and nightly cry is "Avenge me of mine adversary," which just means "Come, Lord Jesus, come quickly." And this is her cry because she is desolate and has no hope but in his coming, "for the Scribes and Pharisees have devoured her house, and she hath cast into the offerings of God all that she had, even all her living.[1]

We cannot join her cry until we also are desolate, but as soon as we truly hear that word, "Christ crucified for thee, and risen for thee," we shall find that it is a word which maketh desolate after a godly sort; we shall find that it has the same power as that word which was spoken to Abraham, "Get thee out of thy country and from thy kindred, and from thy father's house, unto a land that I will show thee." Christ was crucified by the sin of that world and that flesh to which we belong, and in which we live; they are our country and our kindred, and shall we not get us out from them? They are the murderers of our Lord, and shall not our souls be wearied because of these murderers, and shall not we long more than they who wait for the morning, for him who is the desire of all nations, that he would come and deliver the world, which he hath redeemed with his own blood, from that murderous oppression under which it is now so willingly, but so miserably, enslaved?

The natural life which we have is poisoned and condemned, and is continually taking part in the murder of Christ, by seeking enjoyment in the flesh and the world which crucified him; and we are enclosed in, and brought into constant contact with that very flesh and that very world. Now what is our resource? Why just this: We have another life in Jesus, a pure, blessed, unassailable life, a life uncondemned and

[1] 1 Tim. v. 5; Luke xviii. 3; xx. 47; xxi. 4; Rev. xxii. 20.

untainted, even that eternal life which is in the Father, and was manifested in the Son. Yes, *we have it*, reader; there is no doubt on this matter; for "this is the record, that God *hath given to us eternal life, and this life is in his Son.*" We have it; it is ours, although the source of it is not *within* our own persons, but in Christ, the head of the body. But it is not the less ours on account of its being not in our own persons, but in Christ for us; it is only safer and more unassailable on that account. We have the natural light of day; it is ours, although the source of it be in the sun, and not in our own persons. We enjoy light by looking to it; even so we enjoy *life* by looking to Jesus, by believing in him as our life. And we are called on and privileged to live out of our natural life, which is in the flesh, and to live in this new life, and in the power of it, even now encompassed as we are by all this dense mass of evil, successfully to contend against it, and to crucify the flesh, crying continually out of the depths unto him who is the source of our strength as well as of our life, and whose cause it is, and who will overcome in us even as he, in the days of his flesh, after having in like manner contended and cried, did in his own person overcome, and thus in patience to possess our souls, until he who is our life shall appear, and then shall we also appear with him in glory. Then shall the victory be complete, and then shall the longings of God be accomplished and the soul of Jesus shall be satisfied, and the groanings of the whole creation shall be stilled.

Now observe the character of this life which is laid up for us in Jesus, and its manner of working in us when received. It is a life rising out of the death of the flesh, and coming to us through death. It is just the life proceeding from the serpent lifted up, the bruised head of the serpent. Not that life comes out of the serpent, or out of death, but it comes *through* death and *through* the victory that the bruiser of the serpent gained over him. Christ himself is our life, and he became so in consequence of his obedience unto death, by which he overcame the serpent. He was not the head of life to man till he had passed through death. This is the character of the life. Its source is on the other side of death, beyond the bounds of this mortal life. Our great head broke through death's prison on the other side, and passed the bounds of this mortal life, in order to obtain it for us. He could not obtain it in any other way; thus it comes to us only through the rent veil of his crucified flesh. He, as our head, has through death entered in within the veil, into the upper sanctuary, the native region of that pure life, where he not only lives it for himself, but is filled with it, as a fountain of life for the whole mass of that nature which he has assumed. For although he is on that side of the veil, and we on this, yet the bond of the flesh by which we are connected with him remains unbroken; we are still bone of his bone, and flesh of his flesh, so that the channel of communication between him and us is still open, and the life which is in him is available to us, and flows into us just according to our faith in him, that is, according to our faith in his death and resurrection, and the character of God revealed in them.

But as it is a life coming to us through death, and from a source lying on the other side of death, it is always a strange and unwelcome inmate in the flesh and in the world lying on this side of death. They hate it, and no wonder, for it is a mortal enemy to them in their present state; it refuses all sympathy with them, it condemns everything in which they delight, it witnesses against them continually as the murderers of Jesus, and its continual working is to crucify them. It is no wonder, therefore, that they hate it, and seek to crucify it. It is no wonder that they hated Jesus and crucified him, for he was *the life itself* manifested. It is here, then, in an enemy's country; it has no rest for the sole of its foot, and so it is ever forced, like the dove, to go back for shelter to the ark whence it came out; and thus it necessarily separates those into whom it enters from the flesh and the world, and forces them up to seek their enjoyment in its own native region, even with Jesus within the veil. They thus become desolate like the importunate widow, and are, like her, compelled continually to cry for the avenger of blood, who is also the kinsman Redeemer, and to live in hope of the glory to be revealed at his appearing. And they are also compelled continually to have recourse to him for present help against their powerful and close besetting enemies, for with them that saying is true, "A man's foes are those of his own house." Close besetting indeed their enemies are, for their own personal flesh, that which is nearest to them in the world, is their greatest and most dangerous enemy. Their flesh is possessed by the serpent; it is his strong-hold; and this new life which is in them is the spirit of the bruiser of the serpent, and, therefore, there is an unceasing warfare between them and their flesh—a warfare which can only be terminated by one or the other spirit being cast out of them. And this warfare can only be sustained by their holding an unceasing intercourse with Jesus by faith, for they never have a moment's stock of life in themselves; it is entirely in him as the fountain, and all that they receive must be drawn from him, moment after moment, by faith.

Jesus obtained this life for us through the death of his flesh. And he did this, not as our substitute, but as our Leader. He led the way through death to this life, and we can only enjoy it by following in the same way. He did not enter into death's prison to dispense with our entering it; but he entered it as our Head, that he might break open a way into the region of life on the other side of it, through which he might draw his body after him. The grave was a fast prison, until he entered it, but when he entered it, he broke its bars, he spoiled the spoiler, "he lay till midnight, and then he rose, and took the doors of the gate of the city, and the two posts, and carried them up to the top of the hill." "He ascended up on high, leading captivity captive."

This life is properly a resurrection life, and cannot

be fully enjoyed, until we have passed through death into the resurrection state. And as it cannot be *fully* enjoyed till then, so it cannot be enjoyed *at all* in the present state, except in so far as the flesh in us is mortified and dead. Jesus was made *perfect* as the *Head* of this life, only through sufferings unto death, and men are only made *perfect* as his *members*, through the same process. It was not till the last moment that he could say, "It is finished;" and until the last moment, Paul continued to say, "neither am I already perfect." A capacity for resurrection-glory is the perfection of which he speaks, and it was to be produced by "a fellowship in Christ's sufferings, and a conformity to his death." He was called to arrive at perfection through sufferings, just as his Master did, that is, through crucifying the flesh, keeping under the body and bringing it into subjection; and he knew that as by following this road he would attain perfection, so by abandoning this road he would become "a castaway."[1] This life, from its very nature, is a life of *hope*. It draws us upwards and forwards, to Jesus *now* within the veil, and *speedily* to be revealed. "It is the anchor of the soul sure and steadfast, because it entereth into that within the veil, whither the Forerunner is for us entered, even Jesus."[2]

When we think of Jesus within the veil, it may sometimes seem to us as if the source of our life and strength were at a great distance from us; but here

[1] Heb. ii. 10; v. 9; John xix. 30; Phil. iii. 11, 12; 1 Cor. ix. 27.
[2] Heb. vi. 19.

the oneness of the flesh comes in to bring him near to us. He is our Head; he is *in* us. "Abide in me and I in you." Blessed be his name for that word, "Christ is in you;" the glorious hope, the coming King is in you. No lower gospel can meet our wants.

Yes, this is the full and glorious gospel of the grace of God, and the purpose of this gospel, with regard to each one of us, is that Christ may so dwell in us by his Spirit, that the flesh, the old man in us, may be crucified, and that it may be no more we who live, but Christ who liveth in us. Our calling is not that we should, under the influence of higher motives and clearer views, correct and improve our characters into a greater conformity to the will of God, but that we should die to ourselves, and yield ourselves to God, as those who are alive from the dead, to be dwelt in by Jesus, yea, to be nothing less than habitations of God through the Spirit, and temples of the Holy Ghost.

This is the life, life from the fountain of life, the everlasting life, the birth from above, without which the kingdom of heaven, when it comes in power, can be to us no other than a rod of iron, breaking us in pieces like a potter's vessel. This life is nothing else than the eternal Spirit of God, one with the Father and the Son dwelling in us and acting in us. This life is laid up for us now in our risen Head; for this was the recompense given to him, after he had finished the work given him to do; he asked life, and it was given to him; he became the fountain of life for men. This same life was in him before his resurrection; it was the life by which he lived, but he was not the Fountain of life, he was not the Head of life until his resurrection. He was born of the Spirit, and he lived *personally* by the Spirit, but it was not till his resurrection that the Spirit dwelt in him *federally*. He was raised by the Spirit, and then the Spirit dwelt in him as the Head of the body. And so to know the power of his resurrection is just to receive that Spirit which raised him from the dead and dwelt in him as the common Head after the resurrection. And here mark that it is only by knowing the power of his resurrection that we can have fellowship with his sufferings. For we can only share in his sufferings by having in us that same thing which made him suffer. And as it was this very life in him, even the Holy Spirit, which made him a man of sorrows and acquainted with griefs, so we can have fellowship with his sufferings only by being filled with that same Spirit as our life. The Spirit of holy love in him grieved over all sin and contended against it; and specially it grieved over and contended against sin in the nature of which he had become the Head; and wherever that Spirit is, there will be the same grieving over sin, and the same contending against it. And so a fellowship in Christ's sufferings is not a grief because Christ suffered, it is not a grieving that Christ grieved so much on our account; no, it is having the *same grief*, and this no man can possibly have until he has in him that very living spirit which grieved in Jesus. A sinner who knows that God in his nature has suffered and bled and died for his sins, will doubtless be ashamed and confounded, and grieved, for having been the cause of so awful and horrible a thing, and he will see that there must be something very evil in sin, which made such an expiation necessary; but the grief arising from these considerations, though a grief most becoming in us, and most due to him whom our sins have pierced, is yet different from a fellowship in Christ's sufferings.

We are not called on to love men because Christ loves them, or to hate sin because he hates it, but we are called on to love men with Christ's own love, and to hate sin with Christ's own hatred; and this we can only do by being filled with the very Spirit of Christ, —by having Christ dwelling in us, and then it will be no more we who love or hate, but Christ loving and hating in us. In like manner we can have fellowship in the sufferings of Christ only by having Christ living in us. And thus he who could say, "I fill up that which is behind of the sufferings of Christ in my flesh, for his body's sake, which is the Church," said also, "I am crucified with Christ, nevertheless I live, *yet not I, but Christ liveth in me.*" Christ dwelling in him, by his Spirit, was his life, and it was this Spirit in him which suffered in his flesh, just as it had suffered in the flesh of Jesus. And this life entered into him, and was maintained in him by the belief of Christ's dying love; and so he adds,—" And the life which I now live in the flesh, I live by the faith of the Son of God, who loved me and gave himself for me" (Col. i. 24; Gal. ii. 20).

It is not by an effort, nor by working ourselves up, that we should either come to love or hate, or suffer with Christ; we must have the very spirit of Christ in us, the very love wherewith God loveth; nothing less will do. "I have declared unto them thy name, and will declare it, that *the love wherewith thou hast loved me may be in them, and I in them*" (John xvii. 26). This love in us, which is life, God's own life, yea God himself, for God is love, will love, and hate, and suffer in us, just as Christ did, because it was this same love dwelling in him, which loved and hated, and suffered in him. It will "believe all things, and hope all things," not from any facility of disposition, but because it stands in the counsel of God, and enters into his mind, and therefore recognises all that he reveals to be indeed the truth, and longs in his own spirit for the accomplishment of his righteous will, and the establishment of his blessed kingdom.

CHAPTER V.

CHRIST THE KING.

When God made man he invested him with kingly dignity and power over all things in the earth, for he said to him, "have dominion over every living thing that moveth in the earth." This dominion over the creatures Adam held under God as his sovereign Lord, and he held it so long as he continued faithful to his sovereign. Whilst this dominion lasted, the earth brought forth to him of herself that which he required; she supplied the demands of her king, and the creatures were his willing subjects. But when he fell from God, the kingdom departed from him, the earth yielded him thistles, and the creatures rebelled against him. Whilst he was faithful to God, and was therefore upheld as God's viceroy, the spirit or power of God was on him, and that power was mighty in him to maintain his dominion. But when he fell by yielding himself to another lord, the power of God left him, and the spirit of that new lord immediately supplanted the spirit of God within him. And the spirit of that new lord is not a spirit of power; he has endeavoured, as we may see in the history of Cain's line, to mimic power by arts and sciences, but the true sovereign of the world is he to whom power alone belongeth, and when man rebelled against him he took the sceptre of power out of his hand, and let him feel that the glory was departed. That new lord was the prince of darkness, who thus became the god of this world, and the prince of this world, for his spirit entering into man, the highest part of the dust of the earth, has through man ruled the rest of the world. And so man has been a tool in the hand of Satan, and a wretched toiling bond-slave ever since in this world, where he was anointed king. And he has been a willing slave; for the bait of the tempter has not lost its power. That bait was, " Ye shall be as gods," ye shall be independent. Ah, he knew not the lie contained in that bait; he knew not that to be independent of God is to be the slave of the devil; and the long and bitter experience of six thousand years has done nothing to undeceive him. He has been a willing slave of the devil, and a willing rebel against God. He has yielded himself to be dwelt in by the devil, and to be the instrument through which the devil has usurped the dominion of God in this world. From that dark day the successive generations of men have successively given themselves up to be inhabited by the evil spirit; and they have taken part with him against God, and under his guidance they have striven to shut God out of his own creation. Yet God maintains his claim, however refused; and the history of the world has just been the history of this strange controversy, in which man insists upon being the devil's slave, when God would give him the liberty of the sons of God. In these circumstances it is manifest that any gospel to man must have been an incomplete gospel which did not contain in it the promise of the restoration of the kingship over the earth. And, accordingly, this promise has been always contained in the gospel. And it has been a gospel which has left man altogether without excuse. For it has been good news of a present strength laid up for us in a Deliverer, through which man might even now resist and overcome the devil, and a promise that this Deliverer, who was to be a man, bone of man's bone and flesh of man's flesh, should finally prevail, and cast the devil out of his usurped dominion, and recover for man the lost sceptre of this world, again to be swayed by him, in the power of God, and under the acknowledged sovereignty of God.

The Deliverer is Jehovah in man's nature. He is even now king—not in right only, but in power, though not in manifestation. All things, even now, in heaven and in earth are committed unto him; but, until the mystery of God is finished, the heavens must retain him. And, therefore, even yet the kingdom of God is in that form upon the earth which it had when he himself said of it, "It cometh not with observation."[1] Now the mystery is working; righteousness is trampled on, and unrighteousness triumphs. God's glory is cast out, and man's glory is exalted. The world, which has been redeemed by the love of God and the blood of Christ, scorns that love, and treads on that sacred blood;

[1] Luke xvii. 20.

and yet the world remains unconsumed, although God, the righteous Judge, the consuming fire, reigns. This is the mystery of iniquity, and the mystery of God.

This mighty mystery is drawing near its finishing; and when it is finished, the kingdom of God shall be no more a hidden unobserved thing, but shall be "as the lightning, that lighteneth out of the one part under heaven, and shineth unto the other part under heaven;"[1] and voices shall be heard in heaven saying, "The kingdoms of this world are become the kingdoms of our God and of his Christ." But whilst it continues unfinished, nothing but the prospect of its glorious termination, and the knowledge that even now, under the control of the true king, evil is working out good, can support a child of God, under the pressure of ungodliness and darkness and misery which he feels, and sees in the flesh and in the world. The awful density of that pressure is now fast increasing, and will increase until the last convulsion, just as the agony of Jesus went on increasing, until he said—"It is finished;" and then the graves opened, and the veil of the temple was rent from the top to the bottom.

[1] Luke xvii. 24. Mark the two comings of the Lord, contrasted through this chapter, on from the 20th verse. The first coming is described in the 20th, 21st, 22d, and 23d; then the second coming is introduced in the 24th. Then there is a return to the first coming in the 25th, and from thence to the end of the chapter there is a description of the awful apathy and carelessness and blindedness in which the second coming will find the world. The four following chapters relate to the same subject, viz., the state of the church and of the world when the Lord returns. Let the reader compare these chapters with the descriptions given of the churches of Sardis and Laodicea in Rev. iii.

But why does the king delay his coming? The answer is, "The long-suffering of God is salvation;" "He willeth not the death of a sinner, but rather that he should turn and live." The finishing of the mystery is accompanied with the pouring out of the last judgments, and with the termination of the day of grace; and the heart of God yearns over the souls of men that they may turn and be saved.

But God is not sitting as a mere looker-on, contemplating this work of desolation. And the bruiser of the serpent, who tasted death for every man, is no unconcerned spectator of the ravage which the serpent is making amongst the souls which he hath redeemed. But how is he proving his concern? What is he doing? What has he been doing during this long dark day of rebuke and blasphemy?

As soon as man yielded to the devil's lie promising a happiness out of God, and independent of God, the spirit of the devil entered into him, and thus the manhood which God had made, and will yet make, to be a glorious temple for his own Spirit, became possessed by the devil, whose spirit moved through, and corrupted the mass. To meet this evil, God sent his own Son into the flesh, in within the precincts of the usurped dominion, that thus there might be continually maintained an open channel and access between the Godhead and the manhood; and that thus the Spirit of God, which, without measure, was lodged in Jesus, might have a place within the manhood, whence it might go forth and wrestle against the powers and principalities of darkness that had entrenched themselves in man's nature. And so the contest for the kingdom is carried on by the spirit of Jesus working in the body against the spirit of Satan. This is the dispensation of the Spirit, during which the kingdom of heaven cometh not with observation, that is, not with the manifestation of an earthly power or dominion. And those only who are born of the Spirit do now see the kingdom, and become sharers in this contest, as they only shall finally enter into it. The spirit in them is the spirit of the bruiser of the serpent, and they are constrained by this spirit to contend against the serpent, and to denounce him as an usurper.

Before Christ appeared in flesh, the word of promise concerning him, when received into any heart, became a sacred lodgment, a little fortress, in which the Spirit of God dwelt and warred, and testified against the world lying in the wicked one. Thus it did in Enoch and Noah and Abraham and Lot, and all the patriarchal pilgrims, and all the prophets. As soon as the word of God's promise entered into them, they were engaged, whether they would or not, in a spiritual warfare against the devil and the world; they were compelled to bear their part in God's controversy; they became "men of strife and contention to the whole earth;" they brought a claim from God upon men, and a charge from God against men, and therefore "every man cursed them;" they were "cast out of the vineyard and slain;" "they were destitute, afflicted, tormented." But yet they were the men "who stood before God in the gap, and turned away his wrathful displeasure, that he consumed not the world." They were the men "who sighed and cried for the abominations done in the land, and God's mark was upon them."[1]

Under the old dispensation, the Spirit of God assuredly strove with man, and dwelt in the servants of God;[2] and thus he left not himself without witness on the earth; but when the Word became incarnate, when the Head *actually* was joined to the body in the bond of the flesh, and, being raised from the dead, became the fountain of the new life, the Spirit was given in a higher and fuller measure; and it was also given *in a different manner*, as is intimated in that word, "The Holy Ghost was not yet given, because Jesus was not yet glorified."

The contest between the spirit of God and the spirit of the devil has become more intense. The serpent has received a deadly wound, but still he has strength, and he has come down in great wrath, knowing that he hath but a short time. Now the enemy has come in like a flood, and yet where is the standard of the Spirit raised against him? God calls on those who know his name to cry for this—to cry unto him that he would be jealous for his own name's glory, and look on the face of his anointed, and avenge us of our adversary.

Satan disputed once with our prince the great arch-

---

[1] Jer. xv. 10; Matt. xxi. 35; Heb. xi. 37; Ps. cvi. 23; Ezek. ix. 4.
[2] Gen. vi. 3; Isaiah lxiii. 10, 11.

angel about the *body* of Moses,—that is, about the Jewish people, to whom God had given Moses as a *head;* and our Prince said, "The Lord rebuke thee, Satan."[1] And now will he not contend for *his own body*, and will he not now say, The Lord rebuke thee, Satan? Yea, he will say it; but he will speak, and plead, and contend by his spirit, through his body, through his members. It is in them that the spirit is to lift up a standard against the flood of spiritual delusion and wickedness which is even now deluging the earth. And this standard can be nothing else than the living power of the Head animating and filling the members; it must be Christ evidently living and moving in them by his own spirit. When he was upon earth, his personal body, that part of the flesh or human nature which he personally possessed, the man Christ Jesus, was ever filled with the spirit (because his faith was ever perfect), and in all his movements and actions fully declared the Father. Wherever he appeared, he appeared as a witness for the righteousness of God, and against all unrighteousness of man. This was the *body* in which he declared the Father at *his first coming;* and when it was perfected through sufferings unto death, endured in this work of declaring the Father, and was thus *prepared* for the heavenly glory, he ascended with it, and took possession of the mediatorial throne, at the right hand of the Majesty on high. This was the *preparing of that* first *body*, or the *boring of the ear*, in virtue of which the faithful servant of

[1] Jude 9; Zech. iii. 2.

Jehovah, as the Head of the human nature, was received into his master's house, on an everlasting covenant, to go no more out.[1] But that body, that personal body, is only the head of life to a more extended body, the Church, which is the *body to be prepared for him against his second coming*. When *this body* is prepared, he will come again, and with it will take possession of another throne, even the throne of David, on which he is to reign a King for ever and ever.

It is only because this body is not yet prepared, that he now delays his appearing. But when it is prepared—when the bride hath made herself ready, then he will come and will not tarry—then will the glorious kingdom be revealed.

But as his personal body was prepared not merely to be an inmate of God's house, but to become verily the habitation of his glorious presence, only by the continual indwelling of the Spirit, and by the continual contending even unto death, in the power of that Spirit, against the devil, the world, and the flesh, so also must the Church, his mystical body, be prepared for glory. And as the preparation of the Head upon the earth was a continual witnessing for God's righteous-

[1] Heb. x. 5 ; Ps. xl. 6 ; Ex. xxi. 6. The *opening* or *boring* of the ear was *after* a service, not before it ; and as this *opening of the ear* is one with the *preparing of the body*, it is clear that the preparing of the body must mean the same thing as *perfecting by sufferings*, and must refer, not to the preparation of our Lord's body in the womb of the Virgin, but to the admission into his Father's house above, to be an everlasting indweller, as Head of the human nature.

ness, and against man's unrighteousness,—and a continual holding forth of the light of his reconciling love,—and a continual opening up of the heart of God as the fountain of life, to which all were welcome,— so must the preparation of the Church be. It must be a contending against the powers of darkness, by a showing forth of the light of life, even the holy love of God, of that love which hath laid on Jesus the iniquities of us all.

The members of Christ are called on to be in this world as Christ was in this world, to take up their cross and follow him, to do as he has done, to be fellow-workers with him in this contest. This is a wondrous calling for worms of the dust, polluted worms, less than nothing and vanity—to follow in the steps of the great bruiser of the serpent. And as it is a wondrous, so it would be an empty calling, were it not that he who calls us is the Lord Jehovah, who is faithful and true, and in whom is everlasting strength. But it is no empty calling, for he *hath given* to us the bruiser of the serpent to be *in us*, and to every one grace according to the measure of this unspeakable gift, and so we are not called on to go this warfare at our own charge, but at the charge and in the strength of him who hath already fought and conquered.

This preparation of the body answers to the "accepted time," and to the "unobserved state of the kingdom,"[1] and to the "dispensation of the Spirit." For it is the work of the Spirit, and the continual object of the

[1] Luke xvii. 20.

longing of the Spirit—of that Spirit who ever looks on the race lying in the wicked one, and possessed by the wicked one, with the yearnings of the love which "tasted death for every man," with the yearnings of the love which "rejoiceth not in iniquity, but rejoiceth in the truth." The desire of the Spirit is to penetrate and quicken the whole mass of the human nature, even as the sap of a tree seeks to penetrate and quicken the whole mass of the tree. But within the limits of this general desire the Spirit has a special charge, marked out for him by the sovereign election of God, and that is the cleansing and sanctifying from out of the human nature a temple for the Lord, a body for Christ. And it is through continual grief and sorrow of the Spirit that this work is carried on; for it is a continual conflict with the spirit of Satan, and in this conflict the evil heart of man is continually taking part with Satan against God and against his own soul. And therefore the Spirit of holy love, which is the Spirit of God, is continually grieved and grieving over man. It was this Spirit dwelling in the man Christ Jesus that made him a man of sorrows and acquainted with griefs. It was this Spirit in him which grieved over the dishonour done to God, and the iniquity that prevailed, and the ruin brought on man. It was this Spirit in him, which bore the burthen of every man's soul, and of every man's sin, and of every man's sorrow. And it was thus that in the power of God the Spirit he witnessed for God what God really is; it was thus that he declared the Father. Oh, what a God! What a Father! And this Spirit, which is the Spirit of Jesus, having been given to him as the reward of his work, and is now laid up in him for us, still bears our griefs, and carries our sorrows; he still is wounded by our transgressions, and bruised by our iniquities; he still bears the iniquities of us all; he takes deep and painful interest in every sin and every sorrow; and as he thus suffered in the Head, whilst the Head was in fallen flesh, and hence was capable of suffering, so he still suffers in the members of his body, whilst they continue in mortal flesh, according to the measure of his indwelling, which is according to the measure of their faith.[1] The living members of Christ do

[1] And thus the prophetic history of sufferings contained in the 53d chapter of Isaiah, though in one sense exclusively applicable to Jesus as the great atoning sacrifice, yet is in another, but perfectly true sense, applicable also to all those who receive the spirit of Christ into them. This may startle at first sight, but any one who sees the true character of our Lord's sufferings, and understands them to have been not a vicarious infliction, but the grieving of his holy love over the sins and sorrows of a nature which he had actually assumed, and of which he was actually the head, and the persecution which such a love would necessarily draw on itself from the unholy enmity of the world, will perceive that whilst the world continues wicked, the spirit of Jesus in a man must suffer as Jesus did. Compare the description of love in 1 Cor. xiii. with this history of suffering in Isaiah, and you will be convinced that in a world like this, such a love could not escape such sufferings. "Love seeketh not her own; rejoiceth not in iniquity, but rejoiceth in the truth; love beareth all things, endureth all things." Is not this the very spirit which is wounded by the transgressions of men, and bruised by their iniquities, and on which the Lord lays the iniquities of all? This is just the spirit which breathes through the Psalms. And thus, although they are properly and originally the prayers of the Head, yet they are also the prayers of all those in whom that spirit dwells.

thus, like their head, bear the burden of the world's sins and sorrows; and they are thus fitted to be intercessors for the world, and to stand before God in the gap.

Christ, when on earth, contended against the kingdom of Satan, by a continual prayer, and by a continual witnessing for God. And the Spirit of Christ in his members contends in the same way. We can understand something of the power of *witnessing*, but *prayer* is a great deep. Is the creature to move the unchangeable God? But it is not the creature, it is the Spirit of God in the creature, which prays. And what is this but a deeper deep—God praying to God? It is, indeed, a great deep. Prayer is the breathing of the Spirit of Christ in his struggle with the spirit of the serpent. It is the expression and utterance of the mind of God in that mighty and mysterious conflict between the powers of light and darkness, on the field of man's flesh. Man is the subject contested for—by the Spirit of Christ to deliver and bless him; by the spirit of Satan to bind him fast in ruin. Prayer is the expression of the Spirit of Christ in this conflict. It is the bursting forth of the holy grieved Spirit of God—the swelling up of the Spirit, into the bosom of God. It is the *holy love* of God appealing to, and taking refuge in, the *omnipotence* of God. Such were the strong cries and tears of Christ, in the days of his flesh. And as the prayers of Christ were just the utterance of the grieved and struggling Spirit, so must also the prayers of his members be. It is not an individual thing; it is one Spirit in all; it is the voice of the one common life-blood, as it circulates through the body, seeking to force its way into the numbed members which resist its entrance, and crying to God for the putting forth of his mighty power to open their closed mouths.

Prayer is the Spirit of God descending into the heart of the creature, and there working desires according to the will of God, and then carrying them up again to God. And as the sphere of the Spirit's interest in this world is the whole human race, with a special charge over the Church of Christ; even so, into whatsoever soul he enters, he carries with him this general interest, and this special charge. And thus that soul will, according to the measure of its faith, be delivered from selfish individuality; it will cease to seek *its own*, and will become an intercessor for the Church and the world with thanksgiving for the unspeakable gift. And as the Spirit longs for the coming of the righteous King, that the glory of the Lord may cover the earth, so will the soul that is born of him cry, Come, Lord Jesus. And it will pray, not as extorting blessings from an unwilling God, but as knowing that he indeed delighteth to bless, and that it is indeed his will that all men should be saved, and that it is his own loving Spirit within it which is even now inspiring these desires, and drawing forth these prayers, for things which he himself longs for, in order thus to prepare for their accomplishment. It is indeed a mighty mystery. For it would seem that something is to be done by prayer which cannot be done even by God (with reverence be it said) without it. What is the meaning of one soul being cast upon another soul, so that that other cannot choose but pray for it, although there may exist little or no personal acquaintance between them, and no tie but this mysterious spiritual necessity? The reply to the whole is, It is God; and who, by searching, can find out God?

The Spirit acting in this way is the *life* of the body, and it is this life animating the members of Christ which fits them to be fellow-workers with Christ and the Spirit against the serpent. It is this which fits them to be witnesses for Christ, as the *head of life*, and it is this which fits them to be intercessors for the body and the world. But this is not all. The *kingdom* must not be left without a witness. The standard of the Lion of the tribe of Judah is a standard of kingly power. Christ is not only a head of *life*, he is a head of *dominion*; he is not only a *living head*, he is an *anointed king*. The Church, his body, with her full endowment, would indeed be fair as the moon, clear as the sun, and terrible as an army with banners!

Oh, we have had low thoughts of the body of Christ! The word preached for long has been only a defective imitation of John's baptism, the doctrine of repentance for the remission of sins—a hope of personal safety; it has not been the glorious gospel of the kingdom. But our head is risen; he is sitting a King at the right hand of the Father; all things in heaven and on earth are committed to him.. He hath ascended up on high, and received gifts for men, even for the rebellious; and now he commands his members to be filled with his own spirit, the spirit of their Head, and in the power of that spirit to go forth witnessing to the world that the promised Deliverer hath indeed reconquered the kingship, and witnessing this not by word only, but by mighty works, which may prove that the life which flows from their Head is a life of power and dominion and kingship. If there be power in the Head, the hand does not witness truly for it, if it is merely alive but manifests no power. The members of Christ are called on to witness for him, not only that he is risen from the dead, but that he has sat down upon a throne.

Understand this, dear reader. If the sap in the root of a tree be a sap capable of producing various kinds of fruit, then a branch of that tree, if it bears only one kind of fruit, is not a full witness of what is contained in the root. Even so, if there be kingly power in Christ, our root and head, then the mere manifestation of holy love in his members, without power, although it be an evidence of the divine life which is in him, and an evidence of a much diviner kind than mere power, is nevertheless not a full witness for him, because it does not witness to his present glorified condition; it is not an evidence of his kingship, and his dominion over the creatures. And therefore it was "with *great power* that the apostles gave witness of the resurrection of Jesus." Great power manifested in the members was a witness of great power residing in the head (Acts iv. 33). There is something very striking in the prayer recorded in this same chapter: "Grant unto thy servants, that with all boldness they may *speak thy word, by stretching forth thy hand to heal; and that signs and wonders may be done by the name of thy holy child Jesus.*" One would be led from this prayer to suppose, that *speaking the word with boldness* necessarily required and included in it the miraculous gifts. And thus in reality the miracles which the disciples performed in the name of Jesus after his ascension were not so much attestations of the gospel, as essential parts of the gospel of the kingdom, because they were indications that the life which flowed from Jesus into his members was a life of power, and thus declared the kingship of the Head. And they are as necessary for this purpose now as ever they were. I do not speak of a power separate from a love, but of a love clothed in power. It was no longer a love manifested in weakness, a love which could do no more than weep with them that weep, but it was a love which healed the sick and raised the dead. The manifestation of this power was in fact preaching the gospel, for it was declaring *love dominant;* and that is the gospel.

Had the faith of the Church continued pure and full, these gifts of the Spirit would never have disappeared. There is no revocation by Christ of that word (Mark xvi. 17, 18): "These signs shall follow them that believe: In my name they shall cast out devils; they shall speak with new tongues; they shall take up serpents; and if they drink any deadly thing, it shall not hurt them; they shall lay their hands on the sick, and they shall recover." And none but Christ could revoke it. In the preceding verse it is written: "He that believeth, and is baptized, shall be saved;" and then immediately comes, "and these signs shall follow them that believe." What right have we to say that one of these declarations is less enduring than the other? We certainly deny the obvious meaning of the words, if we deny that the connection between believing and possessing miraculous powers is as real and permanent as the connection between believing and being saved.[1]

The same thing is taught in Acts ii. 38. Peter is preaching the gospel to the people, and explaining to them the manifestations of the Spirit which they saw in the apostles, after the outpouring on the day of Pentecost. And he tells them that they have only to believe in Christ in order to have the same power manifested in themselves: "Repent, and be baptized every one of you in the name of Jesus Christ for the remission of sins, *and ye shall receive the gift of the Holy Ghost. For the promise is to you, and to your children, and to as many as are afar off, even as many as the Lord our God shall call.*" The gift of the

---

[1] I shall explain, a little further on, how this is consistent with holding that those who have not the gifts may, nevertheless, have salvation.

Holy Ghost is called *the promise*, not only in this passage, but in many others, as Luke xxiv. 49, Acts i. 4-5, Eph. i. 13; and it does not mean regeneration, or sanctification, but the personal indwelling of the Holy Ghost in a man, as in a temple, manifested by actings of supernatural power. Thus it is said, "The Holy Ghost fell upon them, and they spake with tongues and prophesied" (Acts xix. 6. See also ii. 4; x. 44-46). *This*, then, is the promise which Peter tells the people is not confined to the apostles, but is to them also; which is not confined to one generation, but is to their descendants also; which is not confined to one country, but is to as many as are afar off also, even to as many as the Lord our God shall call; which must mean as many as shall believe, for calling must here mean effectual calling. It is impossible to conceive any language more explicit, in declaring that the gift of the Holy Ghost (which *always* means the miraculous gifts) is limited neither to time nor place, neither to Jew nor Gentile; for the term *afar off* is the term for the Gentiles (see Eph. ii. 13); in fact, that it is limited by nothing but want of faith. This passage, therefore, is a strong confirmation that the promise in Mark xvi. should be taken in its literal sense.

Then again it appears from Eph. i. 13, 14, that this gift of the Spirit, which is the earnest of the inheritance, is to continue with the Church, *until* she enters on the inheritance itself: "In whom also, after that ye believed, ye were sealed with that Holy Spirit of promise, which is the earnest of our inheritance, *until the redemption of the purchased possession;"* that is, until the return of the kinsman Redeemer, to take and give possession. And this same thing, as to the duration of the gifts, is implied in another part of this Epistle, where the gifts are said to be distributed amongst the members of the body, "for the perfecting of the saints, for the work of the ministry, for the edifying of the body of Christ : *till we all come,* in the unity of the faith, and of the knowledge of the Son of God, *unto a perfect man, unto the measure of the stature of the fulness of Christ"* (Eph. iv. 12, 13). In the verses preceding this passage *the gifts* are connected with the *offices* of the Church, as if they were essential to them. And in the passage which I have here quoted the apostle speaks of them as *necessary* for edifying the body of Christ, which surely signifies that a church without them is deficient in a most important point. The following verse marks out an evil condition to be avoided by the manifestation of these gifts, viz., "the being carried about with every wind of doctrine." This evil condition is certainly the present condition of the Church ; and it is so because the word of Christ is taught, not in the power of the spirit, but in the power of natural gifts, such as learning or talent. The charge of Rome against us is quite just in this matter, although she herself be an apostate. Yet apostate as she is, her apostasy is not so awful as the apostasy of those who deny that God is love to every man, and that Christ is the propitiation for the sins of the whole world.

Further, the 12th, 13th, and 14th chapters of 1st Corinthians speak of these gifts, and give instructions for the regulation of them, as if they were the permanent endowment of the Church : " Follow after charity, and desire spiritual gifts, but rather that ye may prophesy." " Wherefore, brethren, covet to prophesy, and forbid not to speak with tongues." Their duration in their partial form is pointed out in that verse, "*when* that which is perfect is come, *then* that which is in part shall be done away."

I shall cite one more passage to the same purpose. In John vii. 38, Jesus says, " He that believeth on me, as the Scripture hath said, out of his belly shall flow rivers of living water. But this spake he of the Spirit, *which they who believe on him should receive :* for the Holy Ghost was not yet given ; *because that Jesus was not yet glorified.*" This certainly implies that *after the glorifying of Jesus*, after his exaltation to the right hand of power, the belief of him should always be followed by miraculous gifts. "Therefore being by the right hand of God exalted, and having received of the Father the promise of the Holy Ghost, he hath shed forth this, which ye now see and hear" (Acts ii. 33).

The difference between the miracles performed by the disciples before the gift of the Holy Ghost was poured out, and those performed by them after that took place, is important. Before Pentecost the Spirit was *with* them ; after it, he was *in* them (John xiv. 17). Before Pentecost the miracles were performed by the power of God, *external* to the disciples, to which they appealed by faith. And thus these miracles were like answers to prayer. But after Pentecost the miracles were performed by the power of God, *dwelling in* the disciples, and uttering itself forth from them, as from a shrine. I do not mean to say that after Pentecost the miracles were *always* performed in this way,—for, in the case of raising Dorcas by Peter, it seems by the account to have been in answer to prayer,—but only that, before Pentecost, they never were performed in this way. Until Christ's ascension he did not receive gifts for men; the power of the Holy Ghost was not lodged in him as the Head of the body, and so that power could not flow *internally* from him into the members. The inflow of the power into them was the witness to the world of the exaltation of the Head.

The great and common mistake with regard to the gifts is, that they were intended merely to authenticate or to witness to the inspiration of the canon of Scripture, and that, therefore, when the canon was completed, they should cease; whereas they were intended to witness to the exaltation of Christ as the Head of the body, the Church.

Reader, do you not feel that if these things be so, then there is a nearness to God, and a walking in him, and a downbreaking of the creature, in real Christianity, of which you as yet know nothing?

I may here remark it as a striking fact illustrative of the deep cunning of the Prince of Darkness, that he has not permitted his instruments to press these texts much, nor to argue from them so triumphantly as they might have done, that the absence of miracles from the Church was a refutation of the Bible. The Bible says, " These signs shall follow them that believe ;" and yet here is a Church holding this faith, and nevertheless unfollowed by these signs. The ready conclusion from this fact certainly is, that the Bible is not true; and we might, therefore, have expected that this argument would have been much urged by those who openly deny the Bible to be a divine revelation. But it has not been much urged. And why? The subtle enemy of man saw that there was more danger to his own kingdom to be apprehended from the use of this weapon, than advantage. It might have led to a result very different from that of disproving the divine authority of the Bible. There was another conclusion to which the argument might have led, and that was, *the lack of faith in the Church*. And thus the pressing of this argument might have awakened the Church to a sense of her true condition; and this Satan fears more than the Bible, knowing that a church asleep is his most powerful weapon against the world—much more powerful than any infidel arguments. There has doubtless been a great deal of true life and true living faith in the professing church since these signs have disappeared; but there must be a great and radical defect somewhere, to account for their absence.

The gospel of the kingdom cannot be fully preached without the manifestation of kingly power in the members of Christ. This is clear from the fact, that although our Lord knew that his apostles were converted living believers at the time of his ascension, still he did not hold them to be as yet fully qualified to be his witnesses, for he commanded them "to tarry in Jerusalem until they were endued with power from on high." " And ye shall receive power after the Holy Ghost is come upon you : and ye shall be witnesses unto me, unto the uttermost parts of the earth." [1] This power from on high must be again manifested in the members of Christ before *the kingdom of Christ* can be rightly witnessed for. And the word of God clearly declares that it will again be manifested. For although that prophecy of Joel, cited by Peter in explanation of what took place on the day of Pentecost, applied to that occasion, inasmuch as it was the commencement of a dispensation which was to continue until the great and terrible day of the Lord; yet its full and proper application is to a period just before the coming of that great day; *and we have thereby the assurance, that whatever interruption may occur in the manifestation of the gifts, there will be a reappearance of them at that period.* This is determined by its position in the context, where it stands connected with the restoration of the Jews, and the judgments on the Gentiles, and with certain signs in the sun and the moon, which, through the other Scriptures, uniformly designate the termination of the present dispensation. The reader may compare the passages. " And it shall

[1] Luke xxiv. 49; Acts i. 8.

come to pass in the last days (saith God), I will pour out my Spirit upon all flesh : and your sons and your daughters shall prophesy, and your young men shall see visions, and your old men shall dream dreams : and on my servants, and on my handmaids, I will pour out in those days of my Spirit; and they shall prophesy : and I will show wonders in heaven above, and signs on the earth beneath ; blood, and fire, and vapour of smoke : *the sun shall be turned into darkness, and the moon into blood*, before that great and notable day of the Lord come : and it shall come to pass, that whosoever will call on the name of the Lord shall be saved" (Acts ii. 17). Now this is just the language of the sixth seal, "*and the sun became black as sackcloth of hair, and the moon became as blood*" (Rev. vi. 12). And it is also the language used in all the Gospels for setting forth, not the destruction of Jerusalem, but the final overthrow of antichrist (see Matt. xxiv. 29 ; Mark xiii. 24 ; Luke xxi. 25). As therefore this outpouring of the Spirit is connected in the prophecy with these signs, we are certainly bound, according to the principles of fair interpretation, to hold it to be connected in point of time with the event which these signs indicate.

According to this interpretation of the prophecy of Joel, the outpouring therein foretold will correspond to, and synchronise with, the *sealing* which is described in Rev. vii. For that sealing is also to take place *just before the last judgments ;* and that it refers to the *miraculous gifts and indwelling of the Spirit* seems abundantly evident from other parts of Scripture in which it is spoken of. The seal certainly is not regeneration : it is God's mark to be put on those who are already regenerated. The persons to be sealed are *the servants of God.* Let us see what is elsewhere said of this seal.

In Eph. i. 13, 14, it is written, " In whom also, *after that ye believed,* ye were *sealed with the Holy Spirit* of promise, which is the earnest of our inheritance until the redemption of the purchased possession." Compare this with an account given in the Acts of the Apostles (xix. 1-6) of Paul's finding certain disciples at Ephesus, whom he recognised as believers, and of whom he inquired "if they had received the Holy Ghost since they believed?" they answered that they had not so much as heard of there being any Holy Ghost. He then asked them, "Unto what then were ye baptized? And they said, Unto John's baptism. Then said Paul, John verily baptized with the baptism of repentance, saying unto the people, that they should believe on him that should come after him, that is, on Christ Jesus. When they heard this, they were baptized in the name of the *Lord* Jesus. And when Paul had laid his hands upon them, the *Holy Ghost came on them, and they spake with tongues and prophesied."* This is the seal. They were believers before, they had spiritual life before, they were regenerate persons before, but they were not sealed before, they had not received the Holy Ghost before. The Holy Ghost had been *with* them before, but now he was *in* them.[1] It

---
[1] John xiv. 17.

was *after* that they believed that they received this seal. So also it was after that the hundred and forty-four thousand had believed, that they were sealed; for the charge committed to the angel was to seal those who were already *the servants of God*. I am anxious to press this, lest any one should confound the work of the Spirit in regeneration with the gift of the Holy Ghost, which appears to be the sealing. And mark, the seal is an *earnest* of the inheritance: that is, a foretaste of it. Now, the inheritance is described under two forms, first, as consisting in God; "they shall have no possession amongst their brethren, *the Lord* is their inheritance," and also "heirs of *God;*" not God's heirs, but "heirs of God." Secondly, as consisting in a kingdom: "Come, ye blessed of my Father, inherit the *kingdom* prepared for you."[1] Now, the seal, to be a true earnest or foretaste, ought to embrace both these forms of the inheritance. And this it does by being the actual indwelling of the *personal Holy Ghost* exercising the *power* of God from out of the man.

I may observe further on this passage in Acts xix., that the baptism of John was distinguished from the baptism of the apostles in this respect, that his was a baptism in the name of the Christ who was to come after him, and whom he pointed out as the Lamb of God that taketh away the sin of the world; and theirs was a baptism in the name of the *risen and exalted King*. "They were baptized in the name of the *Lord Jesus*." The Holy Ghost given to believers was a

[1] Deut. xviii. 2; Rom. viii. 17; Matt. xxv. 34.

witness of the *Lordship* of Christ; thus, Acts v. 31, "Him hath God *exalted* to be a *Prince* and a Saviour, for to give repentance unto Israel and forgiveness of sins. And we are his witnesses of these things, *and so also is the Holy Ghost*, whom he hath given to them that obey him."[1]

But let us look at another instance of sealing. It is written in John vi. 27, "Labour not for the meat which perisheth, but for that meat which endureth unto everlasting life, which the Son of man shall give unto you; for him hath God the Father sealed." Any one who consults the original will see that the last

---

[1] These disciples at Ephesus had *the life* of God in them before they received the Holy Ghost, *and they consequently had salvation:* but they could not witness to the resurrection and exaltation of Christ, for they were not endowed with *power from on high*. The belief that their sins were taken away by the Lamb that taketh away the sin of the world, was a belief which contained *life*, but it did not contain *power*. Now, I do not think that we need go much further than this fact to account for the absence of the gifts from the Church. In the doctrine which has been long preached, the prominent, and, I may say, exclusive subjects, have been the remission of sins and the duties of holiness. We have fallen back to John's baptism, yea, behind it, into an Egyptian bondage; for he preached the Lamb that taketh away the sin of the world, whereas we are urged by our teachers to be still seeking an offered but ungranted forgiveness, and thus to be making bricks without straw. Where is the gospel of the kingdom preached? The death of Christ is spoken of, but who hears of his resurrection or of his exaltation to the right hand of power? Who hears of his exaltation as a head either of life or of power? Indeed, the precious doctrine of his headship, and of the special membership of believers, and of the general membership of men, may be said to have been forgotten. May the Lord revive his work in the midst of the days! I am sure that the consciences of both preachers and hearers must witness to the justness of what is here written.

clause of this passage might be rendered thus, "for him hath the Father sealed, *God*."[1] "God" is the seal, or the impression of the seal, wherewith the Father sealed Jesus. Jesus here calls himself the Son of *man*, to mark that it is as Son of *man* that he is sealed " God ;" to mark that the seal is the Jehovah personally inhabiting and acting in the human nature; according to what he says in another place, "And the words which I speak, I speak not of myself, but the Father which dwelleth in me, he doeth the works." And therefore he says in another place, " I am one that bear witness of myself, and the Father that sent me, he beareth witness also."

This also is the seal wherewith the hundred and forty-four thousand of Israel are sealed before the four winds are loosed, that is, before the judgments come; for when they appear with the Lamb on Mount Zion, we find their seal thus described; "they have his *Father's name* on their foreheads." And let me repeat it; this seal cannot be regeneration or the holy image of God, for those who were to be sealed had previously received this blessing; they were " the servants of God."

I earnestly entreat the attention of my readers to this. This special sealing is to take place just before the coming forth of the last plague, the pouring forth of the last vial, the battle of Armageddon ; or, as it is called in Joel, the great and terrible day of the Lord.

---

[1] The distance between the words Father and God in the original, makes this translation probable, but still there is a difficulty from "God" being in the nominative. But if Θεός be considered as the *device* of the seal, it may be regarded as an indeclinable word, which in some measure lessens the difficulty.

The sealing in the Revelations and the outpouring of the Spirit in Joel are one thing. And that thing is the re-endowment of the Church with the miraculous gifts, just before the great day of the Lord. And that day is near; it hasteth greatly. The judge standeth at the door. We are even now touching on the last scene of this awful mystery, and therefore we ought to be looking for the immediate appearance of the gifts.

The sign which marks our place in the prophetic history and chronology is the gradual wasting of the Turkish empire, which has been going on during the last few years. That empire is spoken of in prophecy under the figure of the river Euphrates. And, therefore, as it is by the pouring out of the sixth vial that the Euphrates is dried up, we have a clear indication that the present time is the time of the sixth vial.

And mark now. We have here set before us in the prophetic record a sealing of the servants of God on their foreheads with his own name, a manifestation of the power of the living Jehovah in these worms of the dust. Now, this is the lifting up of the standard by the Spirit of the Lord against the enemy. And what is that enemy doing in the meantime? that crooked serpent, Leviathan? He is not idle. He is coming in like a flood. Read what the Spirit says of this flood, which is to flow in during the pouring out of the sixth vial, which, as we have seen, is the present point of time : "And I saw three unclean spirits like frogs come out of the mouth of the dragon, and out of the mouth of the beast, and out of the mouth of the false prophet;

for they are the spirits of devils, working miracles, which go forth unto the kings of the earth, and of the whole world, to gather them to the battle of that great day of God Almighty."[1] The enemy is indeed coming in like a flood, he is preparing for the last struggle; and though he knows that his time is short, and that he can neither escape nor resist the might of that arm which is now lifted up against him, yet will he endeavour to solace his malignant spirit in the contemplation of this catastrophe, by drawing in the world to be partakers with him in the fire prepared for him and his angels, and thus to revenge himself on the bruiser of his head, by destroying the souls which he has bought with his own blood; the souls for which his soul has travailed. He will come in like a flood. The usurper will mimic the true King; he will have his sealing too, and so cunningly devised a sealing, that it will deceive, if it were possible, the very elect, for he will forge the seal of God; and as God, he will sit in the temple of God, showing himself to be God; and he will seal his followers also, " he will cause all, both small and great, rich and poor, free and bond, to receive a mark in their right hand or on their forehead;" and he will have his miraculous gifts also; " for his coming is with all power and signs and lying wonders." These are awful prospects, for how shall we distinguish the side of truth from the side of error, if they both possess miraculous power? The only security lies in having ourselves the seal of God, that gift of the Holy Ghost,

[1] Rev. xvi. 13, 14.

by which we may detect all the lying wonders of Satan.

The prayer of the Church ought then to be for this sealing, not only because the very stability of believers will depend much on the possession of it, but also because thus only will they be enabled to bear a full witness for Jesus as the Lord's Anointed, and as the bruiser of the serpent. The magicians were not able to stand before Moses with their enchantments.

This is the state of things which is now fast hurrying on. The mighty contest is drawing to its close, and the two parties are putting forth their strength. The bruiser of the serpent is just about to put his foot on the head of his proud and furious adversary, and that adversary is summoning up all his means of resistance. And, in the meantime, this world, the subject of conflict, remains fast bound in the chains of Satan, lulled asleep by his delusions, and even the Church, even those who know something of the love of Jesus, seem perfectly insensible to the awful circumstances in which they stand, and to the awful crisis which is just at the door. But though men are insensible to their danger, they are not neutral. There are no neutrals in this conflict, and there can be none. Those that have not the life of God in them are really the soldiers of Satan. Reader, are you awake to this awful truth? Do you realise that at this moment, whilst you are reading these lines, you are either contending on God's side against the serpent, or contending on the serpent's side against God? You are engaged in a mighty controversy whether you know it or not. You are a soldier either of God or of Satan, either of light or of darkness. Do you know which side you are on? If you don't know, you pronounce sentence on yourself, you prove yourself to be on the side of darkness; "for he that is in darkness *knoweth not whither he goeth.*" Those who are on God's side are children of the light, they know whither they go. Take warning now before it be too late. And what shall be said of those who, standing in the place of ambassadors for Christ, and speaking in his name, do yet hold forth a false light to the world, and deliver a false message, denying that God is love, and that Christ hath tasted death for every man? This is the very hiss of the serpent, who is even now combining the powers of this world against the rightful King, just as he combined Pontius Pilate, and Herod, and the people of the Jews against him at his first coming. And as the result then was the complete destruction of Jerusalem, so the result now will be the complete destruction of the nations at present occupying the platform of the Roman empire.

Any one at all conversant with the prophetic Scriptures must be satisfied that the period of twelve hundred and sixty days, which was to intervene between the full growth of Popery and the judgment of the Gentile nations, must be either already run out, or must at least be running its last sands. The general outline of prophecy has been that the Deliverer should first be sent to the Jews, and that they should reject him and put him to death, and afterwards in like manner reject his gospel, as preached by his disciples after his ascension; and that therefore they should fall under the judgments of God; dying by the sword, and scattered amongst the nations as a reproach and a hissing; that then the gospel should be declared to the Gentiles, and that they also should reject it, though not in the same way; that their rejection of it should have two steps: that it should first appear, not in refusing the name of Jesus, as the Jews had done, but in corrupting the substance of his gospel, and making out for themselves a monstrous fiction, under the name and form of the truth of God, which we have seen and still see realised in Europe, chiefly under the Papacy, though in a great degree under Protestantism also; and secondly, that it should break forth in the form of direct and avowed infidelity; and that, in consequence of all this, great and heavy judgments should come upon them also, as distinct scourges and punishments for both these forms of rebellion, the infidel power being latterly made use of to scourge and destroy the false Christianity; and that, finally, this infidel power, having risen to great strength and dominion over the nations, and having been thereby puffed up to defy the living God, shall be broken to pieces and consumed by the personal appearance of our Lord Jesus Christ, who shall then return to reign on the earth. Then Israel shall be brought back to his own land, and the mystery of God shall be finished, and the throne of David established, and all things restored.

We have seen the rise of the infidel power, and we

have seen the Papacy scourged by it. But the work is not yet done. The cup of the Lord's right hand is again to go round the nations, and they shall be compelled to drink it to the dregs; they shall be dashed one against another, like the vessels of a potter. The three unclean spirits are now about their work, they are now going forth to the kings of the earth, to gather them together against the Lord and against his Anointed.

It is impossible to look on the world at present without seeing that it is decidedly atheistical. The world says, No God; and for this God will judge the world. Where is God acknowledged as the governor of the nations, as the orderer of events, as the fountain of wisdom, and the fountain of power? Men think that they can do without God, and that by their own prudence and policy and confederacies they can maintain themselves in peace and civil order. Is it not true that second causes, the talents and dispositions of men, the temper and political circumstances of nations, are regarded as the moving principles which determine events? Who looks to the Lord of hosts, to him who sitteth on the circle of the earth, before whom the inhabitants thereof are as grasshoppers? Yet he also is wise—he also is mighty. The language of the 2d Psalm is very awful. It is the voice of God to the rulers and nations of Europe at this very time, for all the prophecies are now meeting upon us, upon whom the ends of the world are come. "The kings of the earth set themselves, and the rulers take counsel together, against the Lord, and against his Anointed :[1] He that sitteth in the heavens shall laugh : the Lord shall have them in derision. Then shall he speak to them in his wrath, and vex them in his sore displeasure; (you think to govern yourselves), yet have I set *my* King upon my holy hill of Zion. I will declare the decree : the Lord hath said unto me, Thou art my Son ; this day have I begotten thee. Ask of me, and I shall give thee the heathen for thine inheritance, and the uttermost parts of the earth for thy possession. Thou shalt break them with a rod of iron ; thou shalt dash them in pieces like a potter's vessel. *Be wise now therefore, O ye kings ; be instructed, ye judges of the earth.* Serve the Lord with fear, and rejoice with trembling. Kiss the Son, lest he be angry, and ye perish from the way, when his wrath is kindled but a little. Blessed are all they that put their trust in him."

O that all those who know the meaning of that word, "Ask, and ye shall receive," would now ask that the Lord would pour into the heart of our king and our rulers the spirit of wisdom and of the fear of the Lord, that so they may be led to seek unto him from whom we have as a nation deeply revolted, and to ask counsel

[1] Peter cites this Psalm (Acts iv. 25) as a prophecy fulfilled by the combination of Herod and Pilate and Caiaphas against Jesus, just as he cites Joel's prophecy as a prophecy fulfilled by the outpouring on the day of Pentecost, and as our Lord himself cites the prophecy of Malachi iv. 5 as a prophecy fulfilled in John the Baptist. In all these instances, the events to which the prophecy was thus applied are to be regarded but as commencements of certain trains or orders of events which in their consummation will give their plenary fulfilment to the prophecies.

at him and to trust in him, and not in man's wisdom nor in the arm of flesh. " Say ye not, A confederacy, to those to whom this people shall say, A confederacy; neither fear ye their fear, nor be afraid, but sanctify the Lord of hosts himself, and let him be your fear, and let him be your dread, *and he shall be a sanctuary.*"[1] And there is no other sanctuary : " Blessed is the people whose God is the Lord." And there is the curse on the other side : " Cursed is the man that trusteth in man, and maketh flesh his arm, and his heart departeth from the Lord." O that the Lord would now pour out upon both rulers and people a spirit of grace and supplication, that the whole land might " cry mightily unto God, yea that they might turn every one from his evil way and from the violence that is in his hands. Who can tell if God will turn and repent, and turn away from his fierce anger, that we perish not?"[2]

Look at the 21st chapter of Luke. From the 6th to the 25th verse there is a prophecy of the punishment to fall on Jerusalem for the rejection of the Messiah. The last clause of the 24th verse contains her history from the time of Titus down to our own days. " And Jerusalem shall be trodden down of the Gentiles, until the times of the Gentiles be fulfilled." Now, there can be no doubt that the fulfilment of the times of the Gentiles is the same period as the conclusion of the 1260 days of the papal apostasy. Mark then what is to take place *when* the times of the Gentiles *are fulfilled*, verse 25, " And there shall be signs in the sun, and the moon,

---

[1] Isaiah viii. 12.   [2] Jonah iii. 8.

and the stars, and upon the earth distress of nations, the sea and the waves roaring; men's hearts failing them for fear, and for looking after those things which are coming on the earth, for the powers of heaven shall be shaken; and then shall they see the Son of man coming in a cloud with power and great glory." In prophetic language, the sun and moon and stars represent either civil or ecclesiastical authorities and constitutions, and the sea and waves rolling represent popular commotions. Such a scene of things has already passed over the earth in the events of the French Revolution, and the present state of affairs proves that the mass of the European world is ripe for a recurrence of them in a still more desolating form. The cement which has hitherto kept the social edifice together is falling out, and the parts thus detached will be dashed together with violence. Reverence for established authorities has disappeared, and we have nothing but self-interest to take its place. And self-interest is no cement; it is a principle of enmity, not of union.

This late shake amongst the nations, which even now agitates them, is a voice in the wilderness, proclaiming the coming of the great day of vengeance. It is a voice joining in with many voices, which are now witnessing that that great day of the Lord is near. And it is felt to be so, even by those who say, " Where is the promise of his coming ?" There is a strange foreboding of evil mixed up with the recklessness which characterises the age. Men's hearts are failing them for fear, and for looking to the things which are coming on the earth.

And what is it that even now hinders the jarring elements from universally rushing to the conflict? Is it any unpreparedness in these elements for the work that lies before them? No; it is that the four angels are still holding the four winds, for the servants of God are not yet sealed on their foreheads. When that is done, the awful seventh vial is ready to be poured out, which is to finish the mystery of God.

My dear reader, do not begin to put it away from you by saying the world has survived many such storms and many such prophecies. We are certain that the present state of things is sooner or later to be terminated by a mighty convulsion, which is to prepare the way for the kingdom of Christ. We are therefore certain that every day brings that convulsion nearer; and thus, that such an expectation must *now* be nearer truth than ever it was before. I am not specifying any precise number of years; but yet I must say that the prophetic record, when compared with the signs of the times, seems to indicate that we are arrived at the brink of the precipice. Certainly we are fast approaching to it; and therefore those who know the Lord ought to be waiting for him: and those who know him not, ought to be warned of their danger, and urged by the terrors of the coming judgments to take refuge in him whilst the day of grace lasts. Hear, then, what God hath spoken concerning the fulfilling of the times of the Gentiles.

"Behold, the day of the Lord cometh, cruel both with wrath and with fierce anger, to lay the land desolate: and he shall destroy the sinners thereof out of it. For the stars of heaven, and the constellations thereof, shall not give their light: the sun shall be darkened in his going forth, and the moon shall not cause her light to shine. And I will punish the world for their evil, and the wicked for their iniquity; and I will cause the arrogancy of the proud to cease, and will lay low the haughtiness of the terrible. I will make a man more precious than fine gold; even a man than the golden wedge of Ophir. Therefore will I shake the heavens, and the earth shall remove out of her place, in the wrath of the Lord of hosts, and in the day of his fierce anger."[1]

"Thus saith the Lord, Take the wine-cup of this fury at my hand, and cause all the nations, to whom I send thee, to drink it. And they shall drink, and be moved, and be mad, because of the sword that I will send among them. (Then took I the cup at the Lord's hand, and made all the nations to drink, unto whom the Lord had sent me.) All the kings of the north far and near, one with another, and all the kingdoms of the world, which are upon the face of the earth: and the king of Sheshach shall drink after them. Therefore thou shalt say unto them, Thus saith the Lord of hosts, the God of Israel, Drink ye, and be drunken, and spue, and fall, and rise no more, because of the sword which I will send among you. And it shall be, if they refuse to take the cup at thine own hand to drink, then shalt thou say unto them, Ye shall certainly

[1] Isaiah xiii. 9.

drink. Therefore prophesy thou against them all these words, and say unto them, The Lord shall roar from on high, and utter his voice from his holy habitation; he shall mightily roar upon his habitation; he shall give a shout, as they that tread the grapes, against all the inhabitants of the earth. A noise shall come even to the ends of the earth: for the Lord hath a controversy with the nations; he will plead with all flesh; he will give them that are wicked to the sword, saith the Lord. Thus saith the Lord of hosts, Behold, evil shall go forth from nation to nation, and a great whirlwind shall be raised up from the coasts of the earth. And the slain of the Lord shall be at that day from the one end of the earth even unto the other end of the earth: they shall not be lamented, neither gathered, nor buried; they shall be dung upon the ground. Howl, ye shepherds, and cry; and wallow yourselves in the ashes, ye principal of the flock: for the days of your slaughter and of your dispersion are accomplished, and ye shall fall like a pleasant vessel."[1]

" Proclaim ye this among the Gentiles, Prepare war, wake up the mighty men, let all the men of war draw near, let them come up: Beat your ploughshares into swords, and your pruning-hooks into spears: let the weak say, I am strong. Assemble yourselves, and come, all ye heathen, and gather yourselves together round about: thither cause thy mighty ones to come down, O Lord. Let the heathen be wakened, and come up to the valley of Jehoshaphat; for there will I sit to judge

[1] Jer. xxv. 15.

all the heathen round about. Put ye in the sickle; for the harvest is ripe: come, get you down; for the press is full, the fats overflow : for their wickedness is great. Multitudes, multitudes in the valley of decision : for the day of the Lord is near in the valley of decision. The sun and the moon shall be darkened, and the stars shall withdraw their shining. The Lord also shall roar out of Zion, and utter his voice from Jerusalem; and the heavens and the earth shall shake : but the Lord will be the hope of his people, and the strength of the children of Israel."[1]

All these prophecies refer to the fulfilling of the times of the Gentiles—a period which has either already arrived, or is just at the door. At that period the rightful owner of the world is coming to claim it,— the Lord's Anointed is coming; he has been absent, having gone to a far country to receive for himself a kingdom, and to return, and now is the time of his return, and now will he take account of his servants, and will say of his enemies who would not have him to reign over them, Bring them hither and slay them before me. He will take account of his servants, those to whom he had committed the charge of his house and of his cause, during his absence, the stewards of his mysteries; he will reckon with them. At his first coming those stewards were the very men who rejected him. They were the builders who set at nought the true corner-stone. They were the husbandmen who cast the heir out of the vineyard, and slew him.

[1] Joel iii. 9.

Let our pastors take this history as a voice saying, "Satan hath desired to have you that he may sift you as wheat;" for assuredly his chief effort will be against them, that through them he may delude the people. Let them remember that the history of Jerusalem is the prophetic history of the Gentile Church. Let them read the history of the chief priests and the scribes, as the history of a work which Satan desires to accomplish in them. And may the Lord now give them, at this awful crisis, hearts according to his own heart, that they may deliver their own souls, and the souls of their people, in the day of recompence. May he put into their hearts a holy love for souls and a holy jealousy for his great name, that they may indeed travail in birth for souls, and blow the trumpet in Zion; and that they may be like Ezekiel, "signs of sighing," warning the people of "the tidings, for it cometh," and that they may weep between the temple and the altar, and say, Spare thy people, O Lord. "Who knoweth if he will return and repent and leave a blessing behind him?" The command left to them, and to all, was, "Watch, for ye know not when the master cometh, lest coming suddenly he find you sleeping." God is even now looking for intercessors, for it is written, "He wondered that there was no intercessor," and he thus reproaches the foolish prophets, "Ye have not gone up into the gaps, neither made up the hedge, for the house of Israel to stand in the battle in the day of the Lord."

This is the dark cloud which is even now hanging over the world. And now is the time, the set time, for the pouring out of the Spirit on all flesh, and the sealing of the servants of God. Now is the time for prayer, and for humiliation, and for witnessing. On the other side of the cloud is the glorious kingdom. But the cloud must be passed through; and the cloud is to be a time of darkness, and desolation, and woe, such as never was upon the earth. It is the treading of the wine-press of the wrath and fierceness of Almighty God. It might be expected that the signs, and the forebodings, and the warning voices, would prepare the world for the event, but it is not to be so. It is to come as a snare on all the inhabitants of the earth, except the children of the kingdom. "As it was in the days of Noah, so it shall be also in the days of the Son of man. They did eat, they drank, they married wives, they were given in marriage, until the day that Noah entered into the ark, and the flood came and destroyed them all. Even thus shall it be in the day when the Son of man is revealed."

Reader, are you prepared for these things? Are you on the Lord's side? Are you born again? Are you watching for the return of your Lord? Are you of those who will cry to the mountains to cover them, or of those who will lift up their heads with joy, knowing that the time of their redemption is come? Don't let these questions be unanswered now; very soon they *must* be answered at the bar of Jesus.

Yes, brethren, the signs of the times are running out, and the day of the Lord is at hand. And there probably never was a period when there was a more decided unpreparedness for it. In the times of intellectual darkness, man's rebellion takes the forms of superstition and idolatry; in the times of intellectual light, it takes the form of atheism, which is the more daring sin. And that is the character of our period and of our religion. Even of our religion, I say, although in saying it I may seem to speak an absurdity. Men have always imagined false things concerning God. But we find that in the earlier ages and amongst uncivilised men, there has always been a more real recognition of a *personal power* in God, a present, acting, controlling, *personal power*. Their doctrines were lies, and therefore had a poisonous influence, but still there was a sense and recognition of an unseen and supernatural being, who, himself a person, acted towards men as persons; and this was good. But where the living personality of God is lost, there is atheism. And this is the case now. And here is the great subtlety of the evil—the name of God, and the forms of religion and many of the forms of morality are retained, and therefore the age thinks itself a religious and God-fearing age, but it is not the *living God* that is worshipped. Men have *a religion* instead of *a God*. This is their atheism, this is their shield against God. And so we find that everything that brings God near to them as a *living power*, everything supernatural, is rejected. They will have a God with whom they can be at ease, they like not to retain in their knowledge a God who is near, and living, and making continual demands on them, and who is not bound by the laws of nature.

And so they shrink from the thought of the voice of God being again heard on the earth, and from the thought of the personal advent of Christ, to execute judgment and to reign in righteousness, and they prefer even a continuance of present evils. And in like manner they shrink from the doctrine of the necessity of personal assurance, because it calls on them to meet God's eye. They would have no objection to the doctrine of God's universal love, if that love were the benevolence of the philosophers; but they cannot bear the mention of a love of God unto death for every man, that looks every man intensely in the face, and demands from him a continual response, and a continual sympathy in abhorrence of evil, and that brings against him a continual charge of baseness, and ingratitude, and wickedness, when he looks away, and ceases to respond to it, and to sympathise with it.

O for the voice of the mighty God of Jacob to come forth and awaken out of their deep sleep the Church and the world. They are like men asleep on the top of a mast, and they know it not; for they listen to that word, "all things continue as they were from the foundation of the world," and they are lulled by it to their destruction; for even now the deep openeth her mouth for them. And oh! ye watchmen, hear this word, "If a man die unwarned, his blood will I require at the watchman's hand" (Ezek. xxxiii. 6). Give warning now; listen to the voice of the day of the Lord, and proclaim its coming. It hasteth greatly; it is even at the door. Cry aloud, "Fear God, and give him glory, for the hour of his judgments is come." Even now is the Lord rising out of his place to plead with all flesh, and to punish the world for its iniquity. His sword is even now lifted up, it is made bright for the slaughter. Now will he do his work, his strange work. Oh, then, come under his shadow now, and call others to come under it; for there is no help, no refuge but in him, even in him of whom it is written, "*A Man* shall be a hiding-place from the storm, and a covert from the tempest." He will not forsake his people, for his great name's sake, because it hath pleased him to make them his people.

CHAPTER VI.

GOD THE SOVEREIGN.

ON the other side of that darkness is the glorious light. The light is to arise out of the darkness. The kingdom of light is to be manifested in the destruction of the kingdom of darkness, and as rising out of its ruins. And thus the great mystery of God will be unfolded, and the ways of God will be justified.

The permission of evil is the great mystery. Is it not a mystery that God should be *omnipotent love*, and yet that the world should be just a vast caldron boiling over with violence and pollution and misery? It is no wonderful thing that a world of sin should be a world of sorrow; this requires no explanation. The creature away from God is necessarily away from blessedness, and it is right that it should be so. But the existence, the permitted and prolonged existence, of a sinning and sorrowing world, is a riddle; and the triumph of darkness over light is a riddle; and the affliction of God's children is a riddle. *Can* God not help this, or *will* he not? We are living and moving and having our being in the midst of this mighty riddle—it meets us everywhere—it encloses us as a net on every hand, and man's wisdom can find no outlet, no solution. And amongst the many marvels that are to be found in man's character and condition, there are few greater than this, that he should be able to contemplate himself and his condition without astonishment, and as if there were nothing in them to be wondered at. It is indeed a mighty riddle. It is God's riddle, and none can solve it but God. God's word contains the solution of it. This is the *secret of the Lord*, which is with them that fear him: and it consists in the knowledge of God and of Jesus Christ whom he hath sent.

Man charges God with the existence of evil, and exculpates himself. God declares that evil has arisen from the creature's seeking to be independent of God, and so shutting God out from it. God is not the author of evil. He is good, and he abhorreth evil, and desireth its destruction. The death of Christ is the expression of God's abhorrence to evil, of God's incompatibility with evil. If God were the author of evil, there would be no hope for man. But although God is not the author of evil, although he created all things very good, yet he has permitted evil to enter and mar the good. Now, why is this? A good rising out of evil is the solution of the mystery,—a higher, and nobler, and more blessed good than that which the evil had destroyed, and a good which could be produced only by the destruction of evil. The whole Bible is just a varied unfolding of this mystery—a varied revelation of this purpose, in order that man, by the knowledge of it, might be carried forward through and beyond the present evil, to embrace a future good, which is to arise out of it. This hope is the anchor of the soul; it is the hope by which we are saved. Now mark how this hope is set before us in the brazen serpent.

The first word of gospel to man, after he had yielded to the serpent's temptation, and so had opened his heart to the inflow of evil, was, "The seed of the woman shall bruise the serpent's head." Although the serpent has prevailed against you, and has brought you under the power of that word, "thou shalt surely die," yet there is hope,—ye *shall* surely die; but there is a strong Deliverer coming, who will open the house of the prisoners,—who will deliver from death, and destroy him that had the power of death, even the devil, and give a better life than that which was lost. The serpent lifted up in the wilderness is just a confirmation and a carrying forward of this promise. For here we see the serpent with his head bruised, and health coming out of him, as a foreshadowing of that life which is to arise out of the victory of the woman's seed over him.

The same gospel was repeated to Noah in these words: "And surely your blood of your lives will I require: at the hand of every beast will I require it, and at the hand of the man; at the hand of every man's brother will I require the life of man. Whoso sheddeth man's blood, by the man shall his blood be shed: for in the image of God made he man." What is the meaning of God's requiring man's blood at the hand of *every beast?* Hear what Daniel says: "I saw the four winds of heaven strive upon the great sea, and four great *beasts* came up from the sea:" and this is the interpretation, "These great *beasts*, which are four, are four kings, which shall arise out of the earth" (Daniel vii. 2, 17). They are, in fact, human dominations set up by the devil, and used by him against the Lord's Anointed. These are the beasts at whose hand God will require the blood of man. We are now living in the time of the last beast—the most powerful and the most wicked of them all. His history is the great subject of the Revelations of John. He contains all the evil of the former beasts. In fact, they all survive, and are summed up in him. And so it is said, that "he is like a leopard, and his feet as the feet of a bear, and his mouth as the mouth of a lion; and the *dragon, the old serpent*, gives him his power, and seat, and great authority." With his destruction the mystery of God is to finish, and at his hand God will require the life of man; he hath shed man's blood; his history has been a history of blood; the spirit of Satan, who hath been a murderer from the beginning, has been in him, and God will take vengeance on him, and he will take it through the hand of him who is every man's brother, and the avenger of every man's blood. "By the *man* shall his blood be shed" (Rev. xix. 19; Gen. ix. 6). He is to make war upon the saints, and to overcome them. But his fate is sure. The avenger of blood will require it of him. That this is the meaning of the word spoken to Noah will be evident to any one who will compare the passages. In Genesis it is said of the beast, "He that sheddeth man's blood, by man shall his blood be shed" (Gen. ix. 6); and in Revelations it is said of him, "He that killeth with the sword, must be killed with the sword" (Rev. xiii. 10). And in the Revelations also we have the fulfilment of this prophecy, in the account of the last conflict, in which *the man* overcomes *the beast.* "And I saw heaven opened, and behold a white horse; and he that sat upon him was called Faithful and True; and he treadeth the wine-press of the fierceness and wrath of Almighty God. And I saw the *beast,* and the kings of the earth gathered together to make war against him that sat on the horse, and against his army: and the beast was taken, and was cast alive into a lake of fire, burning with brimstone" (Rev. xix. 11). And *the man* who thus overcomes the beast shall reign upon the earth, for his name is *King of kings* and *Lord of lords.* He will put down all power of man which has been moved and used by the serpent, and will establish the reign of God on the earth, and of man under God.

When man yielded his power to be used by the devil, this word passed upon him, "Let his heart be changed from man's, and let a beast's heart be given unto him." And when the Deliverer shall have overcome the beast, this word also shall be verified, "At the same time, even at the end of the days, my reason returned unto me, and I was established in my kingdom, and excellent glory was added unto me" (Dan. iv. 16, 36).

The beast rose out of the waters; that first flood had

not drowned him, but he is to be cast into the lake of fire even now, before the thousand years commence, into that same lake into which, after the thousand years are ended, the serpent himself, and death, and hell, are to be cast at the final judgment. The blessedness of the millennial reign is to arise out of the destruction of the beast, as the blessedness of the permanent glory after the millennium is to arise out of the destruction of the serpent. Whilst the serpent remains, death remains. But when they are cast into the lake, then the world shall be baptized with fire, and the new heavens and the new earth, in which dwelleth righteousness, shall appear, as rising out of their defeat. This is just a better life coming to the earth out of the death of the serpent, as the healing came to the Israelites out of the brazen serpent lifted up.

The defeat of the devil himself, the old serpent, foretold to Adam, was the first gospel. The defeat of the beast, that is, of all earthly power used and animated by the serpent, foretold to Noah, was the second form of the gospel, and was really the *gospel of the kingdom*. The flood had washed the earth of her abominations, and a new earth had risen out of the destruction of the old earth. Through death, the earth had received a new life. That new life was to suffer from the oppression of the beast; but this promise of the destruction of the oppressor, this renewal of the gospel, was an anchor of the soul.

The more the reader considers the expressions containing the threat of *requiring man's blood at the hand of every beast, and at the hand of every man's brother*, along with the circumstances in which they were spoken, and the references made to them in other parts of the Scriptures, the more, I am sure, he will be convinced that the interpretation which has now been given has nothing fanciful in it, and must be the true one. They fill the chief place in the blessing with which God blessed the second father of men when he descended from the ark to take possession of the new world which had just emerged from the flood. The blessing to Adam, immediately after the fall, was summed up in that word, "The seed of the woman shall bruise the serpent's head." This was the one hope of the fallen race, there was no hope out of it, and therefore any blessing which did not contain this promise in it must have been defective in the chief element of blessing. Now, can we suppose that this mighty thing was omitted in the blessing pronounced on Noah and his family? And yet unless the interpretation given of *the beast* and of *every man's brother*, is the true one, it is omitted. The faithfulness of God, which had already given this promise to the race, and the necessities of man, which continued the same, required that this promise concerning the serpent and the seed should reappear, under one form or other, in every blessing pronounced by God on man. And it is so, for in Noah's blessing the serpent appears under the form of, or is represented by, *the beast*, to whom " he gives his power, and seat, and great authority;" and the seed of the woman appears under the form of *the man*, and of *every man's brother*. At the hand of *the man*, at the hand of *every man's brother*, will I require the blood of man's life shed by *the beast*. As the *beast* is the name for the serpent's usurpation, or for human domination under the guidance of the serpent, so the name of *every man's brother*, which is given here to the overcomer of the beast, suits well with that seed of the woman who is also the Lord's Anointed, whose type in Israel was to be elected according to this law, " one from among thy brethren shalt thou set king over thee ; thou mayest not set a stranger over thee, *who is not thy brother*" (Deut. xvii. 15). He is not only the rightful king, but he is also the avenger of the blood of his brethren, as being their nearest kinsman, and he will avenge it on that enemy who has been a murderer from the beginning, and on his instruments. And see what is prophesied of this king, " And I the Lord will be their God, and my servant (David), the beloved one, a *prince* among them ; I the Lord have spoken it. And I will make with them a covenant of peace, and will cause the *evil beasts* to cease out of the land." " And they shall no more be a prey to the heathen, neither shall *the beast* of the land devour them, but they shall dwell safely, and none shall make them afraid" (Ezek. xxxiv, 25, 28). And when "a king shall reign in righteousness," then this shall be true of the earth, " No *lion* shall be there, neither shall any ravenous *beast* walk there" (Isaiah xxxv. 9).

Everything had been forfeited by the fall, because *life*, in which all other things are included, had been forfeited. This was the great loss with which Adam was threatened, and no other loss was specified. The promise of the Deliverer, therefore, would be to his mind, specially, a promise of the restoration of immortality. The blessing would just meet the forfeiture; and the preservation of his life after the forfeiture had been incurred would be to him a pledge and a confirmation of the full accomplishment of the promise of the bruising of the serpent's head by the woman's seed, as a promise of the restoration of immortality. Nothing had been spoken to him by God of the loss of the dominion, and nothing was spoken to him concerning its restoration. Life was the blessing which had been lost, and which was to be restored. Death was the curse which had been pronounced, and which was to be removed. But though nothing had been spoken of the forfeiture of the dominion, yet it had been forfeited; and though nothing had been spoken specially of its restoration, yet it was to be restored. And the promise of this restoration is actually contained in the blessing pronounced upon Noah. Adam's blessing before the fall ran thus, "Be fruitful and multiply, and replenish the earth, and have *dominion* over every living thing that moves upon the earth." Noah's blessing has the same commencement, but the dominion had been forfeited by the fall; and therefore, instead of the gift of the dominion, we find in Noah's blessing the promise of him through whom the dominion is to be recovered. In the promise made to Adam, the Deliverer appears as the Head of life. In the promise made to Noah, he appears as the Head of dominion. In the promise made to Adam, he is the Destroyer of him who had destroyed life. In the promise made to Noah, he appears as the Destroyer of him who had usurped the dominion of the earth. In both of these first blessings, it is remarkable that the blessing to man is couched under the form of a curse on man's enemies—the serpent and the beast.

The blessing on Noah then is just *the gospel of the kingdom*. It is the promise that the true King shall overcome the usurper, and avenge man's blood upon him, and establish the kingdom of righteousness and peace and joy in the Holy Ghost; that is, cast out the evil beasts. And so we find the types of that true King foreshadowing his victory by the destruction of evil beasts. Thus Samson, the mighty Nazarite of Dan, rent the lion ; and David, the shepherd of Israel, slew, in the defence of his father's flock, both a lion and a bear. And when he offered himself as the champion against Goliath, he said, " And this uncircumcised Philistine shall be as one of these."

The serpent himself appears as the first enemy, and he is revealed as the seducer of man from God as the fountain of life, and thus as the destroyer of man's life. He is the first enemy, and he is last to be destroyed. For it is not until after the thousand years are finished, that he, along with death and hell, are to be cast into the lake of fire. The beast is the second enemy, and he is revealed as drawing men from God as the fountain of power. He is the dragon's anointed, even as Jesus Christ is the Lord's Anointed. For the dragon had " given him his power, and seat, and great authority." He is to be overcome, and cast into the lake of fire at the commencement of the thousand years, by that King of kings who is the avenger of man's blood, and the brother of every man.

And as the final victory of the woman's seed over the serpent, and the blessed immortality which is to result from that victory, are typically foreshadowed by the serpent lifted up in the wilderness, and by the health proceeding out of it; so the final victory over the beast, and the sweet peace which, during the thousand years, is to result from that victory, are typically foreshadowed by the rending of the lion by the judge of Israel, and by the honey which came out of his dead carcass. "Out of the eater came forth meat; out of the oppressor came forth sweetness." This was Samson's riddle; and it is, in truth, the shadow of that great mystery of God in which we are all enclosed. Our mighty Nazarite hath also rent the lion, and hath put forth his riddle, "Blessed are they that are persecuted for righteousness' sake, for theirs is the kingdom of heaven," which is just Samson's riddle; and even after the *third day*, which might well have given the answer to it, his companions cannot expound it; but the *seventh day* of the feast is coming, the true seventh day, the rest of God, the glorious kingdom of our Lord Jesus Christ, and then the earth will flow with the honey, and the riddle will be solved. "And she wept before him the seven days while their feast lasted; and it came to pass on the seventh day that he told her, because she lay sore upon him."[1] The prayer of the Church will yet prevail

[1] Judges xiv. 17.

and the fruit of the travail of the soul of Jesus shall yet be manifested in her, to the praise of the glory of God.

The same gospel was preached in another form to Abraham. In it the promise of the seed is renewed, and in the seed a blessing is promised to all the families of the earth; but neither the serpent nor the beast is mentioned. In God's dealings, however, with Abraham respecting this promise, and in the way in which it was confirmed to him, there is an indication given of another enemy, out of whose death it is that the blessing is to come. It was from Abraham's "body now dead, and from the deadness of Sarah's womb," that the seed was to spring. The seed of life was to spring out of this death of the *flesh*, out of this *grave*, as it were; and as it is in him that all the families of the earth are to be blessed, we have the indication given us that it is through the death of the flesh that the new life is to be obtained. Now it is through the flesh—the natural life —that the serpent and the beast chiefly exercise their power over us. For no sooner had Adam yielded to the devil's lie, than the spirit of the devil entered into his flesh, his natural life, and took possession of it, and has still continued to hold it, and to use it as armour against the Spirit of God in man, and against that witness which God has placed for himself in the conscience of every man. And thus it is that the *seed*, through the *death of the flesh*, gains the victory over the serpent and the beast, and spoils the strong man of the armour in which he trusted.

The fallen flesh, thus occupied by the spirit of Satan,

is the third enemy of God and man to be vanquished by the great Deliverer. It is the evil counsellor that is continually urging man to seek life in the gratification of self, and thus it is continually repeating the serpent's lie, that God is not the fountain of life ; and, by the influence of this lie, it is continually leading him from God as the fountain of authority also, and drawing him into a confederacy with the beast. It is the false prophet, it is Balaam the son of *Bosor* (*the flesh*), who counselled Balak to set a stumbling-block before the children of Israel, so as to cause them to commit a trespass against the Lord in the matter of Peor, and thus to draw down upon them the anger of the Lord. It was a carnal counsel, and a carnal temptation. He was the prophet of the flesh, and he came to the help of the beast, the king of Moab, against the armies of the living God. He was however, notwithstanding his own evil purposes, constrained, by the mighty power of the Spirit, to bless Israel; thus showing forth in shadow, that it was through the Spirit's taking possession of the fallen flesh that the blessing was to come. After this he gave his evil counsel, and joined the armies of the beast, and was slain with them on the day of Midian. This is that false prophet who, along with the beast, is overcome, and cast into the lake of fire, at the beginning of the thousand years, by him who sat upon the white horse, and whose name is King of kings and Lord of lords.[1] This fallen flesh, this false prophet, is always

---

[1] See Numbers xxii. xxiii. xxiv. xxxi. 8, 16 ; Rev. xix. 20; 2 Peter ii. 5.

throughout the Epistles contrasted with the Spirit of God, the true Counsellor, the true Comforter,—the spirit lusteth against the flesh, and the flesh against the spirit; and as it is by his Spirit that God is ever present with the souls which he has made, so it is by the flesh that Satan is ever present with all men, and thus, in some degree, possesses the attribute of omnipresence. And thus the flesh appears as the third person of the antitrinity, the dragon, the beast, and the false prophet, the devil, the world, and the flesh, the dragon being opposed to God, as the fountain of life, the beast being opposed to Jesus, as the anointed king, and the false prophet, who continually urges on us the delusions of the dragon and the beast, being opposed to the Spirit, who takes of the things of Christ, and shows them unto us.

The death of the *flesh* of Christ, the anointed Head of the body, was followed by the dispensation of the *Spirit;* the casting of the *beast* into the lake of fire shall be followed by the millennial reign of *Jesus;* the casting of the *serpent*, along with death and hades, into the lake, shall be followed by the giving up of the kingdom into the hand of the *Father*, and the subjecting of the Son to him, that God may be all in all (1 Cor. xv. 26-28). There is surely a mighty mystery contained in these contrasts and connections, and a mystery which we ought to search into, for it cannot be in vain that God has given us these traces of it in his word. It is written, that "the wise shall understand;" and Jesus says to his disciples, "All things that I have heard of my Father I have made known unto you." It is not a true humility which draws back from the counsel of God. The entrance of thy word giveth light and understanding to the simple. It giveth light and understanding. It not only presents truths to us, but gives us light to see them by, and understanding wherewith to apprehend them. The word of God is a living thing; it is a stream issuing out from God; it is God's life. "My word is spirit and life." God is in the word; open then thy mouth wide, and be filled with God. "The river of God is full of water;" "Drink, yea drink abundantly, O beloved." We are exhorted not to satisfy ourselves with the outside meaning of the word, but to dig in it for the treasures hid in it. I understand very little of what is contained in the things of which I have been writing in the last few pages, but I am sure there is much of God's truth in them, for I cannot but recognise his seal in the magnitude and mightiness with which they span creation and grasp its history. Verily they bear the stamp of him who sitteth upon the circle of the earth, and the inhabitants thereof are as grasshoppers. They are the living elements of the word of God, and they are continually appearing and reappearing throughout it, under various forms, in all its histories and prophecies, and prayers and thanksgivings. They are the seeds of things; and all events are but the unfoldings or reappearances of them. The Bible is the book of the wars of the Lord; it begins with setting forth and describing his enemies, and declaring his purpose in them and for them, and it concludes with a glorious vision of the accomplishment of his purpose, in the establishment of a holy, and blessed, and enduring kingdom arising out of their defeat; and the intermediate part just contains the history of the warfare, which consists in a continued unfolding and discovery of the goodness of God, and the evil of his enemies.

It contains the whole history of the world, and of the race, for there is no event which takes place in this world, or which has relation to any partaker of the one flesh, that does not form a part of the wars of the Lord. This world and this flesh are both the field of the conflict and the subject of it. They have been occupied by a usurper, and God is reconquering them. And why has he made the history of this warfare known to us? Why has he thus opened his heart and his counsels to worms of the dust? It is not only that when the work is accomplished, there may be a record to prove that as it was God who foretold it, so it was God that hath done it, and that whilst the work is in progress there may be a continual witness that the Lord's hand is in all; it no doubt answers, and will answer, these purposes, but there is another purpose, God's love hath purposed for us that we should be his sons and daughters, that we should be sharers in his plans, yea, and fellow-workers with him in their accomplishment; and therefore he says, "Shall I hide from Abraham that which I do?" He has chosen the human nature to be his battle-axe and weapons of war, for it is the seed of the woman that is to bruise the serpent's head; and he would have it a conscious instrument, a willing weapon; and it is to become so by his *word* abiding in it. It is wonderful to think how God has lavished his confidence upon us, and has laid open to us the secrets of his government, and has called us into a fellowship of interest with himself. It shows us that the calling to be the sons of God is no vain thing—no empty title; that he means what he says, when he calls us to be sons. Christ, the seed of the woman, the first-begotten son, is the personal *word* in flesh; he is the Captain of salvation, the Captain of the Lord's host; and Christians, the members of his body, are those in whose flesh the *word* of Christ dwells; and thus it is that they become weapons of righteousness unto God, and good soldiers of Christ. The word is the utterance of God, the eternal wisdom expressed, the shining forth of the invisible glory, the intelligible mind of God. And it is this which is now dwelling in our flesh, and dwelling as a fountain-head, from which streams flow forth, seeking to fill the whole mass. He hath shown us the end from the beginning, and hath thus invited us to stand in his counsel, and to see things even as he sees them. It is just one thing with the gift of Christ. He treats us even as if he were Christ; he tells us everything. "All things that I have heard of my Father, I have made known unto you." This confidential disclosure of the heart of God in his word, is just the pouring forth of his mind into the human nature, out of which he would make to himself a Church to be as a transparent vessel, through which the light of his mind might visibly and intelligibly shine forth upon the creation.

This fatherly familiarity of God toward man is a

mighty mystery. And the reception which it hath met with from man is the opposite mystery. Man has despised the confidence of God. As the Incarnate Word was crucified, so the spoken word has been trodden on. And even to those who acknowledge its authority, it is a sealed book, for they enter not in by the door, and they yield not themselves to the Spirit. A love of God towards man, which seeks oneness with him, is the first principle of the Bible, and is indeed the only reason which can account for the existence of the Bible. Now this is the door, and as it is the door, so it is the light by which alone we can see what is within. No wonder then that the Bible is a sealed book, since this love is denied; and men think that they are to understand it by their own wisdom and learning, and thus the Spirit has been grieved and quenched: and in this way "the vision of all is become unto you as the words of a book that is sealed, which men deliver to one that is learned, saying, Read this, I pray thee: and he saith, I cannot; for it is sealed: and the book is delivered to him that is not learned, saying, Read this, I pray thee: and he saith, I am not learned. Wherefore the Lord said, Forasmuch as this people draw near me with their mouth, and with their lips do honour me, but have removed their heart far from me, and their fear toward me is taught by the precept of men: therefore, behold, I will proceed to do a marvellous work among this people, even a marvellous work and a wonder; for the wisdom of their wise men shall perish, and the understanding of their prudent men shall be hid." We are now lying under the power of this word, and yet we say that we are increased in goods, and have need of nothing. And this state of thick darkness is to continue until the day of Christ: "In that day the deaf shall hear the words of the book, and the eyes of the blind shall see out of obscurity, and out of darkness" (Isaiah xxix.). May the Lord speedily rend the veil!

The prophetic history of this warfare and its result is the gospel. It is the good news of a glory and a blessedness which are to rise out of the present scene of things. The gospel has always been a promise, because it has been a word going forth and travelling on to its accomplishment. And thus it at once declares the source in the heart of God from which it comes, and the object which it is to execute. It declares a present character in God, as well as a future event; for the future event rises out of the present character.

The gospel preached to Adam was the promise of the destruction of the destroyer; the promise of the undoing of him who had introduced sin and death. This promise looks forward to a far future event; but it declares also a present character in God as the source of the promise, and that is a forgiving holy love; and thus the promise of "the Seed" contains a declaration of the present reopening of the access to God as the fountain of life. This renewal or reopening of the access to God as the fountain of life, which had been closed up by the rebellion, is what is meant by the forgiveness of sin, inasmuch as the exclusion from God constitutes the condemnation of sin. No creature that is permitted to drink out of God can be said to be under condemnation. For the fountain is the love of God, and the permission to any creature to enjoy the love of God (which is drinking out of the fountain) is certainly a permission to it to believe itself loved by him; for how else can his love be enjoyed? But the permission to believe this is a declaration of its truth, for it is impossible that God could expressly permit any creature to believe a lie. And thus God's invitation to men, " Ho, every one that thirsteth, come ye to the waters," is a declaration of universal forgiveness, for it is an assurance that no one is excluded from his love, nay, that all are called to enjoy it. This reopened access to God is the inheritance to which every man is now born, as much as the original access was the inheritance to which Adam was created; and it is the knowledge of this forgiveness of sin, this reopened access, which gives a man *confidence* before God, and thus enables him to drink of the fountain. Whilst he does not know it, he has no confidence before God, he cannot drink out of God, and so " he is *alienated* from the *life* of God through the *ignorance* that is in him." He cannot live to God, or before God, until he knows himself forgiven. And therefore it is Satan's grand weapon of destruction to persuade men that they are not forgiven, but that forgiveness needs yet to be obtained before they can look to God as loving them. His lie to the unfallen man was that God was not a sufficiently liberal fountain of life, and his lie to the fallen man is that he is not forgiven, and thus that the fountain of life is closed to him.

The nakedness, through the consciousness of which Adam and Eve were afraid to stand in the presence of God, was a symbol of the fearfulness and want of confidence which they felt whilst they knew themselves to be sinners, and knew not that their sins were forgiven; and the coats of skins, which must have been the skins of animals slain in sacrifice, are types of their confidence restored through the knowledge of the great sacrifice for sin.[1] It is worthy of remark that these coats, made of the skins of the victims, have substantially the same meaning as the sprinking of the blood of the victims under the law. Neither the coats of skins, nor the sprinkling of the blood, made any addition to the sacrifice; the sacrifice was finished by the death of the victim, and the sin was put away by the finishing of the sacrifice; but it was needful that the worshipper should *know* that the sacrifice was *finished*, in order to have *confidence* before God; because, until he knew that sin was put away, he could not have confidence. The skin and the blood of the victim were proofs of its death; they were, therefore, proofs that the sacrifice was finished, and that the sin was put away; and thus it is that the belief of that word, "it is finished," is to us both the covering of our nakedness with the coats of skins, and the

---

[1] The wedding garment is another type of the same thing. The intruding guest had some other ground of confidence than the sacrifice for sin.

sprinkling of us with the blood; because it is the assurance that the sacrifice is completed and sin put away, and thus it gives confidence before God, and boldness to drink of the fountain of life which is in his love. That sacrifice hath finished transgression and made an end of sin, whether a man knows it or not; but his conscience is not purged till he knows it; he has not on the wedding garment till he knows it; he is not a true worshipper; he is not drinking out of God; he is not trusting in God till he knows it. He may have confidence, but it is not a confidence in God; it is not a confidence that God will acknowledge. The coats of skin, and the sprinkling of the blood, are both of them figures of the necessity of a personal confidence towards God, founded on that sacrifice which hath put away the sin of the world, in order to qualify a fallen man to serve God, and enjoy him as the fountain of life.

Thus the coats of skins were part of the gospel preached to Adam; they declared the forgiveness of sins, and so they gave boldness to drink of the fountain of life revealed in the promise of the bruiser of the serpent's head. As I believe that this is the meaning of the coats of skins, so I am also much disposed to believe that the Hutchesonian interpretation of " the cherubim and the flaming sword to keep the way to the tree of life," is the true interpretation—namely, that the cherubim were symbols of the divine presence, and that the flaming sword, or, as it is literally, the fire and knife, were symbols of the great sacrifice which hath taken away the sin of the world; and that the truth here taught was, that the access to the tree or fountain of life was kept open through the shedding of blood acceptable to God; the knife meaning the shedding of the blood, and the fire meaning its acceptance with God.

The gospel preached to Adam in the promise of the destruction of the serpent, thus contained these two things—the assurance of the final destruction of sin and death, when the kingdom shall be delivered into the Father's hand; and the revealing of the fountain of life as reopened to man by the forgiveness of sin through blood.

The gospel to Noah was specially, as we have seen, the gospel of the kingdom; and this, I believe, had its symbol in Noah's planting the vine and drinking of its fruit, even the new wine of the kingdom, the wine that maketh glad the heart of man. There is a connection between the first chapter of John's Gospel and the gospel preached to Adam. For there we read both of the fountain of life and of the new access to it, revealed in the *Word*, who is also the *Lamb* that taketh away the sin of the world. And there is a connection between the second chapter of John's Gospel and the gospel preached to Noah. For there we read of the purging of the temple, and then of the water of the purification being changed into the wine of the kingdom. Noah had risen out from the flood, and out from the death of the old world into a world purified of its pollutions, and into a life which was typical of the resurrection-life, and being thus *born again, he saw the kingdom of God*, and was glad. Thus, the gospel preached to him, although specially the gospel of the *kingdom*, yet embraced the gospel of the *life*, as its foundation; and thus he and his family represented the Church of the first-born, the blessed ones who have part in the first resurrection, and are the heirs of the glorious kingdom.

Noah was also a type of Christ, the first of the firstborn. For before the flood came, Noah knew that it was coming; he knew that the world, of which he was himself one, lay under this threatened judgment; he felt as a man burdened with a sentence, and who had to undergo and pass through the infliction of it. But when the flood had come, and was past, and when he descended from the ark, he felt as one who had undergone and survived his sentence; he felt as a free man, unburdened by any condemnation, against whom no claim existed, and over whom no evil impended. And to his heart thus lightened the kingdom was revealed, and he planted the vine and drank of its fruit.

So Christ, before his death, was burdened by a sense of an impending judgment; he had become the partaker and the head of a nature which, being a sinful nature, was, on account of sin, subject to the punishment of death, and he knew that he had to undergo and pass through his punishment, and that the life which he had was a condemned life. But when the sentence was executed, and when he rose from the grave, he felt as a free man, over whom no evil impended, and against whom sin had no claim; he knew that he had nothing now before him but the glorious kingdom. Now, as we were all included in Noah, so are we all included in Christ, the head of the nature : and thus baptism into his death and resurrection is the antitype of Noah's safe passage through the flood; for our baptism into his name is an ordinance by which God declares that we are of one body with him, and that, as he had earned remission of sin by passing through the penalty, we are, through our natural connection with him, partakers of that remission. And the knowledge of this saves us, because it purges our consciences before God, by setting us free from the sense of imputed sin, and thus begets us into a living hope of the coming kingdom.[1]

As Noah was the type of the first resurrection, so he was in some measure the type of the election. Now wherein did his election consist? It consisted simply in this—that he was made to know the truth of a thing, which was as true to every individual that perished as it was to him; he was made to know that God would bring a flood upon the earth for its wickedness, but that he willed not the death of the wicked; he

---

[1] See 1 Pet. iii. 21. If the knowledge of Christ's resurrection ought to give a man the answer of a good conscience towards God, it must be because he ought to know himself to be included in Christ. Christ's resurrection was Christ's clearance from condemnation, and it is also the clearance of all who are included in him. But unless the union of Christ with every man be admitted, how is any man so to ascertain it in his own case as to rejoice immediately on knowing of the resurrection of Christ?

willed not that any should perish, but that all should go into the ark and live. He was appointed to be the preacher of these tidings, and by preaching them he condemned the world that refused to hear. If the ark had not been as free to all as to him, his preaching could not have condemned them. He could never have condemned them by telling them of any particular privilege which had been bestowed on himself and his family. Their condemnation consisted in this, that the same long-suffering and forgiving love which had watched over Noah, and had warned him of the coming danger, and had provided a refuge for him, had come forth upon them, and had been despised. In reality, the doctrine of election, as taught by the history of Noah, amounts to this, that the glorious kingdom which is to come, is a kingdom of which none can be partakers except those who have first been partakers of a new life, a resurrection-life, a life which has risen out of an exhausted condemnation. "To him that hath shall be given;" to him that hath the life shall be given the kingdom; it shall be said to him, "I will make thee *ruler* over many things." "And from him that hath not, shall be taken away even that he hath;" from him that hath not the life, shall be taken away even that provision of life, and that hope of the kingdom which he hath despised. The gospel of the *kingdom* can only be truly known and welcomed by those who know the gospel of *life*, which to the fallen man is the gospel of the Lamb of God, which taketh away the sin of the world.

The ark and the vine, the water and the wine, were the symbols of the gospel preached to Noah just as the coats of skins, and the sacrificial access to the tree of life, were the symbols of the gospel preached to Adam.

Noah's drunkenness[1] and David's dancing before the ark were manifestations of the same spirit, and were, like the day of Pentecost, foretastes of the glorious day of Christ's kingdom—the day of his espousals—the day of the gladness of his heart. And Ham's looking on his father's nakedness, and Michal's despising David, and taunting him with "*uncovering himself* as one of the vain fellows shamelessly uncovereth himself," and the mockery of those who said, "These men are full of new wine," were also manifestations of one spirit, even the spirit of him who hateth the mention of Christ's kingdom, because his own kingdom is then to have an end. The Spirit of God *in* the creature prostrates it in the dust, although it gladdens it, and therefore it is that the carnal mind has such a repugnance to it, and such a contempt even for the manifestation of it. The gifts of the Spirit are connected with Noah's vine.

The gospel preached to Abraham included both the promise of the life and of the kingdom. Its peculiarity consisted in its indicating that the enjoyment of the life and of the kingdom was to come through the death

---

[1] I do not believe that Noah's drunkenness was sensual drunkenness; its resemblance, in point of *reproach*, to the other two cases mentioned, leads me to believe that it resembled them also in *principle*.

of the flesh, and through the quickening of the dead flesh by faith, that is, by the Spirit received by faith. Its symbols were: the promise of Canaan, to be enjoyed after his death, *i.e.* in a resurrection-life; the birth of *Isaac* in the land of pilgrimage, indicating the *joy* of faith, even in our present condition of expectancy; and the receiving of Isaac from the dead, by a figure shadowing the death and resurrection of Jesus, through which the blessing was to come. Now Abraham is the full type of the election. He was the first person to whom, as the head of a separate family, and as the representative of only a part of the world, the great promise was made. This is a very important thing, for we are hereby taught wherein the election consists, and wherein it does not consist. And God has been very gracious in this matter, for this same Abraham, who is set forth as the type of the election, is also set forth as the pattern of believers, whereby we are taught that all men have a right to believe, and ought to believe, what Abraham believed, and thus, that the difference between the elect and the unelect does not consist in the one being loved and forgiven in Christ, and the other not; but in the one being taught by God to believe this forgiving love, and the other being permitted to put it from them. Men are elected not to the *shedding* of the blood, but to the *sprinkling* of the blood, which means the purging of the conscience through faith in the atonement.

There is nothing to hinder men from believing but their own self-will. " Ye believe the testimony of men;

the testimony of God is greater." And yet, in point of fact, none do believe except those who are acted upon by this supernatural influence. Men pervert this truth to their own destruction. They say that they *actually cannot* believe the testimony of God without this electing grace, and thus they speak peace to their own consciences, and throw from them the charge of wilfully frustrating the counsel of God, and the condemnation of unbelief, which God lays upon them. They say the truth when they say that we can do no good thing of ourselves; but their error lies here, that they do not understand that God has already given Christ to every man as a head of life, and that it is in the power of this life already given that we are called on to serve God in any way. That life is the Spirit, and it is already given to us in Christ; and thus, as we are forbidden to do anything by the flesh, that is by our own strength, so we have no need to do anything by it, seeing we have the Spirit of Christ given to us whereby to do all things to the glory of God. The old life of the fallen flesh is under a condemnation; it cannot serve God—it cannot approach him; and one of the radical errors in all false religion lies in an ignorance of this, and in an endeavour to force this natural life into the service of God. This is impossible, and the endeavour is as fruitless as it is sinful; and when this impossibility is felt, man begins to throw the blame upon God, and to say, I am willing to believe if God would give me faith, and thus he says to God, "Thou art a hard man, reaping where thou hast not sown." But God answers: Out of thine own mouth will I judge thee; where is that talent which thou hast hid in the napkin? He *hath given* to us eternal life. He *hath given* to us Christ, and in him the ability to glorify God.

Abraham is also the figure of the visible Church, which is the enduring and ordained type of the true election. In the visible Church there is an evident setting forth and affirming of a relationship between her and God, that rests simply on declarations of God, which apply to every human being as well as to her; and the difference between her and the world is this, that she believes, or professes to believe, the reality of these declarations, and the world does not. She declares her members to be the beloved children of God, bought with the precious blood of Christ, in whom they have the Spirit, and the promise of an inheritance in a glorious kingdom, which is to rise out of the death of this fallen flesh and the destruction of the rebellious powers of this world; and in declaring this, she is declaring no more than what is true of every human being, and thus she is a light to the world, and a condemnation to the world who reject Christ, in whom all these things are given. And further, if she walks in holy love and joy, as a stranger here and an expectant of the kingdom, she witnesses also for the blessed power of that truth which she declares, and thus she condemns the world, which ought to walk as she does, having as much the power of doing so as she has; the Lord Jesus being God's gift to the world, and not to the Church. Unless the universality of the love and the redemption be declared by the Church, she is neither a light to the world nor a condemnation to the world, because she represents her own circumstances as exceptions to the general rule, and as more favourable than those of the world, and thus she exculpates the world, because they cannot be called upon to be filled with holy joy and love on any lower grounds than the Church herself. And even though she may declare somewhat of the truth in words, yet if she is not walking as a stranger and the expectant of a kingdom, she is bearing a false witness to the power of that truth which she speaks, and thus she sins against God, and against that purpose of love for which he called her, viz., to be a light to the world, that they seeing the light may give glory to God.

The doctrine of election is connected with the sovereignty of God, which, according to its ordinary acceptation in theology, is just a name for what is *unrevealed* of God. He hath revealed to us his holy love and righteousness in Jesus Christ, and he claims from us that on the ground of that which he hath revealed of himself, and of the explanation he hath vouchsafed to give of the principles of his government, we should, in things which are not explained, trust in him as the same God, assured that though we cannot trace his ways, yet he is not changed. He is *one* and his name *one;* and that name is revealed in Jesus Christ to be a love which tasted death for every man. Men will blindly seek to explain the revealed part of God's government by the unrevealed; instead of explaining the unrevealed by the revealed; and they think that they honour God by dwelling much upon his sovereignty as distinct from love and holiness, as if the glory of God consisted in his being above the control even of a principle. The glory of God is his goodness, and our Father would have us trust his goodness even in the dark, seeing he hath vouchsafed us such a marvellous light.

The false prophet is not merely the fallen flesh under the influence of the spirit of Satan; he is the fallen flesh assuming to do of itself that which the Spirit of God alone can do; he is the fallen flesh rivalling the Spirit as the beast rivals the true King. And thus the false prophet is connected with the Church. The false prophet is manifested in the substitution of selfish, carnal, worldly objects in religion, for the glory of God, and in the substitution of ceremonies or doctrines, or talents or learning, for the Spirit; and in this way he seeks to shut God even out of religion, and to set up man in his place—" the *man* of the earth," as the beast is called in the 10th Psalm (between which 10th Psalm and 2 Thess. ii. there is a remarkable harmony) that beast "whose number is the number of *a man*" (Rev. xiii. 18). Where is wisdom? who has faith to ask and receive the knowledge of this mystery? We shall need to know it. "Here is wisdom." Alas! The second beast spoken of in Rev. xiii. 11, that had two horns like a lamb, and that spake as a dragon, seems to be the same as the *false prophet*, or to be a reappearance of him. For he will fully assume the office of the Spirit in regard to the dragon's anointed, and perform miracles to deceive men in his behalf, and will cause the earth and them that dwell therein to worship him, even the first beast, whose deadly wound was healed. The Roman empire, with its agents, is the beast. In the time of our Lord, Pilate was the manifestation of the beast, and Caiaphas, I believe, was the manifestation of the false prophet. Like Balaam, he was compelled to speak a great truth by the Spirit of God, but his own counsel was against the Lord's Anointed.

The gospel preached to Adam was preached to all his descendants, who were all then enclosed in him, even as an oak is enclosed in its acorn. Thus it was a universal gospel; there was no limitation nor exception in it. It declared the fountain of life to be open to every human being, and thus it declared the love of God, and the remission of sins, to every man through the bruiser of the serpent. As it is the first promise to man, so it has the greatest breadth and the greatest length; it has a wider compass, and looks farther forward than those given afterwards. It embraces the whole race, and the whole history of the wars of the Lord, and has its fulfilment only in the absolute destruction of the first and last and greatest enemy of God and man, and in the full and final restoration of all things under the Father's reign. It looks beyond the millennium, for it is not till after the millennium that the serpent and death are to be cast into the lake of fire. The serpent was and is the enemy of man as man; *he is the enemy, not of the Church only, but also of the world;* he is the head of the general revolt, and the introducer of the general condemnation, namely, death, which is common to all. Now, the gospel to Adam is the promise of the destruction of this common enemy. And thus it has not its fulfilment in the millennium, for though the Church will then be immortal, yet the world will yet be mortal, and the greatest portion of mankind will be lying in the grave under death. After the millennium, the world is to be baptized with fire, and it is out of that baptism that the new heavens and the new earth are to rise. The two last chapters of the Bible describe that state of things. It is the conclusion of the wars of the Lord.

The gospel preached to Noah was preached also to his descendants, no doubt, and in this respect it also was universal; but it was universal only in so far as it was the repetition of Adam's gospel; that is, in so far as it repeated the gospel of the *life.* But there was a speciality in Noah's gospel, as there was a speciality in his history. He was *elected* out of the old world. He was the type of the first resurrection. He emerged from that flood which was the grave of the rest of the race; he rose out of a death which lay on all mankind besides; *he rose from among the dead;* and being thus raised, the gospel of the *kingdom* was preached to him. The gospel of the kingdom is contained in the promise of the destruction of the beast. *This gospel is a promise to the Church, to those who are born again; it is not a promise to the world,* for during its fulfilment, which is during the millennial reign, the rest of the world will either be actually dead, or liable to death; and those last will not be partakers of the kingdom, but subjects of it.

The beast and the false prophet are the enemies of the *Church*, not of the *world;* and, therefore, when the Church is perfected, which is at the commencement of the millennium, they are cast into the lake of fire. Although the world is liable to be oppressed by ungodly power, and deluded by the spirit of Satan, yet the name of the beast and the false prophet do not apply to such oppression and delusion, otherwise we should not read of the beast and the false prophet being cast out at the perfectionment of the Church, which is at the commencement of the millennium, but only of their being bound, as Satan was. At the commencement of the millennium, Satan and death are actually destroyed, as far as the Church is concerned, for they have no more dominion over her; but as they are the enemies of the world, as well as of the Church, and as their power over the world still continues all through the millennium, they are not cast into the lake of fire until after the final judgment, which follows the millennium.

Now, why does the reign of Christ precede the casting of the serpent along with death into the lake? It is for the glory of Christ, that he himself, along with a Church, composed of fallen mortal men, should appear in a state of glory and immortality upon the earth, even whilst death still exercises power there, over all besides. This is to the glory of the second man, who is a quickening, a life-giving spirit; for thus it will appear that the immortality of his Church does not proceed from death having been abolished, but from her being *his body*, from her being united to him, and thus partaking in his life. The world is not to be all converted, or at least upheld in holiness, during the millennium, as is proved by the rebellion that takes place at the conclusion of it, and over these unregenerated or lapsed persons death will continue to exercise his power, as well as over those of former generations who died unconverted; and thus the immortality of the Church will be a glorious exception, and the reason of the exception will also be distinctly manifested to be her union to the quickening Spirit. As it is to the glory of Christ that even now, during the continuance of the power of the beast and the false prophet on the earth, he should have a Church, which is upheld by a simple faith in him, in the refusal to worship the beast and to yield to the suggestions of the false prophet; so it is to his glory that, in the face of death, and during the continuance of his power, there should be a manifested Church, glorious and immortal, rescued from his grasp, and rescued from him not by his having been cast out by an omnipotent word, but by her being indwelt by the Spirit of Christ, and upheld in her glorious immortality simply by that Spirit. She will have been rescued, and will continue to be defended from death, not by the power of God warding off death from her, but by a life communicated to her and dwelling in her, which being the life of God, is stronger than death, and lives in the presence of death, and cannot die.

The manifestation of God is made by contrast and exception. Christ declared the Father in the presence, and in opposition to the acting domination, of all his enemies, and as an exception to the rest of the race to which he belonged. Whilst he was yet in fallen mortal flesh, and dwelling amongst men of like flesh, he declared the mind and will of God by a life of holy love, in opposition to their unholy enmity; and in this he gave glory to God as a God of holy love, because the reason of the difference was, that he was born of the Spirit of God, and they were born only of the flesh. And, in like manner, he declared the Father and witnessed for him, as the fountain of power, even in the presence and during the reign of the beast, by the mighty works which he wrought by the Spirit of God dwelling in him. Why did he alone of all men perform these works? Why was he mighty and all others weak? He was of the same flesh with them. What made the difference between them? The Spirit of God was in him and the spirit of the world was in them. And thus he proved that power belongeth unto God, and that the creature is weak, and thus he disproved the lie of the beast, who had denied that God was the fountain of power, and had taught men to say, "Our lips are our own; who is Lord over us?" In like manner, he witnessed for God by his resurrection. If it had been the general law of nature for men to rise again after they were dead, Christ's resurrection would have been nothing; but when the general law was that men should not only die, but remain dead, his resurrection moves the question, Why does he rise more than the rest of the race? Now the answer is, that he alone of all mankind never, in thought, word, or deed, departed from the living God; that he never sought good but in God; that he drank of the fountain of God's love continually, by a perfect and uninterrupted faith; and that he thus wrought a perfect righteousness, which the Father rewarded by raising him from the dead. This answer declares that God is the only fountain of life, in opposition to the lie of the serpent who had denied it. Thus he witnessed for God before his resurrection and by his resurrection. The Church is, in like manner, called on to witness for Christ now, as he did for the Father before his death. She is called on not only to manifest the holy love of God, but to do mighty works in opposition to the domination of the beast, and in contrast to the weakness of those who do not acknowledge Jesus as their King, and therefore have not his Spirit. And she will be called during the millennium to witness for the virtue of his quickening Spirit by her glorious deathless life, in the presence of the power of death still reigning over the rest of the race.

We have only to compare the life and works of Christ on earth, with the life and works of the Church at present, in order to see how lamentably she frustrates the counsel of God in her calling. Oh for humiliation and brokenness of heart! But alas! when her shortcomings are declared, she stirs herself up, not in the way of repentance, but in the way of self-defence or self-justification. The false prophet's counsel is listened to, and he counsels confidence in the flesh; he wars against the spirit, yea, he counselled to put Lazarus also to death, whom Jesus had raised from the dead.

There is an important lesson taught in the priority of the serpent to the beast, and of his temptation to the beast's temptation, and in his being, as it were, the God and parent of the beast; for we are thus taught that the denial of God as the fountain of *life*, which is the serpent's temptation, is the grand lie of the enemy, and must precede the denial of God as the fountain of *power*. We are thus taught that the departure from God as the fountain of life constitutes the fall, and that the departure from him as the fountain of power and authority springs out of that first root of bitterness. Whilst the creature knows God as the fountain of life, it is qualified to honour him as the fountain of power, and it will assuredly so honour him. But when it does not know him as the fountain of life, it cannot honour him as the fountain of power; and thus it is that no mere belief of the power or authority of God will, or can, ever make a man honour or obey God. God must be first known as the fountain of life, that is, he must be known as *love*. For it is in knowing God's love that men receive God's life, and enter into his counsel and honour his authority. And therefore it is that the Ten Commandments are prefaced by that word, "I am the Lord thy God that redeemed thee," therefore obey my voice.

And this same lesson is taught by the serpent's surviving the beast, and raising an insurrection against the reign of Christ at the conclusion of the millennium. Although the power of Christ will then be manifest, and though his reign will have been one continued act of righteousness, and though there will be no apparent power in opposition to him under which men may range themselves, yet the instant they again receive the serpent's grand lie, that God is not the fountain of life, they will not be restrained from again casting off his authority. The glorious, and holy, and blessed security of the Church, at that time, against both the seductions and the violence of the serpent, in contrast with the readiness of the rest of the world to yield to him, will be another bright manifestation of the power of the Spirit of Christ within them, to overcome all evil. The insurrection described seems to be that of a tumultuous unorganised mass of individuals. The beast will then be gone, who now heads the war against Christ. But they will rise, from pure hatred, even without a head. Thus also the devils now war against God, although they know that it is hopeless, and that they are increasing their own condemnation. But they know not God as the fountain of life, as the fountain of love, and therefore they cannot cease from warring against him. For nothing but God's life in the creature can truly bind its obedience to God, and nothing makes God the fountain

of life to the creature except his love. Love is the only
fountain of life; and therefore the tempter began his
work of darkness by sapping man's confidence in the
love of God. 'Ye shall not surely die; the fruit will
not hurt you; it is not from regard to you that God has
forbidden you to eat it; it is because *he grudges* you the
advancement you would gain by eating it; he pretends
care of you in this thing, but it is jealousy of you. *He
may kill you, but the fruit* will not; nay, it will advance
you; ye shall be as gods, knowing good and evil. The
provision which God has made for you is a narrow
stinted provision; if you would know happiness, you
must go out from him; ye shall not surely die by going
out from him; on the contrary, you will get into a higher
and fuller life.'[1] He that believed this lie disbelieved

[1] Oh what an answer the cross of Christ gives to this lie of the
devil! Did God indeed grudge us the fruit of a tree? The cross
answers, Nay, he grudges us not himself; "He loved us, and gave
himself for us." And then again it says, "Ye shall surely die."
For why does *he* die who hangs there? Simply because he has assumed the nature which was poisoned by the fruit of that tree. No
guile has been found in his mouth, but he took the poisoned nature,
and see the result; he cannot escape death. And then again it
says, Did God indeed grudge our being as gods? Nay, he has
suffered this, "that we might be partakers of the divine nature."

When God forbade Adam to eat the fruit of the tree of knowledge
of good and evil, he at the same time gave him the reason of the prohibition, In the day that thou eatest it thou wilt die; it is poison; it
will kill thee. This was not the exercise of bare arbitrary authority,
it was the authority of love watching over Adam's wellbeing. It
is quite evident that the serpent understood the prohibition in this
sense, for it is against this sense of it that the whole weight of his
temptation is directed. His object is to persuade Eve that the prohibition is an act of arbitrary authority, barring them from a real

God's love, and thus having rejected God as the fountain of life, he soon fell under that other temptation: " All these things will I give thee if thou wilt fall down and worship me." But he who knew his Father's love, and had found it a full fountain of life, answered that first temptation by, " It is written, Man shall not *live* by bread alone, but by every word of God;" and was prepared to repel the second temptation by, "Get thee behind me, Satan; for it is written, Thou shalt worship the Lord thy God, and him only shalt thou serve." So also the three children in Babylon, who refused the king's provision of *life*, finding their God's provision sufficient, resisted the beast's command to worship his golden image, and said, " We are not careful to answer thee in this matter. Our God whom we serve is able

---

benefit, under the pretence of caring for them. And so when he says, Ye shall not surely die, he does not mean to say, God is too good to punish you, but, It is not goodness in God to forbid you. He means to say that the prohibition is entirely arbitrary, for the fruit itself is not only harmless, but beneficial, and therefore that any evil consequences which may follow the eating of it will not come from the fruit, but from God himself. This is the real lie of the devil, That the evil of sin arises from God's having forbidden it, and from the punishment with which God visits it, and not from the nature of the thing itself. And so men who receive this lie wish that such and such things had not been forbidden, thinking that, if they had not been forbidden, there would have been no harm in them. Whilst this thought is in the heart, obedience is impossible.

I believe that the general way of interpreting both the prohibition and the temptation corresponds with the feeling of the carnal mind, and with that system of religion which dreads the proclamation of a general forgiveness, as if the fear of an infliction were the only barrier against sin.

to deliver us from the fiery furnace, and he will deliver us out of thy hand, O king."

Let me here remark, that the truth concerning God which the serpent denied was not that God is *a* fountain of life; he did not venture to deny that, but he denied that God was *the only* fountain of life. And this is the form in which the serpent's lie is generally found amongst men who profess religion. The daring denial that God is at all a fountain of life is the last triumph of the enemy.

As it is love which makes God a fountain of life to his creatures, so it must be a love which forgiveth sin that can alone make him a fountain of life to a fallen creature. And as the devil's lie to Adam was, that God was not a fountain of life to him, because he loved him not, and grudged him a happiness, so his lie to the fallen man since that day has been that God is not a fountain of life to the sinner, because he loves him not, and has not forgiven him. And the devil well knows that those who believe this lie cannot acknowledge God's authority, and must fall under the beast; and therefore it is that he is so zealous to propagate it, pretending even that he is influenced to do so by a regard for the honour of God and for the good of souls.

In the serpent lifted up in the wilderness, we have not merely a repetition and confirmation of that first promise which was made to Adam concerning the bruising of the serpent's head, but we have also, in the healing thence derived to the people who had been wounded by the bites of the fiery serpents, a typical manifestation of the ultimate and glorious effects of that bruising. The voice of the sign was this: Assuredly the serpent's head shall be bruised, and assuredly life shall proceed out of his death; fear not, the time is coming when God shall smite the head of Leviathan (the crooked serpent) in pieces, and give him to be meat to the people inhabiting the wilderness; the time is coming when man is again to be blessed, and holy, and immortal. Thus the serpent lifted up looks back to the fall of man, and forward to the reign of the Father; it looks back to the first promise, and forward to the glory which is to arise out of its accomplishment. It marks the source of all sin and all sorrow, and it points to the termination of all sin and all sorrow. It is a symbol of wonderful vastness. It contains the *secret* of the Lord.

The devil is said to be "he who has the power of death;" he is the author of death; he introduced sin into the world, and, through sin, death; and as he is the author of death, so he is the author of disease, which is just a form of death; and which, as well as death, is a work of the devil. And therefore Jesus, whilst he was upon earth, healed the sick and raised the dead, not merely to typify a spiritual healing and quickening, but to prove that he was indeed the promised Deliverer, by his destroying these works of the devil; and also to give a foretaste and a shadow of the ultimate effect of his redemption upon the whole man, body and soul. And thus we find in the New Testament that the healing of the sick, and the preaching the gospel of the kingdom, are almost always conjoined, and are even spoken of as if they meant the same thing. Thus, "Jesus went about preaching the gospel of the kingdom, and healing all manner of sickness, and all manner of disease amongst the people" (Matt. iv. 23). And the charge to the apostle is, "As ye go, preach, saying, The kingdom of heaven is at hand. Heal the sick, cleanse the lepers, raise the dead, cast out devils" (Matt. x. 7). Compare these passages with Luke ix. 1, 2, and x. 9. And it was for this reason that he so often chose the Sabbath-day as the time for performing these miraculous cures. For the Sabbath was a type of the rest of God, the true seventh day, the millennial period, during which disease and death shall be unknown in the Church, but the saints shall reign with the Lord upon the earth in glorified bodies; and it was for this same reason also that he so often required faith in the subjects of his miraculous cures; not that faith was necessary for these temporary cures, as indeed he often performed them without it, but he thus taught them that the real and permanent restoration of the body was inseparable from a spiritual relation to himself, as, in fact, it was to be produced by the Spirit of God dwelling in them, which could only be their condition by faith in him. The reign of Christ upon earth during the thousand years, and the binding of Satan at that time, and the ultimate bruising of his head, are the events pointed to, both in the cures by the serpent in the wilderness and in those by Christ when on earth, for then shall that word have its fulfilment, "The inhabitant shall no more say, I am sick; the people that dwell there shall be forgiven their iniquity" (Isaiah xxxiii. 24). I may remark that the *forgiveness* spoken of here by the prophet is not the non-imputation of sin, but the removal of the *curse* of death, the original condemnation.

Then God will have glory from this earth, and from our nature—the glory of a manifested goodness, of a victorious love; and that glory shall endure for ever; the Lord shall rejoice in it; he shall joy over it with singing, and all those in whom his Spirit dwells shall enter into his joy.

This joy is a higher, and holier, and more glorious joy than that which was marred by the entrance of sin. God hath taken advantage of that evil thing to make a greater good. Compare that little picture of happiness contained in the end of the second chapter of Genesis with the glory of the New Jerusalem, described in the concluding chapters of the Bible, and say, Verily God counted the cost when he permitted the triumph of the serpent. "Out of the eater hath come forth meat, out of the oppressor hath come forth sweetness." But this is not the strongest nor truest way of marking the difference between the loss and the gain; compare the unfallen Adam, the living soul, with the glorified Christ, the brightness of the Father's glory : these are the two heads, and the bodies are in proportion. Blessed be his great and glorious name for ever and ever. The whole earth shall be full of his glory. And I think that I see also how this blessedness could not have been otherwise produced preserving the responsibility of man, though I would desire to tread softly on such ground. But I see that that word of God, or that putting forth of the character of God, which sustains the creature in existence, is the proper internal life of the creature; it is that which surrounds it, and by which it lives; it is the atmosphere which furnishes its breathing. Now the word by which man was sustained before the fall was a meagre putting forth of the Divine character, in comparison of that full word which is uttered in the gift of Christ; and therefore it was, in comparison, a meagre life. The manifestation of God to the unfallen man was the manifestation of a bountiful Creator and Preserver. The *manner* of God's love—the holiness of his love—the righteousness, the entire unselfishness of his love—was not declared. The fall drew forth that full manifestation of his character. And as that manifestation is made *in a man*, who is the root of the nature, and so connected with every individual of the nature, the character so declared is more than a manifestation; it becomes an infusion; it is a new sap. It is laid up *in that man*, as in a fountain, that it may flow through the rest of the members, just as they open their mouths to receive it. In this way whatever is manifested of God in his dealings with us, when *known*, enters into us, and becomes *life*. And thus it is that life eternal consists in the *knowledge* of the only true God, and Jesus Christ whom he hath sent. And thus also it is that we become partakers of the divine nature, even now, through the knowledge of those promises which declare the character of God. And thus we see how God hath not only made darkness light, and crooked things straight, but hath taken occasion of the wrath of the enemy to make a brighter light, a more excellent glory, than that which the enemy had obscured.

Reader, you see that in these three first forms of the gospel preached to Adam, to Noah, and to Abraham, we have the promise not only of the defeat of the three great enemies of man—the devil, the world, and the flesh—but the prospect also of blessings to arise out of their defeat. These are the powers and principalities which have drawn man away from God, and which shut man's heart against the love of God, and over them it was that Jesus triumphed, and of them that he made an open show on the cross, having through death overcome him who had the power of death, even the devil. As yet, we see but little fruit of this mighty work, but the day is at hand when he will accomplish his work.

In these promises, the Revealer of secrets has, from the very first, given a solution of his own riddle fitted to be life and strength to the souls that were enlightened by his Spirit to understand them. In fact, when we rightly understand the threatenings against the serpent and the beast, and the promise of life out of the flesh now dead, we shall perceive they have the same meaning as that word, "The earth shall be filled with the glory of the Lord;" for that glory has been hindered and excluded by the machinations of the serpent, and by the dominion of the beast under the guidance of the serpent, and the suggestions of the flesh, and thus the promise of their destruction is the promise of the removal of the barriers which have so long prevented God's glory from flowing forth upon the earth.

But their destruction is no light matter. The world and the nature are possessed by them. It is a real demoniacal possession. And as, when Jesus cast the devil out of the demoniac at the foot of the Mount of Transfiguration, the devil cried and rent him sore, so that he lay as dead, so it will be now. The world and the nature will be rent by the convulsion. And the time of that convulsion is drawing near.

We are on the eve of seeing the awful realities foretold by all the prophets actually appear. We are on the eve of that last conflict between the beast and him who is every man's brother, which is to precede the glorious kingdom. Reader, it is an awful prospect, for the whole world is following the beast. There is an universal rejection of the true King—the Lord's Anointed. Men have forgotten that the world and themselves belong to God, and have been bought by the blood of Christ. And in the midst of this rejection, the King is coming. "Behold, he cometh in clouds, and every eye shall see him." He is coming to judgment; he is coming to plead with all flesh; he is coming to plead with those who have rejected his love. "These are the days of vengeance." O reader, come under his shadow, for he is a sure refuge. He yet waiteth to be gracious. Give him your confidence; that is what he asks of you: and has he not earned it? He has tasted death for you; these hands were pierced on the cross for you. "*Abide in me*," saith the Lord. *That* is the place of strength—*that* is the munition of rocks. And soon, very soon, there will be no other place of security; for the day is at hand when all the earth shall be devoured with the fire of his jealousy. Save yourselves from this untoward generation. "Believe on the Lord Jesus Christ, and you shall be saved." "Hear, and your soul shall live." "He loved us, and gave himself for us." "He died because we were sinners, he rose because we were justified." He hath thus declared the Father, that our faith and hope might be in God; he hath thus declared himself, that we might rejoice before him at his coming.

And now I commend this book to God; I cast it upon him. May he forgive in it whatever is amiss; and may he put a rich and holy blessing upon it, as far as it is according to his own mind. May his own voice speak by it, and may his own Spirit work by it unto the salvation of men's souls, for Christ's sake. Amen.

NOTE.

WITH reference to what is written in the 2d chapter of this book on the subject of *substitution*, let me beg the reader's attention to a few lines more. In the first place, *Substitution is not a Bible word*, but I do not wish to contend either for or against *words;* I wish to contend for the truth of God, and if ever I have *unnecessarily* jarred against the feelings of any child of God, by my use of words, I grieve for it as a sin. But I am satisfied that I have not been guilty of this sin, in objecting to the word *substitution* as characterising the relation in which Christ stood to us in his sufferings, because I am satisfied that there is a dangerous error connected with the word. Substitution always supposes that the person suffering in the place of another is quite distinct from that other, and quite free from all righteous liability to the doom under which that other is sentenced to suffer. This is, I believe, the idea generally associated with substitution, and it is as conveying this idea that I object to the word, for this idea really controverts the true humanity of our Lord Jesus Christ. For though, whilst he was yet in the bosom of the Father, before he took our nature, he was free from all liability of suffering, and was under no call to suffer for men, except the importunate call of his own everlasting love, yet after he took our nature, and became the man Jesus Christ, he actually stood himself within the righteous liability of suffering, not indeed on account of any flaw in his spotless holiness, but as a participator of that flesh which lay under the sentence of sorrow and death, and being now engulfed in the horrible pit along with all the others, he could only deliver them by being first delivered himself, and thus opening a passage for them to follow him by; as a man who casts himself into an enclosed dungeon which has no outlet, in order to save a number of others whom he sees immured there, and when he is in, forces a passage through the wall, by dashing himself against it, to the great injury of his person. His coming into the dungeon is a *voluntary* act, but after he is there, he is liable to the discomforts of the dungeon by *necessity*, until he breaks through. This is one man suffering for others, but it is not substitution.

Every pang that Jesus endured, he endured exclusively for others, for he was God and needed nothing; he was love and sought not his own things; only by taking part in our suffering flesh he became capable of suffering, and of suffering in a way which might be available to the salvation of men.

But further, the great mystery of the manifestation of God in the flesh is not limited to the person of the incarnate Word. That mystery has its root and origin in him, but he is the head of a body, in which the mystery is continually to be developed. The manifestation of God the Holy Ghost, as the spirit of the Son, in the members of Christ, is the continual showing forth of the mystery of godliness until the end, and this proves that the work of Christ was the work not of a substitute but of a Head, for it was the fountain of that manifestation of God in the flesh, which is to flow through the body, the Church, marking its oneness with its head, because declaring the presence of the head in every member. But if it had been the work of a substitute, the fountain would have been cut off from the stream, and the oneness of Christ with his members would have been lost.

ON LOVE, PERSONAL ASSURANCE, ETC.

ON LOVE.

WE can only have love in us by knowing that God hath loved us first, and yet this love is not gratitude, and of course not selfish. The knowledge that God has loved us and forgiven us, is necessary to our having confidence in God, and so opening our hearts to let God in. But this knowledge does not produce the love, it only opens the door of the heart to let it in ; God is himself the love. And when he enters us, we shall love him with himself, with his own love, just as we see the sun with his own light, that is, with himself. We love God because he first loved us ; as we see the sun because he first shone on us. There is no other light by which we can see the sun but his own light, and there is no other love by which we can love God but his own love. There is no other love ; everything else which takes the name of love is a spurious thing. "Love is of God," and he who has not God dwelling in him cannot love truly ; he has no love wherewith to love ; and therefore, when we are commanded to love, we are in fact commanded to receive God into us. We are not called on to love our fellow-creatures, *because* God loves them, but *as* God loves them, with the very same love, that is, with God in us loving them. God's love is entirely and essentially different from anything which goes by the name of love in the creature, just as different as God is different from the creature. And therefore we mistake the matter altogether when we confound God's love in the heart with the gratitude and affection produced by the kindness of our fellow-creatures to us.

God's love cannot be separated from himself, and so it is written, "He that dwelleth in love dwelleth in God, and God in him." A man's having real love in him can be accounted for only in one way; he must have God dwelling in him; he could not have love otherwise, for there is no other love; and so the love of God in the creature is not a mere readiness to do the will of God *when known,* as the love of an earthly parent is just such a readiness; the love of God is *knowledge* of his will and *conformity* to it, as well as readiness to do it; the love of God is actually the fulfilling of the law, *because it is God himself who is the law, dwelling in the creature.* Love is the blessing of the new covenant, "I will put my law in their hearts," and not a mere readiness to do it. This is the meaning of the dispensation of the Spirit. The Spirit is love. And so, when it is written that "love believeth all things and hopeth all things," it is not meant that there is a facility or proneness in love to believe or hope anything; but the meaning is, that love, which is God's own Spirit in the creature, stands in God's counsel and knows his mind, and therefore recognises all his revelations, and hopes or desires all that he purposes; the meaning is the same as when it is said, "The Spirit searcheth all things, even the deep things of God." Man's love flatters its objects; man's love suffers sin in its objects; man's love comes forth on those who have qualities fitted to attract it; it comes forth on those who are agreeable to him, on those who are estimable in his eyes, on those who flatter his selfish feelings in some way or other. God's love is the opposite of all this. He loves, not because any object attracts his love, but because he is love. "He commendeth his love to us, in that whilst we were sinners, Christ died for us." This greatest proof of his love is the very thing which declares his unutterable abhorrence of the characters of those whom he thus loved. His love spares not the feelings of its objects; it is a consuming fire; the cross declares the love; this love crucifies those whom it loves, because " it rejoiceth not in iniquity, but rejoiceth in the truth;" " it loveth righteousness and hateth iniquity." It is love which hateth iniquity; nothing else can hate it. Love is the fulfilling of the law, and one part of the law is, Thou shalt not suffer sin in thy brother. Love is the fulfilling of the law, and what is holiness but a conformity to the law? So love is holiness, and holiness is love; there is no other love and no other holiness. Love is that fire of which it is written, "Who among us shall dwell with the devouring fire?" The answer given is, "He that walketh righteously," he and he only can dwell with this love. Love is a state, and it may exist without any object, and so it is said, "*He that loveth is born of God.*" "*He that loveth,*" without even supposing an object. Loving what? just loving. The man is supposed to be living in a state of love. And so enmity is a state, it is the condition of the natural man. Let no one say, that if another meaning is to be attached to the word *love* in the Bible, than its ordinary meaning amongst men, then the whole Bible becomes unintelligible to us, and speaks to us in an unknown tongue; for the truth is, that the whole Bible is written just to explain this very matter to us, just to show us what love is, and to show us how entirely different it is from what man calls love. Love is the birth from above, the everlasting life, and enmity is the natural and universal condition of fallen man, until born of the Spirit. Love is the Spirit. " God so *loved* the world as to give his Son," and he that believes this love receives it into him, he receives the Spirit, he is born of the Spirit, he hath everlasting life. Love is the bruiser of the serpent. The serpent was a murderer from the beginning; love alone can bruise his head. And love is of God alone. Love is the name of God, and for that name's sake Jesus was hated by men, " For my love, they are my adversaries," and in that name it was that Jesus overcame, "They came about me like bees, but in the *name* of the Lord will I destroy them." And it is for this name's sake also that his disciples are to be hated of all men, as it is in this name that they are to set up their banner.

We are living and moving and having our being *in* this love, in the midst of it. We are surrounded and embraced and pressed upon by it, and it is a grieved and grieving love, it is the very love which wept and groaned and agonised in Jesus. The sufferings of Jesus were not a manifestation of a passing temporary thing; they were the manifestation of the mind of the unchangeable God towards sinful man. Reader, this is a mighty and an awful reality; we are living enclosed in the substance of a loving omnipotent God, whose Spirit is continually grieved by the madly wicked resistance that we make to be dwelt in by him, and so to be made partakers of his nature, of his sorrow, of his joy.

ON PERSONAL ASSURANCE.

PERSONAL assurance means a knowledge that God is now looking on me with a Father's love, and that he is not imputing sin unto me, because he hath given me the righteous One, who hath finished transgression by tasting death for every man, to be my Head. This personal assurance, therefore, is the same thing which is called, in the Epistle to the Hebrews, "being made perfect as pertaining to the conscience," and "having the conscience purged from dead works," and "having our hearts sprinkled from an evil conscience" (Heb. ix. 9, 14; x. 22). Without this it is impossible "to serve the living God," or to draw near to God; for until a man has this, all that he does in relation to God must be in the spirit of bondage, and fear, and selfishness, and in order to obtain a personal safety. The man must know himself loved and forgiven before he can serve God. This same truth is contained in that word,

"There is forgiveness with thee that thou mayest be feared;" that is to say, no man can fear God with a godly fear until he knows himself forgiven; until then, he will fear him with a slavish fear. No man, then, can do a single act which is not in itself sinful, until he knows himself forgiven. Now, how is he to know that he is forgiven? Just because God testifies in his word that Jesus "hath tasted death for every man," and that thus he hath made "propitiation for the sins of the whole world." The personal confidence is founded on the general atonement. He who believes in the general atonement has the personal assurance; and thus it is only by rejecting God's testimony, and so making him a liar, that any man is without personal assurance.

The personal assurance does not add to the sacrifice; it is only the purging and perfecting of the conscience by the knowledge of the sacrifice. The man is not a true worshipper without it, but his sin has been atoned for without it.

The law of Moses is full of types wherein both the atonement and the personal assurance are represented; and it is of great importance to see them in their proper relation to each other, without mixing them and confounding them. The death of the victim puts away the condemnation; but the ultimate purpose of this being that the man should "serve the living God," and this being impossible until he knows himself forgiven, the sacrifice has not its real purpose answered with regard to him unless he knows that it is really slain, and that it is for his sin that it is slain, because, until he knows this, he cannot know *himself forgiven*. Now, the laying the hand on the head of the victim is typical of a man's recognising that the victim is slain for *his sin*, and the sprinkling of its blood upon him is a typical assurance that the *sacrifice for his sin is finished*.

These two things, viz., the laying the hand on the head of the victim, and the sprinkling with its blood, correspond to the two witnesses which the blood of Christ bears to every man; 1*st*, that he is a sinner; 2*d*, that he has eternal life. For that blood having been shed for every man is a testimony to every man that he is a sinner; and as it is the blood of the Lamb of God that taketh away the sin of the world, it testifies to every man that his sin is forgiven. And the two ways in which man makes God a liar are just the denials of these two testimonies. (See 1 John i. 10; and 1 John v. 10-12.)

Thus personal assurance is nothing else than faith in the gospel. It is nothing added to faith; it is neither more nor less than being sure that the gospel is true. For the gospel is a personal word "to every creature," and therefore the belief of it must be a personal belief, or a being personally sure of its truth.

Further, personal assurance is the faith which God *reckons righteousness*, "Abraham believed God, and it was counted to him for righteousness." Now what was the character of his faith? "He staggered not at the promise of God through unbelief, but was strong in faith, giving glory to God, *therefore* it was imputed unto him for righteousness" (Rom. iv. 3, 20, 22).

Abraham's faith was an unstaggering faith, a perfect confidence, a personal assurance, and this faith God reckoned or imputed for righteousness. This expression does not mean that God, as it were by a fiction of law, agreed to take faith instead of righteousness, or put anything to Abraham's account which really did not exist in him; but it means that God then declared it to be an eternal truth, that the only righteousness of the creature is personal confidence in the Creator, as revealed in Christ, the promised seed. *Imputation* here means the same thing as *estimate*. This is God's estimate of the creature's confidence in the Creator; he says that such confidence is righteousness; he imputes it, or reckons it, or accounts it, or estimates it to be righteousness. And the reason of this estimate is, that the creature can only be of one mind with God whilst it is giving him its entire confidence. " Being justified by faith," in the beginning of the fifth chapter of the Epistle to the Romans, just means having the righteousness of faith, having personal assurance, having personal confidence. It is most wonderful to see how much false theology has been built on the misunderstanding of that word, *justification by faith*, a theology which makes the judicial act of God, warranting every man through the work of Christ to rejoice in him as his forgiving God, to be dependent on the faith of man, whilst its true meaning, viz., personal confidence in God, from a knowledge of what he is, has been cast out as heresy. (See the foot-notes at pp. 88 and 158.)

In Rom. x. 3, where it is written, " they being ignorant

of God's righteousness, and going about to establish their own righteousness, have not submitted themselves to the righteousness of God;" *God's righteousness* evidently means *a ground of confidence* in God's character, and *their own righteousness* as evidently means *a ground of confidence* in their own character. *Justification by faith* is an improper expression; it does not occur as a substantive in the Bible (see note, p. 88); it ought to be the *righteousness* of faith, and it means confidence in God, or having the conscience purged through faith in the atonement, which is the principle of confidence.

In Acts xiii. the 38th verse announces a *general* forgiveness of sins through Christ, and the 39th verse declares that those only who believe in this announcement can have their consciences purged so as to have confidence before God, seeing there are so many offences for which there is no atonement provided in the law of Moses. These two verses do not contradict each other; the first declares the unlimited forgiveness, the second, the personal assurance founded on it in those who believe it. "Through this man is preached unto you the forgiveness of sins, and every one who believeth in him (this is the true and literal rendering) is justified (*i.e.* has his conscience purged) from all things," etc. God's will concerning us, revealed in the work of Christ, is our sanctification, and therefore the man who knows this to be the will of God concerning him, and enters by the faith of it into God's purpose, will confidently put himself into God's hands to accomplish his own will in him, assured of the result. This confidence is personal assurance and the righteousness of faith.

TEXTS ILLUSTRATING THE MEANING ATTACHED TO THE WORDS *RIGHTEOUS* AND *WICKED* IN THE BIBLE.

In Psalm ix. 17, it is written, that "The wicked shall be turned into hell, even all the nations *that forget God.*" And in 2 Peter i. 9 it is written, that those who lack any right thing, as godliness, brotherly-kindness, charity, lack them *because* they are blind, shutting their eyes, *having forgotten that they were purged from their old sins*, or rather, and more literally, having forgotten that by which they were purged from their old sins, viz. the atonement through the blood of the cross. These two passages are parallel, the forgetfulness of God being in fact the forgetfulness of the atonement. It is the same forgetfulness, forgetfulness of God meaning forgetfulness of his character, and his character being only fully manifested in the atonement. And the forgetfulness is just ignorance, ignorance of the forgiveness of sin through the Lamb of God, it being a matter of little importance whether the persons *so forgetting* have *always* rejected this forgiveness, or having once known it, or seemed to know it, have *again rejected it*. In the Psalm quoted, the first class seem to be spoken of, and in the epistle, the second. The *wicked*, then, are those who know not, or who forget, that God hath forgiven sin through an atonement. In Psalm xxxii. 10, the characteristic feature of wickedness is evidently supposed to be *a want of confidence in God*, for the wicked man is directly contrasted with *him that trusteth in the Lord*, " Many sorrows shall be to the wicked, *but he that trusteth in the Lord, mercy shall compass him about.*" And who are they that trust in the Lord? The answer is given in the same Psalm ix. 10, "They that know thy name will put their trust in thee." And what is the name of God? Just the *character of God* manifested in the atonement of Christ, as Christ himself says in Psalm xxii. 22, " I will declare thy *name* unto my brethren," just the same name which was proclaimed to Moses, Exodus xxxiv. 6 : "The Lord God, forgiving iniquity, transgression, and sin, yet by no means clearing the guilty." This name of God Christ did declare, when on him was laid the iniquity of us all (Isaiah liii. 6), for God then was manifested as forgiving iniquity without clearing it, as forgiving iniquity, not by passing it over, but because he had already condemned and punished it in the blood of Christ. This is the name of God, which gives confidence to all who know it. "They that know thy name will put their trust in thee." They that forget not that by which they were washed from their old sins, will put their trust in thee. But it is a characteristic of the wicked that they trust not in God. Now why is it that they do not trust in him? Just because they know not his name; they forget God, they know not *that atonement* by which they were washed from their old sins; they know not, or they have forgotten him on whom their iniquities were laid; they deny the Lord that bought them (2 Pet. ii. 1). The wicked shall be turned into hell, even all the nations that forget God. They know not the atonement, which magnifies the holiness and justice of God in the forgiveness of the sinner, and therefore they regard the holy and just God as their enemy; they say unto him, Depart from us; they say, Who will show us any good?—they forsake the fountain of living waters, and hew out to themselves broken cisterns, which can hold no water; they tread under foot the Son of God, and count the blood of the covenant wherewith they were sanctified an unholy thing, and do despite unto the Spirit of grace. These are the wicked with whom "God is *angry* every day" (Psalm vii. 2); just as he who declared the Father "looked round him with *anger*, being *grieved* at the hardness of their hearts," being grieved that they would not believe that he was the gift of God's love to them, and that he was the Lamb of God, that had come from heaven to take away their sins. Yet the heart of the Father and the Son yearned over them. The anger was not the anger of hatred, but of a love that longed after them. The wicked addressed in Isaiah lv. 7 are the same persons. The waters to which there is a general invitation given in the 1st verse, are the blessings flowing from the sufferings of Christ, and the glory which should follow, as described prophetically in the two preceding chapters. And the wicked are those who, instead of drinking of these waters, instead of giving God glory for that holy love which laid on Jesus the iniquities of us all, and thence looking forward to the glorious return of the King of glory, spend their money for that which is not bread, and their labour for that which satisfieth not; and whilst they are thus occupied, it is said, "Let them forsake this way, and these thoughts, and let them return unto the Lord, and he will have mercy on them, and to our God, and he will multiply to pardon them;" let them return to the waters, and they will find them still flowing, not stinted in consequence of their forsaking them; they flow from a full fountain, the holy love which laid on Jesus the iniquities of us all. The wicked here are desired to drink of the waters which flow from that well-head; "The Lord hath laid on him the iniquities of us all." Could any man be desired to drink of that water unless it could also be said to him, "The Lord hath laid on Jesus thine iniquities?" I trow not. For otherwise I should think that God mocked the man. And when God invites the wicked to drink of these waters of forgiving love, knowing the narrowness of man's heart, and his indisposition to believe in this undamped graciousness, He adds, "For my thoughts are not your thoughts, neither are your ways my ways, saith the Lord." The wicked are wicked, simply because they know not God, because they forget that the blood of Christ hath been shed for them, and that that blood cleanseth from all sin. This ignorance, this forgetfulness, is the very essence and source of wickedness. And as it is life eternal to know thee, the only true God, and Jesus Christ whom thou hast sent; so men are "alienated from the life of God through the *ignorance* that is in them" (Eph.

iv. 18). And they are saved " by coming to the *knowledge of the truth*," by coming to know their true relation to God, just by coming to know what had always been true.

The terms *righteous* and *unrighteous* always have reference to a judgment. Thus, " And these (the wicked) shall go away into everlasting punishment, but the righteous into life eternal."

" The ungodly or wicked shall not stand in the judgment, nor sinners in the congregation of the righteous." " Like sheep they are laid in the grave ; death shall feed on them ; and the upright (the righteous) shall have dominion over them in the morning (of the resurrection); and their beauty shall consume in the grave. But God will redeem my soul (the soul of the righteous) from the power of the grave ; for he shall receive me" (Ps. i. and xlix.)

The members of the *righteous* Head, those who are one spirit with him, shall be partakers of the first resurrection ; their righteousness shall be declared and acknowledged by the fact of their being raised at that time, to reign with Christ during the millennium. The wicked shall then be lying under the power of death ; and their unrighteousness shall be thus declared and condemned.

www.ingramcontent.com/pod-product-compliance
Lightning Source LLC
Chambersburg PA
CBHW022105230426
43672CB00008B/1285